THE TWO VERSIONS OF MARIANO AZUELA'S LOS DE ABAJO:

A COMPARATIVE STUDY

THE TWO VERSIONS
OF
MARIANO AZUELA'S
LOS DE ABAJO:
A COMPARATIVE STUDY

BY
THOMAS W. RENALDI

STUDIES IN THE LITERATURE OF MEXICO

GORDON PRESS
NEW YORK
1979

GORDON PRESS — Publishers
P.O. Box 459
Bowling Green Station
New York, N.Y. 10004

Library of Congress Cataloging in Publication Data

Renaldi, Thomas Wayne.
    The two versions of Mariano Azuela's Los de abajo.

    (Studies in the literature of Mexico)
    Bibliography: p.
    1. Azuela, Mariano, 1873-1952. Los de abajo.
2. Mexico in literature. I. Title. II. Series.
PQ7297.A9L637   863   78-9927
ISBN 0-8490-1396-8

Printed in the United States of America

ACKNOWLEDGEMENTS

I dedicate this dissertation to Professor René DeCosta, my adviser, who taught me the meaning of purely literary analysis and sharpened my use of English; to my dilligent readers, Professor Kenneth Zimmerman and Professor Francisco Ayala; to my wife Betsy, who typed hundreds of pages and was my constant moral support; and to her family, whose encouragement and favors did so much to further my work.

TABLE OF CONTENTS

INTRODUCTION

Los de abajo is for many reasons considered as Mariano
Azuela's masterpiece. In it he abandons for the first time
the linear continuity of his previous work. The novel, based
on notes which Azuela took while traveling with a troop of
revolutionaries, was published in 1915, in the midst of the
Mexican Revolution. Many incidents and characters are based
on what Azuela saw or heard described. As a consequence, Los
de abajo contains a unique combination of an almost documen-
tary realism in the rendition of action, while Modernist es-
theticism is apparent in the impressionistic rendition of the
scenes.

Latinamericanists who recall the widespread reverence in
which Azuela was held during his declining years, usually over-
look the fact that recognition of his masterpiece came late and
grudgingly. In 1923, when the novelist celebrated his fiftieth
birthday, he had written almost all the works now recognized
as his best. In the maturity of life, with his finest writing
behind him, Azuela had still received almost no applause nor
even recognition from Mexican critics. Manuel Pedro González[1]
documents in detail the critical silence which greeted everything that Azuela produced through 1918. María Luisa (1907)
was reviewed only in Cuba and Los fracasados (published in
1908) gained recognition from only one Mexican critic, Heri-
berto Frías, a figure of little prestige. Another minor literary critic, José G. Ortiz, commented upon Los fracasados and
Mala yerba (1909). The prestigious critics of the Revista
Moderna steadfastly ignored Azuela. A similar reception awaited Andrés Pérez, maderista (1911) and Sin amor (1912); the former received only anonymous mention in a provincial journal.
Los de abajo, first published in Texas, was for many years un-
recognized in Mexico. The last four novels of the Revolution
(Los caciques, 1917; Las moscas, 1918; Domitilo quiere ser
diputado, 1918, and Las tribulaciones de una familia decente,
1918) gained no plaudits for the author.

The existence of Los de abajo for ten years before it was
acclaimed was due in part to the scarce numbers and poor quality of the early editions, which were printed in undistinguished
publishing houses and in meager issues.[2] One edition, for
example, consisted of just two hundred copies.[3]

Early in 1925, Francisco Monterde published an article[4]
which led to nationwide recognition of Los de abajo. In January, 1925, El Universal conducted a poll on the question,
"¿Existe una literatura mexicana moderna?" In partial reply,
the distinguished critic Eduardo Colín wrote a review of Los
de abajo. His article, dated January 30, 1925, marked the

first time the novel had ever been considered by a prestigious critic.[5] Colín's favorable review prompted a succession of new editions of the novel, as recorded in Leal's bibliography of Azuela.[6]

El Universal Ilustrado re-published Los de abajo in serialized form in February, 1925, and the government of the state of Veracruz issued an edition in 1927. The first prestigious editions, though, were issued in Spain by Espasa-Calpe and in Chile by Zig Zag, in 1930. No other editions appeared in Mexico until 1938 (Editorial Pedro Robredo). Finally there was issued a prestigious edition in Mexico, that of Botas in 1939.

An indication of the worldwide popularity of Los de abajo is the number of translations which have appeared.[7] The first documented foreign-language rendition was into French, under the title L'Ouragan, in serialized form in the Parisian newspaper Le Monde, in 1928. The next translation was into English (The Underdogs), issued in New York by Brentano's in 1929. An interesting feature of that edition is José Clemente Orozco's illustrations. An English translation appeared in Britain in 1930. Another French version also came out in 1930, this time in book form, with the title Ceux d'en bas. The novel appeared in German (1930), in Serbian (1933), in Brazilian Portuguese (1934), in Czech (1935), in Italian (1945), and in Swedish (1952). Tajimi Kitagawa translated Los de abajo for Mexico Shimpo, a Japanese-language newspaper of the Capital, in 1932. In another Mexico City newspaper, Samuel Glicowski partially translated the novel into Yiddish.[8]

The rendition into Russian merits a special explanation. La Gaceta Literaria, of Madrid, announced in 1927 that the Russian version would soon appear. Joaquin Maurin, who translated Los de abajo into French, wrote to Azuela in 1929, saying that the novel had appeared in Russia. The title was the equivalent of The Hurricane (III, 1299). Thus Azuela, who felt deep admiration for Gorki and Tolstoi,[9] was recognized in Russia perhaps as early as 1927. Indeed, that little-known translation may have been the world's first. That Los de abajo has earned a place in Western literature is demonstrated by the above bibliographical history and by the extensive studies devoted to Azuela and his work.[10]

Azuela wrote three plays: Los de abajo, El buho en la noche (adaptation of El desquite) and Del Llano hermanos, S. en C. (adaptation of Los caciques). The date when any of the above works was adapted for theater can only be surmised. Azuela himself does not divulge that information in his memoirs, and none of his biographers records even an approximate date of composition. The only known dates are 1938, publication of the three plays;[11] February 22, 1929, debut of Los de abajo;[12] November 20, 1936, debut of Del Llano hermanos;[13] and August 31, 1938, radio presentation of El buho en la noche.[14]

The theatrical version of Los de abajo is dedicated "A Francisco Monterde; vieja deuda de gratitud" (III, 9); it represents, then, Azuela's first public acknowledgement of his emergence into the literary limelight as a result of

Monterde's article. It is therefore strange that the play
has received only a minimum of critical attention. Professor
Leal dismisses it with one sentence:

> En la pieza teatral, la novela Los de abajo
> es reducida a seis escenas sin relación alguna.[15]

Englekirk and Kiddle devote but a paragraph to the adaptation,
subjectively concluding that the play:

> . . . follows the novel quite faithfully in a series
> of six scenes. The dialog is taken almost verbatim
> from the novel, and Solís is the only important minor
> character omitted. The play falls infinitely short
> of the book, however, and no final scene could ever
> be so effective in its arrangement as the closing
> passage of the novel.[16]

No critic to my knowledge has compared the novel and the play
in order to discern what were Azuela's esthetic criteria for
novel and for theater. Such a study seems both necessary and
lacking because of the singular importance of Los de abajo
and the author's pronouncements on both genres. Therefore, of
central interest to the comparative study I am attempting are
some observations Azuela made in "Mi experiencia en el cine y
en el teatro," an article contained in El novelista y su am-
biente (1949), where he confesses that a writer viewing the
stage or film adaptation of his novel:

> . . . está viendo, oyendo y palpando no su propia
> obra, sino la que se construyó con elementos tomados
> de ella, pero modificados y dispuestos conforme a
> una sensibilidad y a una técnica que no son las de
> su novela. Y esto no llegará a reconocerlo sino en
> sucesivas representaciones, cuando pueda captar
> serenamente los nuevos personajes, la acción, el
> ambiente, los efectos dramáticos y cómicos y pueda
> formar un concepto exacto y preciso de lo que hay de
> ajeno en la obra y de lo que ha quedado en pie de la
> primitiva. . . .
> Una bella descripción requiere muchas páginas
> del escritor y muchos minutos de atención del lector,
> en tanto que en el tablado o en la pantalla pasa con
> la rapidez de un relámpago dejando el mismo o mayor
> efecto. Un gesto bien logrado, la atinada inflexión
> de la voz, un ademán oportuno dejan huella más profunda
> y duradera en el público que los prolijos renglones o
> páginas que el novelista ha menester para dar análoga
> impresión. Los diálogos en el teatro requieren rigur-
> osamente concisión, precisión y sentidos. Ni una
> palabra más ni menos. En hora y media o dos horas
> hay que obtener lo que en la novela se produce en
> días y hasta semanas de reposada lectura (III, 1149).

It is hoped that a thorough study of the dramatization of
Los de abajo will elucidate specifically how Azuela dealt with
the immediacy of images and how he created a scenario tailored
to the new work. Comparison and contrast of the play and the
novel will bring to light which episodes of the novel Azuela
considered so indispensable as to transfer them basically unchanged to the play, which he adapted with extensive modifications,
and which he did not adapt at all. Such a study will reveal
the author's methods of solving three types of esthetic problems: those created by the respective art forms, those occasioned by the different organizations of the two versions, and
those which he himself created through his volition.[17]

This dissertation examines the thesis that Azuela the novelist followed certain esthetic criteria in his novel Los de
abajo. Adapting the novel for theater, he decided to present
no more than one major incident in each of the six cuadros,
in order to make each one stand out clearly. He preferred those
incidents which contribute to the long-term development of the
characters' personalities. Aware of the visual and auditory
immediacy of theater, Azuela employed them to present in a new
way incidents which he had decided to adapt from the novel.
Creating a scenario for the play, quite different from the narrative arrangement of the novel, involved the alteration of
some incidents to fit that scenario and also the creation of
some new episodes.

My exposition will proceed from a detailed analysis of the
techniques employed in the novel to a parallel analysis of the
play in order to examine the differences between the two versions and to explain the esthetic reasons for those differences.

Problems which must be overcome, in the exploration of
Azuela's novelistic and dramatic criteria, are classifiable into
two groups: separation of observations pertinent to the dissertation from those which are not, and isolation of the reasons for the differences between the two versions. Comparison
of the doctrinal message of the respective works, immaterial
to a study of literary techniques, is therefore omitted, as
is examination of Azuela's experiences as a medic in the Revolution, as they may have affected the work. Likewise, no
attempt is made to trace evidence in the play of Azuela's experiences during the years which intervene between the two
versions. After isolating the significant differences between
novel and play, it was decided to determine which are due to
the demands of each genre, which obey the requirements of each
work's organization, and which reflect the author's artistic
volition.

The approach employed in the dissertation is one of separate but parallel analyses of the novel and the play, beginning
with the process through which Demetrio Macías is mythified
and then humanized. Other characters are also examined, insofar as they affect Demetrio. Careful attention is given the
hero's awareness of the political forces which make his death
inevitable. Therein lies much of the tragic pattern of both
works.

In order to contrast the structure of the two versions,

it is necessary first to define Azuela's use of the chapter
or the <u>cuadro</u> as a basic unit. Then the structure of each
work as a whole can be meaningfully examined. In the case of
the novel, the essence of each of the three parts is established. In the play, there is no structural division other than
the six <u>cuadros</u>.

The settings which form the background for the events of
each work are also analyzed, with particular attention to the
illusion of space, a problem critical to the play and not absent from the novel. The chronology of the action, more extensive in the novel than in the play, is also considered.

Consequently, the first aspects studied, for the most part,
concern the novel more directly than the play. Of course,
those next introduced (visual and auditory effects, costuming,
stage directions or narrative description, and dialog versus
animation or versus narration) more directly involve the theatrical adaptation.

Last to be considered in each chapter (novel, play and comparison) is characterization. In the analysis of the novel,
that study deals with the dramatized narrators. In the play,
the corresponding section examines characterization.

Throughout the dissertation, the similarities between the
two versions of <u>Los de abajo</u> are established first, in order
to set forth the valid and pertinent differences in an effort
to determine the essence of Azuela's narrative and dramatic
art.

Footnotes

[1]Manuel Pedro González, <u>Trayectoria de la novela en México</u> (México, 1951), pp. 164-165.

[2]El Paso, Texas, 1916; Tampico, Tamaulipas, 1917; Mexico, 1920. The first edition and one other were serialized in newspapers.

[3]John E. Englekirk, "The 'Discovery' of <u>Los de abajo</u>," <u>Hispania</u>, XVIII (1935), 57-59.

[4]Francisco Monterde, "Los de arriba y <u>Los de abajo</u>," <u>Universal Ilustrado</u>, February 2, 1925, quoted in Englekirk, "The 'Discovery' of <u>Los de abajo</u>."

[5]Englekirk, "The 'Discovery' of <u>Los de abajo</u>," p. 60. The article is reprinted in Eduardo Colín's book, <u>Rasgos</u> (Mexico, 1934).

[6]Luis Leal, <u>Mariano Azuela: Vida y obra</u> (Mexico, 1961), pp. 135-166.

[7]Listed <u>ibid</u>., pp. 144-145.

[8]Bibliography in Mariano Azuela, <u>Obras completas</u>, with a Foreword by Francisco Monterde (3 vols.; México, 1958-1960), III, 1299. (Hereafter all references to this work will be given in the text, in parentheses, by volume and page number.)

[9]"La novela mexicana," <u>ibid</u>., p. 1265.

[10]See bibliography in Leal, <u>Mariano Azuela</u>, pp. 145-165.

[11]<u>Ibid</u>., p. 140.

[12]<u>Ibid</u>., p. 81.

[13]<u>Ibid</u>.

[14]<u>Ibid</u>., p. 88.

[15]<u>Ibid</u>., p. 81.

[16]John E. Englekirk and Lawrence B. Kiddle, Foreword to <u>Los de abajo</u> (New York, 1939), p. xxxiii.

[17]It once seemed that the theatrical version of <u>Los de abajo</u> might represent a resolution of Azuela's vanguard crisis, during which he wrote <u>La Malhora</u>, <u>El desquite</u> and <u>La luciérnaga</u>. Such a hypothesis, on the surface substantiated by chronology, cannot be proven stylistically. It is more likely that the play is simply an acknowledgement of Azuela's recently-gained acclaim; the dedication to Monterde supports that notion.

CHAPTER I

LOS DE ABAJO, THE NOVEL

Mariano Azuela's best-known novel consists of forty-two chapters divided among three parts. The chapters describe varied material: military action, romantic crises, philosophical expositions, and scenes of cruelty, plunder and debauchery. They relate fictional incidents inspired by authentic events which Azuela witnessed or heard second hand during his participation in the Mexican Revolution.

Incidents, performed by characters typically Mexican in their speech and dress, take place in a specifically Mexican milieu. The characters' actions and the settings in which they are performed are, then, realistic. One character, General Pánfilo Natera, is historical. Time flows as in life: during the nearly two years which are to elapse in the course of related events, the characters evolve both physically and psychologically. In the later chapters, several characters bear traces of incidents which have earlier befallen them.

The novel tells the story of one man, the protagonist Demetrio Macías, as his life as affected by the Mexican Revolution in the years 1913-1915. Huertista troops visit Demetrio's hut and burn it. He sends his wife to his father's house and escapes to the nearby mountains, where he calls together a ragtag army. They fight the federales the next day and defeat them as Demetrio is wounded in the leg. His loyal men carry him on a stretcher through the mountains until they come to a village where they stay until Demetrio recovers from his injury. While in the village they capture Luis Cervantes, deserted from the huertistas, a medical student who gains Demetrio's favor by healing his leg. A girl of the village, Camila, who brings Demetrio his meals, will later accompany him as his mistress.

After Demetrio is cured, the troops depart for Fresnillo, where they will join forces with part of Pancho Villa's army. On the way they score a resounding victory over the federales in the garrison of a small town. They arrive at Fresnillo where the villista general rewards Demetrio's battle prowess by making him a colonel. In Fresnillo, Demetrio meets a coarse camp follower, la Pintada, who becomes jealous when Camila joins the entourage. Their rivalry culminates in Pintada's murder of Camila.

As Pancho Villa's fortunes turn from good to bad, the war becomes tedious for Demetrio and his men. Tired and discouraged, resented by the peasants because of their looting, they return to their native Sierra. Demetrio is briefly reunited with his wife before he goes out and is killed in a battle with the numerically superior carrancistas.

Patterns of Action

The Hero: Mythified and Humanized

Early in the novel, Demetrio Macías is revealed in his private life. In Chapter 1, Part I, his revolutionary role yet unclear, he seems to be just a peasant. When first presented, he is so unspecific that he lacks even a name:

> . . . un hombre que, en cuclillas, yantaba en un rincón, una cazuela en la diestra y tres tortillas en taco en la otra mano (I, 320).

The choice of the archaic verb yantar echoes the epic tradition of the Spanish romances, while the native tortillas link the activity precisely to Mexico.

The description of the hut surrounds Demetrio with an aura of domesticity:

> . . . En un rincón descansaban un yugo . . . y otros aperos de labranza. Del techo pendían cuerdos sosteniendo un viejo molde de adobes, que servía de cama, y sobre mantas y desteñidas hilachas dormía un niño (I, 320).

Three aspects of Demetrio's private life are presented through symbols. The yoke represents his agrarian occupation, and the bed, his conjugal state; the child might suggest the deepness and permanence of his relationship with his wife. That Demetrio is poor, a notion not insinuated elsewhere in the chapter, is indicated by the rags upon which the baby is sleeping.

Demetrio is described in the following terms:

> . . . de faz bermeja, sin pelo de barba, vestía camisa y calzón de manta, ancho sombrero de soyate y guaraches (I, 320).

Demetrio's clothing denotes his Mexican-ness, while his complexion and lack of a beard establish him as an Indian.

Throughout the novel, Demetrio's Aztec ancestry is reasserted from time to time. For example, in Chapter 15, Part I, his leg is healed and he has embarked on a new military campaign:

> . . . Demetrio se sentía rejuvenecido; sus ojos recuperaban su brillo metálico peculiar, y en sus mejillas cobrizas de indígena de pura raza corría de nuevo la sangre roja y caliente (I, 352).

The narrator ascribes to the Indian race, through Demetrio, traits of physical superiority. The red, hot blood suggests adaptability for combat.

Demetrio also has better-than-average eyesight and a commanding glance. The narrator mentions his "ojos de aguilucho" (I, 374) and "su mirada de ave de rapiña" (I, 376).

The last Indianization of Demetrio is found in Chapter
6, Part III, where he looks at his son:

> . . . reparó en la reproducción de las mismas
> líneas de acero de su rostro y en el brillo fla-
> mante de sus ojos (I, 415).

The description endows Demetrio and the little boy with extraordinary potential. This characterization, establishing Demetrio as a non-public man, also justifies the aura of mystery
which surrounds him. Chapter 1, Part I, gives evidence that
Demetrio's name is sufficient to make his enemies stand in
awe. When he appears in the doorway of his hut, a mysterious
"silueta blanca" (I, 322), the huertista sergeant steps back
in horror and pronounces his name, first and last, like a
magical formula:

> Una silueta blanca llenó de pronto la boca oscura
> de la puerta.
>   --¡Demetrio Macías!--exclamó el sargento des-
> pavorido, dando unos pasos atrás (I, 322).

Demetrio's conduct, in the opening pages of the novel,
contributes to the mythlike quality which surrounds him.
Hearing a barking dog and then the sound of approaching horses,
his wife suggests that he hide outside. Unhurried, he finishes
eating, takes time to drink water from a jug, arms himself and
slips out "paso a paso" (I, 322). Demetrio's unemotional fearlessness is established from the beginning of the novel. When
he returns to confront the federales, it is his aloof silence
which might most impress the reader. He says not one word
while the huertista lieutenant begs his forgiveness, but
simply smiles "una sonrisa insolente y despreciativa" (I, 322).
It is obvious from the lieutenant's frightened monologue that
he tries to shake Demetrio's hand and that he is rebuffed.
Even when the wife embraces Demetrio, begging him not to leave
her, he pushes her gently away and answers impersonally: "Me
late que van a venir todos juntos" (I, 322).
    After showing much of Demetrio's human side in subsequent
chapters of Part I, the narrator returns to his aloof inaccessibility in Chapter 1, Part II. There Demetrio is surrounded
by General Natera's followers, who know him not as a man but
as a famous name. Again, as in Chapter 1, Part I, Demetrio is
taciturn almost to the point of disdain. When Anastasio speaks
in glowing terms of el güero Margarito, introducing him, Demetrio does not bother to remove the cigar from his mouth as he
extends his hand and mutters: "Servidor . . . " (I, 371).
La Pintada, sitting on the bar behind him and grazing his back
with her slippers, tries to present herself. Scarcely glancing
at her, he mumbles: "--A la orden" (I, 371). When she mentions
"el famoso Demetrio Macías que tanto se lució en Zacatecas"
(I, 371), he only nods in acknowledgement. As the narrator
comments, Demetrio " . . . permanecía silencioso y huraño en
medio de la alharaca general . . . " (I, 371).

Demetrio is not again described as a heroic figure.
Narrative preparation for his decline and death takes place
throughout the novel by means of a step-by-step revelation
of Demetrio Macías, the man, with his human shortcomings
and virtues.

The protagonist, as he leaves home, is still an unreal
figure, larger than life. At first he seems above any passion
for revenge. Telling his disciples how the <u>federales</u> burned
his house, Demetrio seems to hold back his <u>rage while</u> the
others vent theirs:

> Hubo imprecaciones, amenazas, insolencias. Demetrio
> los dejó desahogar . . . (I, 324).

He displays emotion for the first time during the skirmish
with the <u>huertistas</u>. Seeing the enemy fording the river in
single <u>file</u>, at the bottom of the canyon, he realizes that
their ranks must be decimated there, lest the first platoons
advance beyond his men and open fire on them from the flank.
Unable to persuade his men to fire downward, he begins to
shout angrily, "--A los de abajo. . . . A los de abajo . . ."
(I, 327). Here, for the first time, Demetrio is shown as
capable of alarm.

Wounded in the leg by enemy fire from the flank, Demetrio
is carried through the mountains by his men, on a makeshift
stretcher. His reaction to the pain humanizes him a bit more;
his rhythmic, monosyllabic moans are the only sound made by
anyone in the platoon (I, 328).

In Chapter 7, Part I, Demetrio reacts more strongly to
Camila than to his wife at the beginning of the novel. He
compliments the girl on her melodious voice, then tries to seize
her wrist (I, 335). More and more the narrator reveals him in
reactions common to most men. Still he is clearly superior
to his disciples. When he decides to have Codorniz pose as a
priest and hear Cervantes' confession, so he can shoot the
prisoner if he is an assassin but spare his life if he merely
deserted from the enemy, Demetrio displays a concern for justice which tries Pancracio's patience: "--¡Hum, cuánto re-
quisito! . . . Yo lo quemaba y ya . . ." (I, 335).

Chapter 13, Part I, dispels any notion that Demetrio is
taciturn. He talks at great length about his past, explaining
to Cervantes his theories about the Revolution (I, 346). Demetrio is no longer a phantom-like figure with no past.

A guerrila who never eats or drinks to excess might be
considered aloof from his conrades. Until Chapter 15, Part I,
Demetrio seems to have no vices. There, for the first time,
after the farewell party in the village, Demetrio is revealed
"bamboleándose un poco" (I, 351). Heretofore none of his weaknesses has been disclosed.

Throughout most of Part I, Demetrio is distinguished by
a refusal to kill in cold blood. He lets the <u>huertista</u> intruders go free, despite his wife's urging that <u>he kill</u> them
(I, 322); he insists on a fair trial for Luis Cervantes and is
exclusively responsible for sparing the prisoner's life. In
Chapter 17, Part I, Demetrio takes revenge for the first time.

Storming the federal garrison and finding an old sergeant whom they met on the road and who lied to them about the strength of the contingent, Demetrio plunges his knife through the old man's ribs (I, 359). The narration evokes in the reader a reaction of horror or disgust at Demetrio's act. The old man has pleaded that Demetrio spare him; Demetrio has paused to study the wrinkled old face and then has murdered him. To further encourage a reaction against Demetrio, the narration mentions that Luis Cervantes turns away in horror (I, 359).

In Chapter 21, Part I, Demetrio's role as a living legend is reaffirmed. Alberto Solís, conversing with Luis Cervantes, tells him about Demetrio's reckless heroics at Zacatecas, how he single-handedly reversed the outcome of the battle (I, 367, 368). The re-mythification of Demetrio serves as a prelude to his renewed aloofness in the following unit, Chapter 1, Part II. There Demetrio remains apart from the raucous festivities for only half the chapter, until his pride swells from the effusive courtesies and compliments expressed by everyone around him. In an expansive mood, he orders champagne (I, 372). His icy reception of Pintada's attentions warms during the night, and he takes her to a hotel room at down, so drunk he cannot walk normally (I, 373). Chapter 1 contrasts Demetrio the legend with the real man, beset by vanity, excessive drink and lust. Still he remains above the conduct of his men, who spend the night galloping through the town, firing their pistols wildly (I, 373). Similarly, in Chapter 2, he lies half asleep while his underlings ransack the former home of a leading citizen, in search of booty (I, 374). Demetrio is shown as more reserved and less greedy and destructive than his followers.

In Chapter 4 of Part II, for the first time, Demetrio's conduct is more imprudent than that of the others. Overcome by drunken lust for a beautiful girl whom Cervantes has brought to the banquet, Demetrio staggers after her. His eyes are red as coals, his lips dripping with saliva. He draws his pistol and tries to kill Pintada when she trips him to prevent his reaching the girl. Anastasio Montañés disarms him from behind, Demetrio begins flailing with his fists. He does not stop until he has knocked down several of the men (I, 379). Chapter 4 describes Demetrio in a moment of exceptional behavior. Though he will not again be presented as so undisciplined, his role as legendary folk hero is once and forever dispelled.

In Chapter 5, Part II, the narrator perhaps balances Demetrio's careless conduct, so recently described. In Moyahua, having broken into his enemy don Mónico's home, Demetrio displays an acute sense of justice. Ordering his men to loot or vandalize nothing in the house, he sets it on fire (I, 383). Remembering the arson committed on his own home by troops called in by don Mónico, Demetrio responds in kind but adjusts his revenge to the offense. He and Mónico are even, their lives spared but their homes burned to the ground.

In Chapter 4, Part III, the narrator shows that Demetrio's efficiency as a military leader has declined greatly. He has

granted rapid promotions to newly-arrived enemy deserters, while
some of his oldest comrades are still privates (I, 413). The
"humanization" of Demetrio is now complete. Militarily vulnerable because his troops' morale is so low, he seems doomed
to lose the imminent skirmish with the carrancistas.

Demetrio's actions, as presented by the narrator, seem
to follow a pattern of prudent and imprudent deeds. Immediately after a reckless act he is shown as just or compassionate.
The narrator does not trace Demetrio's unbroken moral decline
while away from home; rather the protagonist's character is revealed bit by bit, the good with the bad. Demetrio, politically a failure, is briefly returned to his wife and child in
Chapter 6, Part III. In that same chapter his failure as a
family man is intimated. He is, in his defeat, a more human
figure than the inaccessible mythlike individual of the early
chapters. The varied patterns of action contribute to Demetrio's over-all characterization.

The protagonist Demetrio Macías is first revealed surrounded
by symbols of his domestic life. His Indian traits of fearlessness, aloofness and silence contribute to the air of legend or
mystery which envelops him. Demetrio's gradual humanization,
through the disclosure of his human shortcomings, is stylistic
preparation for his decline and death as revealed in Part III.
Subject to rage, drunkeness, lust, vanity and cruelty, he is
de-mythified but not debased. Demetrio's conduct is in nearly
all cases superior to that of his disciples. Humanized by the
defeat and failure made apparent in Part III, he is reunited
with his wife, thereby restored briefly to the circumstances
of Chapter 1, Part I. Demetrio's death closely follows his
homecoming.

The Hero and Women: Camila

Camila is not Demetrio's reason for leaving home, nor is
it she who keeps him away. His prolonged absence is the result
of events beyond his control. Notwithstanding, Camila does
fulfill a specific need which Demetrio feels. Her death,
coinciding with the decline of his political fortunes and his
return homeward, is a symbolic prelude to his own death and
his acceptance of it. Camila first appears in Chapter 4, Part
I, "una moza muy amable" (I, 329) who brings Demetrio a drink.
The narrator reveals her physical unattractiveness and melodious
voice:

. . . la muchacha era de rostro muy vulgar, pero en su
voz había mucha dulzura (I, 329).

Demetrio, badly wounded, must stay for several weeks in the
village, in daily contact with the girl, who leaves a lasting
impression on his memory. Though he never intended to stay
there, fate has thrown him together with Camila.

Before bringing Demetrio and Camila together, the author
drives them far apart. She falls in love with Luis Cervantes;
her affection for him does not turn to hate until Part II,

where he takes her from the village by means of false promises
and delivers her to Demetrio. Despising Luis and seeking protection from the jealous Pintada, Camila turns to Demetrio.

Cervantes deceives Camila because Demetrio has offered
him a fine gold watch. Demetrio, who does not share the avarice of most of his comrades, prefers female companionship to
material wealth. In Chapter 6, Part II, Cervantes offers
Demetrio part of the valuable jewelry he has collected. Demetrio
replies:

> --Déjelo todo para usted. . . . ¡Si viera que no le
> tengo amor al dinero! . . . ¿Quiere que le diga la
> verdad? Pues yo, con que no me falte el trago y
> con traer una chamaquita que me cuadre, soy el hom-
> bre más feliz del mundo (I, 386).

An event of Chapter 5 is a structural prelude to the above
confession. Inside don Mónico's house, Demetrio has demanded
wine, then weapons and finally money. He is about to authorize
the pillaging of the house when the cacique steps out of a
closet. Don Mónico, placing himself at Demetrio's mercy, begs
his old adversary to consider his wife and children. Demetrio
remembers his last night at home:

> . . . con mano trémula, vuelve el revólver a la
> cintura.
>   Una silueta dolorida ha pasado por su memoria.
> Una mujer con su hijo en los brazos, atravesando
> por . . . la sierra. . . .
>   Una casa ardiendo . . . (I, 383).

Demetrio orders everyone outside, leaving the cacique's posses-
sions intact. Returning to the barracks, he instructs Cervantes
to burn the house to the ground (I, 384).

The incident, a stylistic prelude to Demetrio's sending
for Camila, also marks the structural apex of the novel. Geo-
metrically, it occurs somewhat past the halfway point, in the
twenty-sixth chapter of forty-two. Seen from the viewpoint of
plot, it actually fulfills what Demetrio set out to accomplish.
In Chapter 21, Part I, exactly halfway through the novel,
Demetrio has intervened personally to insure the defeat of
Victoriano Huerta, whose eclipse would (in Demetrio's mind)
guarantee an end to his persecution and clear the way for his
return to his wife, removing all obstacles but one: his sworn
enemy, don Mónico. And in Chapter 5, Part II, taking appropriate
revenge on the cacique, Demetrio has effectively accomplished
all that he originally intended to do. Demetrio's career is
already in decline, without motivation, before Camila comes to
him. In a sense, they never have a future together.

Chapter 10, Part II, is a prelude to Demetrio's separation
from Camila and return to his wife. With the brigade camped
nearby, Demetrio and Camila spend the night as guests at a farm.
This brief episode, the author's only presentation of Demetrio
and Camila in a man-wife relationship, is highly ironic. He

sleeps fitfully and gets up at dawn, despite Camila's warm and loving presence. Walking toward camp, his thoughts turn to home:

> Pensaba en su yunta: dos bueyes prietos, nuevec-
> itos, de dos años de trabajo apenas, en sus dos fanegas
> de labor bien abonadas. La fisonomía de su joven
> esposa se reprodujo fielmente en su memoria: aque-
> llas líneas dulces y de infinita mansedumbre para el
> marido, de indomables energías y altivez para el
> extraño . . . (I, 393).

The farm where he stayed has made him think of his own land; apparently his wife is an afterthought. Nonetheless, Demetrio is deeply homesick. When Anastasio tells him they are only three days away from Limón, Demetrio confesses that he would like to see his wife. His words cause jubilation for Pintada and tears for Camila. The narrator, offering no explanation, says that Demetrio does not go to Limón nor does he think about his wife again (I, 394). Demetrio's abandonment of his inten-tion serves a purpose outside the incident. Pintada's jealousy toward Camila, a pre-condition of the forthcoming murder, is sustained by Camila's return to the favor of Demetrio. The brief crisis of homesickness and its abrupt resolution move the action toward a climax of the two women's rivalry.

Camila's death produces in Demetrio a reaction of extreme depression which carries over into Part III. In Chapter 13, Part II, when el güero Margarito promises to find him a pretty girl as soon as they arrive in Lagos, Demetrio answers that he only feels like getting drunk (I, 399). At the end of the evening, when Margarito heads for the houses of prostitution, Demetrio leaves him and returns alone to his hotel (I, 401).

Demetrio's despondency continues in Part III, where he asks Valderrama to sing a sentimental song which brings tears to his eyes (I, 411). Reunited with his wife, he says nothing in greeting. When she asks him to stay, he only looks very somber. Trying to explain to her why he must continue fighting, despite the victory over Huerta, Demetrio takes a stone and hurls it down the canyon. Watching it carrom down, he says: "--Mira esa piedra cómo ya no se para . . . " (I, 416). Deme-trio's discouragement never shows bitterness or violence. The narrator suggests a stoic acceptance of the inevitable, the attitude of a man who no longer has the will to resist.

Of the moments Demetrio spends with women, none denotes lasting satisfaction. With his wife, at the beginning of the novel and at the end, he is always rushed, knowing that he must rejoin his troops for a battle. Likewise, his romantic interlude with Camila is clouded by the danger of Pintada's wrath. Demetrio has told Luis that all he wants from life is drink and "una chamaquita que me cuadre . . . " (I, 386); the narrator reveals that Demetrio enjoys very few happy moments.

Heroic Purpose and Political Insophistication

Adding tragedy to Demetrio's defeat, frustration and death is the fact that he never completely understands why he is fighting. The author presents two philosophies of the conflict, Demetrio's and Luis Cervantes', offering no synthesis of the opposing ideas, both of which are summarized in Chapter 13, Part I. Demetrio says:

> . . . "Usté ha de saber del chisme ése de México, donde mataron al señor Madero y a otro, a un tal Félix o Felipe Díaz, qué sé yo. . . . Bueno: pues el dicho don Mónico fue en persona a Zacatecas a traer escolta para que me agarraran. Que dizque yo era maderista y que me iba a levantar. Pero como no faltan amigos, hubo quien me lo avisara a tiempo, y cuando los federales vinieron a Limón, yo ya me había pelado. Después vino mi compadre Anastasio, que hizo una muerte, y luego Pancracio, la Codorniz y muchos amigos y conocidos. Después se nos han ido juntando más, y ya ve: hacemos la lucha como podemos (I, 347).

Cervantes counters:

> . . . Usted no comprende todavía su verdadera, su alta y nobilísima misión. Usted, hombre modesto y sin ambiciones, no quiere ver el importantísimo papel que le toca en esta revolución. Mentira que usted ande por aquí por don Mónico, el cacique; usted se ha levantado contra el caciquismo que asola toda la nación. Somos elementos de un gran movimiento social que tiene que concluir por el engrandecimiento de nuestra patria. Somos instrumentos del destino para la reivindicación de los sagrados derechos del pueblo. No peleamos por derrocar a un asesino miserable, sino contra la tiranía misma. Eso es lo que se llama luchar por principios, tener ideales. Por ellos luchan Villa, Natera, Carranza; por ellos estamos luchando nosotros (I, 348).

Demetrio, unable to decide if he should follow Luis' advice and ally himself with General Natera, asks Venancio to decide. Venancio, who has understood Cervantes' words no better than Demetrio, accedes because of his enthusiasm for what the young medic has said about "unos cuantos millones de pesos" (I, 348).

In Chapter 14, Part II, Demetrio arrives in Aguascalientes to cast his vote for provisional president. His conversation with Natera manifests his helplessness when confronted by political questions:

--¡Cierto como hay Dios, compañero; sigue la
bola! ¡Ahora Villa contra Carranza!--dijo Natera.
Y Demetrio, sin responderle, con los ojos muy
abiertos, pedía más explicaciones.
--Es decir--insistió Natera--, que la Conven-
ción desconoce a Carranza como Primer Jefe y va a
elegir un presidente provisional de la República.
. . . ¿Entiende, compañero?
Demetrio inclinó la cabeza en señal de asenti-
miento.
-- Qué dice de eso, compañero?--interrogó Natera.
Demetrio se alzó de hombros.
--Se trata, a lo que parece, de seguir peleando.
Bueno, pos a darle; ya sabe, mi general, que por mi
lado no hay portillo.
--Bien, ¿y de parte de quién se va a poner?
Demetrio, muy perplejo, se llevó las manos a
los cabellos y se rascó breves instantes.
--Mire, a mí no me haga preguntas, que no soy
escuelante. . . . La aguilita que traigo en el som-
brero usté me la dio. . . . Bueno, pos ya sabe que
no más me dice: "Demetrio, haces esto y esto . . .
¡y se acabó el cuento!" (I, 404, 405).

Demetrio's long silence indicates his bewilderment. He will
continue to fight for no particular cause, out of loyalty to
Natera and because to quit would seem to him the coward's way.
In Chapter 6, Part II, Luis Cervantes urges Demetrio to
share his booty and go with him to safety outside Mexico. When
Demetrio shakes his head "no," Cervantes asks:

. . . ¿No haría usted eso? . . . Pues ¿a qué nos que-
daríamos ya? . . . ¿Qué causa defenderíamos ahora?
--Eso es cosa que yo no puedo explicar, curro;
pero siento que no es cosa de hombres . . . (I, 386).

Possibly expressing his machismo and pride, Demetrio will fight
on without a cause.
In Chapter 1, Part III, a new idea occurs to Anastasio
Montañés:

. . . lo que yo no podré hacerme entrar en la cabeza--
observó Anastasio Montañés--es eso de que tengamos
que seguir peleando. . . . ¿Pos no acabamos ya con
la Federación?
Ni el general ni Venancio contestaron; pero
aquellas palabras siguieron golpeando en sus rudos
cerebros como un martillo sobre el yunque.
. . . Anastasio, inquieto y terco, fue con la
misma observación a otros grupos de soldados, que
reían de su candidez. Porque si uno trae un fusil
en las manos y las cartucheras llenas de tiros,
seguramente que es para pelear. ¿Contra quién?
¿En favor de quiénes? ¡Eso nunca le ha importado a
nadie! (I, 407).

Men less profound than Demetrio, who never ask themselves
transcendental questions, are never troubled like him by answers
they cannot give.
The narration, offering no synthesis of Demetrio's philosophy and Cervantes', reflects Demetrio's bewilderment. Originally believing that he must fight because of don Mónico's
false accusations, Demetrio follows Luis' advice without
understanding its intricacies nor its consequences.
The narration suggests Demetrio's confusion through very
sketchy presentation of political events, stated in so few
words that they are ambiguous. That Demetrio follows orders
blindly is underlined by the text of Chapter 14, Part II, which
does not state whether Natera wishes him to support Carranza
or Villa.
Only in Chapter 2, Part III, where Demetrio learns of
Pancho Villa's defeat, is there an indication that he is
beginning to see the consequences of his unenlightened course:

> --La verdad, sí, somos desertores--dijo otro--;
> nos le cortamos a mi general Villa de este lado de
> Celaya, después de la cuereada que nos dieron.
> --¿Derrotado el general Villa? . . . ¡Ja!, ¡ja!,
> ¡ja! . . .
> Los soldados rieron a carcajadas. Pero a Deme-
> trio se le contrajo la frente como si algo muy negro
> hubiera pasado por sus ojos (I, 409).

The reader is never told to what extent Demetrio reconstructs
the implications of his past decisions, during the last days
of his life. A part of the protagonist's tragedy lies in his
incomplete awareness of the mistakes which lead to his doom.

Secondary Actions

Some chapters do not specifically move the principal
action along, neither propelling Demetrio further from home
nor bringing him closer again. Such sections, which might
be considered interpolations or interludes, help develop a
secondary action. Examples are Chapter 18 and 21, Part I,
where Alberto Solís expounds his theories about the Revolution, and the cuadro de costumbres of Chapter 9, in which the
village comadres attempt a folk cure of Demetrio's wound.
Chapter 13 contains the exposition of Luis' and Demetrio's
philosophies; Chapter 19 includes a vignette illustrating
the wasteful pillage committed by Demetrio's troops; and
Chapter 20 examines Pancho Villa as a living legend. Such
interludes expand the plot and create dramatic complications.
The interpolations of part II have a more specific function, almost that of a subplot, since they describe irresponsible acts committed by individuals, especially by el güero
Margarito. An example is the comic interlude of Chapter 3,
the raucous banquet scene where Margarito shoots his own reflection in a mirror and Pintada rides a horse into the dining
room. Chapters 9, 11 and 13 contain other excesses committed

by Margarito. Chapter 2 describes the pillage of a wealthy
citizen's home; in Chapter 4, Luis Cervantes recalls Demetrio's
unbridled behavior after the banquet in his honor.

All the units of Part III are directly pertinent to the
principal action except Chapter 3, which contains an impromptu
gathering held to celebrate the discovery of a barrel of tequila.
There is a cockfight and a melancholy song by Valderrama.
Though the episode contributes to the mood of depression so
powerfully evident in Part III, it does not move Demetrio
closer to home or make more imminent the showdown with the
carrancistas.

Though most of Los de abajo describes Demetrio's public
career, he is at the beginning and at the end revealed in the
presence of his family. It is therefore ironic that he dies
a public man, killed in battle by his political enemies.
Early in the novel, Demetrio seems more legend than man. The
federales shrink before him and pronounce his name with awe.
He speaks little and shows no emotion. Throughout the novel,
the author humanizes Demetrio, displaying both his weaknesses
and his virtues, demythicizing him in preparation for his
death.

Fate, in the form of a bullet wound in his leg, places
Demetrio in Camila's village for a long convalescence. The
relationship between them overcomes one obstacle: Camila's
initial infatuation with Cervantes, who has no interest in
her and tricks her into joining Demetrio. Their love does not
survive the second obstacle: the insanely jealous Pintada,
who wants Demetrio for herself and murders Camila when Demetrio
orders her away. Camila's death, marking a decline in Demetrio's
personal fortunes, coincides with his political decline.
Demetrio, when he forms an alliance with General Natera, becomes
an unwilling villista. Shortly after Camila's death, he learns
that Villa has rebelled against Carranza. Villa's defeat,
revealed in Part III, means that the carrancistas will hunt
down and liquidate rebel bands like Demetrio's. His defeat
at their hands is doubly tragic because he has only begun to
understand more than the local aspects of the Revolution. He
does not know in detail why Carranza's supporters have attacked
him.

The novel's plot, Demetrio's journey away from home and
back again, is enhanced by the secondary actions which are
present in all three parts. Some are doctrinal, like Demetrio's
political discussion with Luis Cervantes. Other episodes express ideology, directly in the words of Alberto Solís or indirectly in descriptions of the revolutionaries' excessive acts.
Several cuadros costumbristas fix the action in Mexico, specifically during the Revolution. One episode, Chapter 3 of Part
II, has little value outside its rich humor.

Narrative Organization

Chapter

The forty-two chapters of Los de abajo vary in length
from brief to very brief. Most contain one or two incidents
complete within the chapter. Only a few chapters share a
prolonged incident with one or two others: Chapters 12 and
13 of Part I, which divide a philosophical discussion between
Luis and Demetrio; Chapters 15 and 17, Part I, containing the
massacre of the huertista garrison; and Chapters 3 and 4, Part
II, which describe Demetrio's promotion banquet.

The amount of time represented as transpiring within any
chapter is usually a few hours but ranges from approximately
fifteen minutes to two weeks. The chapters containing the
highest proportion of dialog are quite logically those which
account for nearly every second of the few minutes which
transpire. An example is Chapter 8, Part I, which presents
in great detail a conversation between Camila and Luis.

The chapters can be classified either as episodes,
essential to the principal action, or as interludes of secondary action which orient the reader by providing background
information, and which help to fix the action in time and
place. An example of an episode would be Chapter 12, Part II,
which describes Pintada's murder of Camila. There are several
kinds of interludes: Chapter 2, Part II, which orients the
reader ideologically; Chapter 9, Part I, which orients him
in space; Chapter 20, Part I, which orients him in time; and
Chapter 3, Part II, which contributes humor.

The variable most carefully controlled by the author is
the number of characters who participate in the action of a
chapter. Usually more than two, they vary from one (Luis Cervantes, whose private thoughts are the subject of Chapter 6,
Part I), to twelve (some identified and some not, who take part
in the conversations of Chapter 1, Part II).

In almost every case, episodes of great importance are the
ones in which the least characters appear. Only four figures
intervene in Chapter 1, Part I, where Demetrio is separated
from his wife and his home is burned. Only Cervantes and
Camila participate in Chapters 8 and 11, Part I, which contain crucial conversations between them. In Chapter 6, Part
I, where Luis Cervantes' motives are exposed, only he appears.
Chapter 21, Part I, contains Alberto Solís' thoughts about the
Revolution, told just to Luis. Only Demetrio and Luis participate in Chapter 6, Part II, where Luis promises to bring back
Camila. In the emotionally powerful Chapter 6, Part III,
Demetrio's reunion with his wife, no character except the
immediate family appears. The norm of few characters in the
most significant chapters seems altered in Chapter 12, Part II.
When Pintada murders Camila, in the novel's most tension-
packed episode, there are many witnesses. The circumstances
leading to that murder involve a host of characters. The troops
are ready to leave for Tepatitlán when Camila says she will

not go, for fear of Pintada, and Demetrio sends the woman away. The crowd exacerbates Pintada's fury, laughing gleefully when Margarito refuses to stand by her. Throughout Part II, every chapter except Chapter 6 involves several characters; most involve a large number.

Essentially, the chapter in <u>Los de abajo</u> is not an arbitrary division or mere convenience. Most contain one or two complete actions, transpiring within a day or less and involving a relatively small number of characters. Most chapters are necessary to the plot; only a few are scenic vignettes which do not move the action forward. Some sections of <u>Los de abajo</u> must be considered fragmented because they do not always follow each other in sequence. At times there seem to be unfilled narrative gaps. Luis Leal has explained the illusion of fragmentation in the novel:

> La estructura, . . . más que lógica, es orgánica.
> . . . el novelista ha logrado elevar el tema a un
> plano estético en donde, bajo ese desorden aparente,
> encontramos un orden interno, orgánico, en donde no
> hay escenas o episodios que no tengan una función
> dentro del relato y no nos ayuden a interpretar la
> obra. . . . la estructura de <u>Los de abajo</u> es novedosa
> en la novela hispanoamericana; . . . es el primer
> intento en la creación de una novela estructurada para
> que refleje el mundo que la produce, sin usar figuras
> ajenas al ambiente y los personajes. . . . [1]

The chapter is a functional unit in the structure of the novel.

Part

The division of the novel into parts seems to have a definite purpose. Specific elements of the principal action are developed and climaxed in each part.

Part I reveals the personalities and private problems of Demetrio, Luis and Camilia. During the long pause in the tiny village, a period of rest nearly uninterrupted by the events of the Revolution, the principal characters meet in small groups and speak frankly about themselves. Seldom are there large numbers of characters present at the same time. The last chapters of Part I form a transition from the calm village life to the more rapid tempo and frequent changes of place which characterize Part II. Part I ends climactically with the peaceful but sudden death of Alberto Solís.

Several elements of the plot remain unresolved and, through further development in Part II, form structural links between the two parts. Of most immediate interest is Demetrio's application of Luis Cervantes' theories of personal gain through revolution. Also, Camila has been left behind, her relationship with Luis terminated at his insistence; but he has insinuated that Demetrio can in time win her affection. A long-range problem is Demetrio's absence from home, which links Parts I and III.

As Part I examines the characters' personal lives, Part II develops them in public. What the characters do is nearly always before an audience. External political events, from which the characters were largely isolated in Part I, begin to affect their lives. The fortunes of war move them about Central Mexico, through cities which played a historical role in the Revolution.

The plot elements left unresolved at the close of Part I are concluded in Part II. Demetrio's men take advantage of the opportunity to plunder, with his tacit approval, the obvious result of his conversation with Luis Cervantes. Also, Camila is brought to Demetrio by Luis, who fulfills the promise he inferred in Part I. She becomes Demetrio's lover until separated from him by murder.

Camila's death, the stylistic climax of Part II, is followed by two chapters which form a bridge to Part III. Chapter 13 establishes Demetrio's extreme depression, which his comprades will share in the following part; Chapter 14 summarizes the vastly-changed political spectrum, which will gravely affect Demetrio's fortunes. One plot element remains to be resolved: Demetrio's return home, anticipated by his moment of nostalgia in Chapter 10, Part II.

The brief Part III fulfills three functions: references to the momentous political events of the day, essential to an understanding of the final action; description of the effect those events have on the morale of Demetrio's troops; and resolution of his absence from home, the last remaining plot element.

Part III begins with the only summary found in the novel, concluding all story lines except Demetrio's odyssey. In the form of a letter from Luis Cervantes, it terminates Luis' role in the plot. He is out of the country and Camila is dead; of the major characters only Demetrio remains. His end is revealed in the last paragraph of the last chapter. There is no epilog, just as there was no prolog to Chapter 1, Part I.

In summary, Part I deals with Demetrio's private life and sets the framework for his public career, the apex of which is developed in Part II. Part III treats the consequences of his public decline, giving only the minimum details of that decline, and traces the final steps of Demetrio's journey back to his wife. In this way, the three parts reveal a cyclical pattern. Demetrio's story begins at home, in Chapter 1, Part I, and ends there in Chapters 6 and 7, Part III. He is farthest from home in Part II.

The three parts coincide with Demetrio's three distinct ideological postures. In Part I he is an independent rebel who participates in the insurrection for personal reasons. The historical background is Huerta's last days, culminating in his defeat at Zacatecas, which is described in Chapter 21. In Part II, Demetrio is a _villista_ by accident, having allied himself with Natera, Villa's subordinate. Demetrio's men reap the fruits of the triumphant Revolution. The final paragraphs of Chapter 14, Part II, reveal Villa's repudiation of Carranza. In Part III, Demetrio is no longer a revolutionary but a guerrila outlaw, pursued not by _federales_ but by _carrancistas_.

The historical framework is Villa's defeat at Celaya and Carranza's reunification of Mexico. The tripartite structure of Los de abajo is organized so as to parallel the three historical phases of the Revolution.

Distribution of Incidents

Action is Los de abajo is gradually accelerated by means of the narrative arrangement. The chapters, organized in the aforementioned groups of 21, 14 and 7, are distributed in the declining ratio of 3:2:1. Since the three parts divide Demetrio's career into three approximately equal stages, they relate similar patterns of action in increasingly concentrated presentations.

Part I begins quite rapidly, slows to a halt, and closes at a quick pace. In Chapters 1-4 Demetrio's house is burned, he and his men defeat the huertistas, he is wounded, and they all arrive at Camila's village. Their stay is described in Chapters 5-15, where the pace of action slows markedly. The only physical action is Luis' appearance. The other events described are psychological: Camila's unrequited love for Luis and his persuasion of Demetrio. The last part of Chapter 15, plus 16-17, are high in action and intensely condensed, narrating Demetrio's massacre of the garrison. Chapter 18 contains the arrival in Fresnillo and the alliance with Natera. The rhythm slows again in Chapters 19 and 20, the content of which is mostly psychological. Chapter 19, the aftermath of the rebels' initial defeat at Zacatecas, is a study of plunder which closes with an allusion to Camila. Chapter 20 is an exposition of the legends surrounding Pancho Villa. Chapter 21, the aftermath of the insurgents' victory at Zacatecas, reflects after the fact upon Demetrio's heroism there. Alberto Solís, who tells what he saw Demetrio do, then pauses to philosophize about the Revolution. The action, once again lagging, closes with a sudden cleavage of time: Solís' accidental death.

In Part II, interpolated episodes of pillage and vice, which do little to move the plot along, increase dramatic tension. Episodes illustrating abuses on the part of the revolutionaries are found in Chapters 2, 3, and 4. Chapter 1 introduces Pintada, whose murder of Camila will be the climax of Part II and turning point of the novel. Chapter 5, describing Demetrio's revenge against don Mónico, marks the moment when his original motive for fighting ceases to exist. It begins Demetrio's fatal decline. Chapter 6, philosophical in content, is a rationalization of the continuing struggle. Chapters 7 and 8 contain Camila's arrival and decision to stay. Chapters 9, 10, 11, and 12 heighten the conflict between Camila and Pintada and resolve it in a sea of blood. Chapters 13 and 14 are a bridge between Parts II and III.

As much occurs in Part II as in the longer Part I. The bond between Camila and Demetrio, begun in Part I, is solidified and then severed. Demetrio fulfills his reason for joining the rebellion when he burns don Mónico's house. Luis too accomplishes what he wished, amassing a hoard sufficient to pay his way to safety in Texas. Of the problems planted in Part I, only one remains to be resolved in Part III: Demetrio's separation from his wife. The fourteen chapters of Part II are tension-packed in comparison to the twenty-one chapters of Part I.

The action of Part III is accelerated still further. Chapter 1 is a pause for tying up loose ends of action lines from Part II. Luis Cervantes has fled, el güero Margarito has killed himself, and Pancracio and Manteca have killed each other. The focus of Chapter 2 is political, describing Pancho Villa's defeat. That event, though it took place outside the sphere of the novel, is decisive. Chapter 2 of Part III, crucial to the resolution of Demetrio's fate, contains more dramatic tension than is immediately apparent.

Chapters 3-5 recount Demetrio's journey homeward, a progression toward his tragic end. The three chapters, each a pause in that homeward journey, contain little action in themselves but constitute together a flow toward the climax of action. Chapter 6 contains Demetrio's fleeting reunion with his wife; Chapter 7 relates his death in battle.

Action approaches its peak in Chapter 6, with the allegorical thunderstorm and the carroming stone which Demetrio hurls down the side of the canyon. He must tear himself quickly away from his wife and ride out to battle.

In Chapter 7 tension builds to the breaking point as Demetrio's last battle begins. The enemy gunfire starts up almost without warning; Demetrio's old comrades are quickly killed and he is left alone in a noisy inferno of bullets. The action and the noise subside instantly, heightening the stunning effect which this final chapter has upon the reader. No movement remains except for a herd of grazing cows; there is no sound save that of rasping locusts and softly-cooing doves. The novel opens with the sound of a barking dog and builds to a deafening fury, only to end more quietly than it began. Throughout the novel, action and noise go together in crescendo. The noisiest chapters are 6 and 7 of Part III. The din subsides as Demetrio's end is revealed.[2]

A noteworthy feature of the novel's patterned action is that each part climaxes in a violent death. Alberto Solís, first presented in Chapter 18, Part I, dies at the end of Chapter 21. Camila, present as Luis' unreciprocated lover in Part I, returns as Demetrio's mistress in Chapter 7, Part II, only to be removed by murder in Chapter 12. Demetrio himself, the only character present in nearly every chapter, is revealed in death in the last sentence of the novel. Each death marks the close of a phase of the Revolution and introduces in the novel a mood different from that of the preceding section.

The novel's pace of events is established in Part I, where Demetrio Macías is an independent rebel in the Revolution for personal reasons. More space is devoted to his private life than to his public career. Part II develops Demetrio's public career and Part III traces his incomplete transition back to private life. Independent again as in Part I, he is pursued not by the federales but by the carrancistas, who kill him in battle.

The pace of action is quite slow in Part I, where many incidents take place in the quiet village. Events move faster in Part II and reach their most furious pace in Part III, where brief chapters and abrupt changes in location propel Demetrio closer to home and to his death. The organization of the action of Los de abajo reveals historical continuity within a framework of gradual dramatic intensification.

Narrative Description

The principal narrator of Los de abajo, undramatized, interprets the milieu with esthetic deformation, sometimes lyric and often naturalistic. Fictional and historical events are interwoven to orient the reader in time. Some characters are distorted, revealing only some grotesque quality, while others are sustained in semi-anonymity behind never-disclosed facial details. Nature is viewed as grandiose and man and his works as insignificant in comparison, although at times Nature is used to stimulate or reflect the characters' moods. The undramatized narrator is complemented by four dramatized counterparts and by extensive passages of dialog where a character's revelation replaces narrative exposition.

Settings in Place

The events of Los de abajo usually occur in identifiable places, some indoor and some outdoor. Action may take place in a humble peasant's hut, a corral or courtyard, a quiosco or cantina. Outdoor sites range from small clearings to the open spaces of the sierra or the plains. There are more outdoor locations than indoor, more rural than urban.

The narrator describes some settings in detail. He frequently presents outdoor locations lyrically through metaphors or similes. For example, in Chapter 2, Part I, images denoting the great size and awesomeness of the features of a plateau are preceded and followed by evocations of grandeur and delicacy:

> . . . el sol bañaba la altiplanicie en un lago de oro. Hacia la barranca se veían rocas enormes rebanadas; prominencias erizadas como fantásticas cabezas africanas; los pitahayos como dedos anquilosados de coloso; árboles tendidos hacia el fondo del abismo. Y en la aridez de las peñas y de las ramas secas, albeaban las frescas rosas de San Juan como una blanca ofrenda al astro que comenzaba a deslizar sus hilos de oro de roca en roca (I, 323).

In Chapter 5, Part II, the mountainous landscape is personified, its vastness suggested indirectly through a series of similes:

Vanse destacando las cordilleras como monstruos alagartados, de angulosa vertebradura; cerros que parecen testas de colosales ídolos aztecas, caras de gigantes, muecas pavorosas y grotescas, que ora hacen sonreír, ora dejan un vago terror, algo como presentimiento de misterio (I, 381).

In Chapter 21, Part I, a hillside spendid in itself is made hideous by man's imprint upon it:

De lo alto del cerro se veía un costado de la Bufa, con su crestón, como testa empenachada de altivo rey azteca. La vertiente . . . estaba cubierta de muertos, con los cabellos enmarañados, manchadas las ropas de tierra y de sangre, y en aquel hacinamiento de cadáveres calientes, mujeres haraposas iban y venían como famélicos coyotes esculcando y despojando (I, 368).

A particularly unattractive setting is the interior of Demetrio's headquarters in Moyahua, described in Chapter 6, Part II. There the novelist creates a reaction of distaste through the liberal use of evocative nouns and adjectives:

Sus predecesores en aquella finca habían dejado ya su rastro vigoroso en el patio, convertido en estercolero; en los muros, desconchados hasta mostrar grandes manchones de adobe crudo; en los pisos, demolidos por las pesuñas de las bestias; en el huerto, hecho un reguero de hojas marchitas y ramajes secos. Se tropezaba, desde el entrar, con pies de muebles, fondos y respaldos de sillas, todo sucio de tierra y bazofia (I, 384).

Ironically, the most beautiful setting of the novel is that of Demetrio's death, described in Chapter 7, Part III. The narrator creates images of spendid beauty through a dual device. The loveliness of a wedding day, suggested directly and strengthened by an insistence on the color white, works together with the wild horses, symbols of exuberant freedom:

Fue una verdadera mañana de nupcias. Había llovido la víspera toda la noche y el cielo amanecía entoldado de blancas nubes. Por la cima de la sierra trotaban potrillos brutos de crines alzadas y colas tensas, gallardos con la gallardía de los picachos que levantan su cabeza hasta pesar las nubes (I, 416).

La sierra está de gala; sobre sus cúspides inaccessibles cae la niebla albísima como un crespón de nieve sobre la cabeza de una novia (I, 418).

Just as time is accelerated in each suceeding part of the novel, the narrator speeds Demetrio and his men's journey ever faster. In Chapter 1, Part I, Demetrio leaves his home

and travels all night. In Chapter 2 he gathers his men in a
clearing on the plateau. Chapter 3 describes their battle
with the federales, which takes place on a canyon wall. In
Chapter 4 they travel through the sierra to Camila's village,
where they remain until Chapter 15. Chapters 16 and 17 take
place in and near the garrison which they storm. Chapters 18
and 20 occur in Fresnillo; Chapter 21, on a hill overlooking
Zacatecas; and Chapter 19, on the highway between those two
cities. The twenty-one chapters of Part I are located in just
nine places, counting Demetrio's hut, where the action opens.

The characters move from place to place much more in
Part II than in Part I. Only Chapters 2, 3, and 4 take place
in the same site, and some chapters are split between two locations. The first half of Chapter 14, for example, transpires in a moving railroad car, and the second half, in Aguascalientes. The action of Part II's fourteen chapters takes
place in sixteen different locations.

In Part III the characters are constantly in motion. The
seven brief chapters take place in seven different sites. Even
when Demetrio returns home there is no permanence of place;
his wife meets him along a path. When a sudden storm arises,
they must take refuge in a small cave. Since Part III has no
interior scenes, the characters never seem fixed anywhere
for more than a brief period.

Interior settings in Los de abajo are not specifically
Mexican; the Mexican-ness of the incidents is usually established
by costumes and dialog. Outdoor scenes are detailed, but many
are described through images and not as they naturally appear.
Many of the most realistic descriptions reveal the ugliness
caused by man. The characters, who stay in Camila's village
during eleven chapters of Part I, move about much more in
Parts II and III. The narrator shifts his characters so rapidly from place to place that he creates an illusion of onrushing
events.

Settings and Dramatic Tension

Most chapters of Los de abajo contain one or more actions
which take place in one or more settings. In nearly all cases,
each incident in a chapter takes place in a distinct setting.

The sensation of dramatic tension of crucial episodes is
enhanced by the confined setting in which they take place.
The intrusion of the arrogant federales, in Chapter 1, Part I,
occurs in the highly-limited area of Demetrio's hut. The
small area in which the characters may move contributes to an
impression that Demetrio's wife is a virtual prisoner of her
unwelcome guests. Other high-tension incidents occur in rather
closed surroundings: the battle in a canyon (Chapter 3, Part
I); Luis Cervantes' trial in the hut where Demetrio lies wounded
(Chapter 7, Part I); and the confrontation with don Mónico in
the cacique's own house (Chapter 5, Part II). An exception to
that norm is the murder of Camila, which takes place at an unspecified outdoor site.

There is a pattern of spatial contraction within chapters
which contain more than one setting. The earlier incident

occurs in the less confining place, and the later event, in
the more restricted setting. An example is Chapter 14, Part
I, which begins with Demetrio and his comrades' evaluation of
the doctrine preached by Luis Cervantes. They are at an unspecified outdoor place, in or near the village. The second
episode, Luis' farewell to Camila, takes place in the relatively more confined setting of a river bank. It is the more
crucial of the two incidents which is more restricted in space.
A parallel example is found in Chapter 12, Part II, where the
final clash between Camila and Pintada takes place on the trail
but the murder occurs at an unspecified outdoor location in the
town of Cuquío. The narrator's insistence upon an actual town
confines the murder more than would a nameless urban place.
Similarly, in Chapter 6, Part III, Demetrio meets his wife
along a mountain path and then seeks shelter with her in a
small cavern, where they wait out a storm and he reveals that
he must leave her again. Demetrio, symbolic prisoner of
political events, is held in by sheer rock and by the downpour.
The most elaborate example of increasing spatial tension is
found in Chapter 16, Part I. There Demetrio and his men,
camped at an unspecified outdoor place, enter the town and procure a guide to take them through the streets. They arrive
at the plaza opposite the fortified church, where they are
ambushed by the federales. Regrouping, they take refuge in
a narrow alley. As dramatic tension mounts, the protagonist
is confined more and more by his circumstances. The chapter
closes ironically, with the comic soliloquy of the enemy cap-
tain, who is in the most restricted setting of the five: the
garrison itself. In this case, spatial tension is increased
as dramatic tension is relaxed.

Tension in Los de abajo is increased through several de-
vices. Three approximately equal segments of Demetrio's life
are examined in three parts of the novel, each much shorter
than the one before. The characters are moved from place to
place at a constantly accelerating rate. Finally, as has been
demonstrated in this section, spatial confinement frequently
coincides with episodes of high dramatic potential.

Chronology

The narrator's periodic allusions to historical events
establish a relative chronology between them and the fictitious
incidents described in the novel. Using real occurrences as
points of reference, the reader may estimate how much chronological time has elapsed in the lives of the characters.

The subtitle of Los de abajo, "Cuadros y escenas de la
Revolución mexicana," orients the reader so that he knows approximately during what period of history the action takes
place. In Chapter 8, Part I, Victoriano Huerta is mentioned
for the first time. His relatives and hangers-on are reported
leaving the country (I, 337). That reference fixes the action
in 1914, near the end of Huerta's rule. In Chapter 12, travel-
ers stopping at the village report that Huerta is making his
last stand at Zacatecas (I, 345). In Chapter 21, Alberto Solís

relates Demetrio's heroics there (I, 367, 368). Only that
one time does the narrator mention a character at the center
of an historical event. The incidents of Part I, beginning
at an unspecific time late in 1913 or early in 1914, coincide
with Huerta's last months.

No historical events are again mentioned until the last
pages of Part II. In Chapter 12, Demetrio receives orders to
leave his troops behind and proceed to Aguascalientes (I, 397).
In the following chapter he asks Luis Cervantes what he is to
do there. Cervantes answers that he must cast his vote for
provisional president (I, 400). That reference fixes the
action at the same time as the Aguascalientes Convention of
1915. The action of Part II takes place between the fall of
Zacatecas and the Convention.

The last reference to an historical circumstance is in
Chapter 2, Part III, where villista deserters tell Demetrio
of Pancho Villa's defeat at Celaya (I, 409). That would be
in the spring of 1915. Approximately two months elapse between
the receipt of that news and Demetrio's death in the carrancista
ambush. In Chapter 5, the narrator mentions that the insurgents
arrive in Juchipila on the Feast of the Sacred Heart of Jesus,
one year after their victory at Zacatecas (I, 414). That would
be in June, 1915. Demetrio's death occurs shortly thereafter.

The amount of time which is to have transpired during the
events related in the novel is not quite two years. The narrator states, in the next-to-last chapter, that Demetrio has
been gone that long (I, 415). Periodic reference to historical
occurrences contributes to the illusion that that much time
goes by in the course of the novel's fictional events.

Characters

The narrator, rather than giving complete descriptions of
the characters, frequently concentrates on one or two unattractive facial features which he magnifies. The description of
human beauty is quite detailed but so rare that it occurs only
twice. In Chapter 11, Part I, Luis Cervantes is revealed as
Camila might see him:

> . . . Camila contempló con embeleso el fresco y radioso
> rostro de Luis Cervantes, aquellos ojos glaucos de
> tierna expresión, sus carrillos frescos y rosados
> como los de un muñeco de porcelana, la tersura de una
> piel blanca y delicada que asomaba abajo del cuello y
> más arriba de las mangas de una tosca camiseta de
> lana, el rubio tierno de sus cabellos, rizados ligera-
> mente (I, 344).

The description of Cervantes' eyes, the allusion to a porcelain
doll and such words as "delicada" and "tierno" lend humor to
the paragraph. The narrator records Cervantes' features in
detail and with comment. The humor is double; not only is Luis
imperfectly handsome, but Camila is blind to his defects.

Only once does the narrator call a character beautiful;
he uses the word "belleza" to describe the girl whom Luis

brings to Demetrio's banquet:

> --Le presento, mi general Macías, a mi futura--
> pronunció enfático Luis Cervantes, haciendo entrar
> al comedor a una muchacha de rara belezza.
> . . . .
> Tendría apenas catorce años; su piel era fresca
> y suave como un pétalo de rosa; sus cabellos rubios,
> y la expresión de sus ojos con algo de maligna
> curiosidad y mucho de vago temor infantil (I, 376).

After assuring the reader that the girl is lovely, the narrator
concentrates on her youth and innocence.

The narrator conceals the facial features of a number of
characters, such as Demetrio, his wife, and Venancio. Those
whom the narrator does reveal frequently have some deformity
or unusual feature which is presented to the exclusion of nearly all others. Anastasio Montañés, for example, appears
frequently in the novel; but his general appearance is not
mentioned except in Chapter 2, Part I, where is is "uno de
barba y cejas espesas y muy negras, de mirada dulzona; hombre
macizo y robusto" (I, 324). Thereafter the narrator narrows
his reference to Anastasio's features: "Sólo Anastasio Montañés
conservaba la expresión dulzona de sus ojos adormilados y su
rostro barbudo, . . ." (I, 327). When mentioning him for
the third time, the narrator de-emphasizes his bearded face:
" . . . en su semblante persiste su mirada dulzona, . . . "
(I, 359). Because many men might have a dark beard and eyebrows, it is Anastasio's sleepy-eyed look that sets him apart
from others. The narrator increasingly concentrates on that
detail.

Pancracio and el Manteca, frequently presented together,
are a study in contrasting physical and moral inferiority.
When first revealed in Chapter 3, Part I, both are screaming
at the federales, who have begun firing on them from the flank:

> . . . Gritaba Pancracio, alargando su cara lampiña,
> inmutable como piedra, y gritaba el Manteca, contray-
> endo las cuerdas de su cuello y estirando las líneas
> de su rostro de ojos torvos de asesino (I, 327).

In Chapter 12, Part I, the two men become angry at each other
because of a card game:

> . . . Pancracio enfrentaba su rostro de piedra ante
> el del Manteca, que lo veía con ojos de culebra,
> convulso como un epiléptico (I, 345).

The narrator, streamlining his characterizations, has formed
one-word associations. Pancracio is like a "rock," and Manteca, like a "snake." Rage is shown at its two extremes,
boiling inside one man and erupting throughout the other's
body.

The most detailed description of the two comrades occurs
in Chapter 6, Part I, where Luis Cervantes watches them as
they sleep:

> Contempló a sus centinelas tirados en el
> estiércol y roncando. En su imaginación revivieron
> las fisonomías de los dos hombres de la víspera.
> Uno, Pancracio, agüerado, pecoso, su cara lampiña,
> su barba saltona, la frente roma y oblicua, untadas
> las orejas al cráneo y todo de un aspecto bestial.
> Y el otro, el Manteca, una piltrafa humana: ojos
> escondidos, mirada torva, cabellos muy lacios
> cayéndole a la nuca, sobre la frente y las orejas;
> sus labios de escrofuloso entreabiertos eternamente
> (I, 334).

The narrator, seeing the men as Luis might see them, points
out the most repulsive feature of each man: Pancracio's
resemblance to a prehistoric man and Manteca's scab-covered
lips, a possible symptom of syphilis.

The narrator, seeing Camila as Cervantes might see her,
possibly suggests racial prejudice:

> Luis Cervantes plegó las cejas y miró con
> aire hostil aquella especie de mono enchomitado,
> de tez broncínea, dientes de marfil, pies anchos
> y chatos (I, 337).

The epithet "monkey" is unsubstantiated by the rest of the
description, which categorizes Camila as a rather typical
Indian. The paragraph, containing only a general description
of Camila, reveals a very specific bias on the part of
Cervantes.

Concentration on the grotesqueness of certain characters
is infrequent after Part I. In Part II it is extended to
nameless figures who appear very briefly:

> Ocho músicos "de viento," las caras rojas y redondas
> como soles, desorbitados los ojos, . . . (I, 388).

The musicians' physical state is not inherent but the result
of long hours during which they have played without rest.
Their red faces and bulging eyes are temporary features.

In Part III, the narrator displays a preoccupation with
scars. He describes a revolutionary veteran with a copper-
colored face and a scar which runs from his forehead to his
chin (I, 409). The proprietress of an open-air restaurant in
Juchipila is " . . . una viejota insolente, con una enorme
cicatriz en la cara, . . . " (I, 415). The scars may symbolize the ravages of war, referred to several times in Part III.

The narrator summarizes the appearance of several characters by referring to just one feature, usually one which
detracts. At times the ugliness symbolizes moral inferiority,
but it may reflect the prejudice with which one character sees
another.

The characters, when their grotesqueness is not magnified,
are frequently made faceless, identifiable by some attribute
other than detailed physical appearance. The narrator de-
personalizes them, at times to the point of dehumanization.

Demetrio, in Chapter 1, Part I, is described in the
following words:

> . . . Alto, robusto, de faz bermeja, sin pelo de
> barba, vestía camisa y calzón de manta, ancho
> sombrero de soyate y guaraches (I, 320).

The narrator, detailing Demetrio's clothing more than his
face, reveals only that he belongs in two categories: he
is Mexican and a peasant. Later in the same chapter, Demetrio
is not only faceless but nearly formless, "una silueta blanca"
(I, 322). As was pointed out earlier in this study, the narrator intends that the "white silhouette" contribute to Demetrio's mysteriousness. The technique is not simply de-
personalization but mythification through abstraction. In
Chapter 2, Part I, is found the supreme de-individualization
of Demetrio. There, deftly scaling a canyon wall, he is
"como hormiga arriera" (I, 323). Comparing Demetrio to a tiny
insect, the narrator makes him seem not only unspecific but
insignificant.

Camila, when first introduced in Chapter 4, Part I, is
presented very impersonally. The narrator uses an auditory
phenomenon to describe her, de-emphasizing any visual image:

> ₒ . . la muchacha era de rostro muy vulgar, pero en
> su voz había mucha dulzura (I, 329).

It is Camila's voice, not her face, which sets her apart.

In the following chapter, Luis Cervantes, presented for
the first time, is so submerged that only his clothing is
recorded:

> Panacracio conducía a un mozalbete cubierto
> de polvo, desde el fieltro americano hasta los
> toscos zapatones . . . (I, 330).

Demetrio's men, when first introduced, are described as
if all were identical, emphasizing the group:

> . ₒ . salieron, unos tras otros, muchos hombres de
> pechos y piernas desnudas, oscuros y repulidos como
> viejos bronces (I, 324).

They are generalized and deprived of faces; only a few will
ever be detailed more. In Chapter 19 they are named "los
gorrudos" (I, 363) because of their wide-brimmed sombreros.
In Chapter 21, Part I, seen from a distance, they seem all
dressed alike, not at all individualized:

> Muchos federales fugitivos subían huyendo
> de soldados de grandes sombreros de palma y anchos
> calzones blancos (I, 369).

Their uniform is all that matters; one individual is presented
like another.

In Chapter 8, Part II, the revolutionaries remain identifiable only through their clothing:

> . . . Los sombreros galoneados de cóncavas y
> colosales faldas se encontraban en vaivén con-
> stante; caracoleaban las ancas de las bestias,
> que sin cesar removían sus finas cabezas de
> ojazos negros, narices palpitantes y orejas
> pequeñas. Y en la infernal alharaca de los borrachos
> se oía el resoplar de los caballos, . . . (I, 388).

Horses and even hats are detailed, while the men themselves
are reduced to "alharaca."
  In the following chapter, the first visual image is dust,
which gives way to detailed descriptions of horses and finally
to less-detailed presentations of the men:

> El torbellino del polvo, . . . rompíase brus-
> camente en masas difusas y violentas, y se destacaban
> pechos hinchados, crines revueltas, narices trémulas,
> ojos ovoides, impetuosos, patas abiertas y como enco-
> gidas al impulso de la carrera. Los hombres, de ros-
> tro de bronce y dientes de marfil, ojos flameantes,
> . . . (I, 389, 390).

Though both horses and men are standardized, the former are more
thoroughly described.
  The expositions quoted above seem based on actual observation, reflecting the instantaneous first impressions of a
theoretical onlooker. Each description seems a "blink of an
eye" impression. In Chapter 4, Part I, the narrator is like
an observer who has peered once into a dimly-lit hut:

> . . . se aglomeraron chomites incoloros, pechos
> huesudos, cabezas desgreñadas . . . (I, 329).

The narrator seems then to have glanced a second time:

> . . . y, detrás, ojos brillantes y carrillos frescos
> (I, 329).

Some nameless minor characters are de-personalized because the narrator employs a symbol to designate them. Insignias of their military rank stand for the two federales who
burst into Demetrio's hut in Chapter 1, Part I:

> Uno llevaba galones en los hombros, el otro
> cintas rojas en las mangas (I, 321).

Nowhere are the huertista intruders described further.
  In Chapter I, Part II, revolutionary officers are described
in symbols only. There is no mention of human beings, only
insignias, articles of clothing and parts of bodies:

. . . Menudearon las estrellas y las barras en
sombreros de todas formas y matices; grandes pañuelos
de seda al cuello, anillos de gruesos brillantes y
pesadas leopoldinas de oro (I, 372).

Demetrio and his men participate in three battles in
which anonymity plays a key role. A day or two after Demetrio's
house is burned, he and his followers ambush a battalion of
huertistas in a canyon. Killing more than five hundred of the
enemy, they inflict their slaughter from across the canyon,
with rifles. Their victims are so far off that they have
become faceless. The narrator describes the federales over
and over again, each time from a different perspective. First
there is "la primera silueta de un soldado" (I, 325), only a
colorless shape. When the sun rises, the silhouettes become
like lilliputians: "hombres diminutos en caballos de miniatura"
(I, 325). Next the narrator calls the enemy "figuritas moved-
izas" (I, 325), as if they were no longer tiny living beings
but puppets. Finally they are only like splotches of color
(" . . . ora negreaban . . . sobre el ocre de las peñas"
(I, 325)) or images sculpted on the canyon wall: "Los demás
. . . permanecían inmóviles, como bajorrelieves de las peñas"
(I, 325).
When Demetrio's men begin placing bets on their marksmanship, they talk as if they were not killing men but simply
knocking targets from the backs of horses:

       --Mi cinturón de cuero si no le pego en la cabeza
al del caballo prieto. . . .
       --Veinte tiros de máuser y media vara de chorizo
porque me dejes tumbar al de la potranca mora . . .
(I, 327).

The narrator reveals none of the gore of battle, so imperson-
nally does he present Demetrio's victims.
The massacre of the huertista garrison, in Chapter 17,
Part I, is also very dehumanized at first. The narrator
describes the enemy's movements after the rebels have thrown
two rounds of grenades:
Aquello no es más que una correría de ratas dentro de la
trampa (I, 359). Demetrio and his men are scarcely more than
light and shadow:

       . . . aquella veintena de espectros de cabeza y
pechos oscuros como de hierro, de largos calzones
blancos desgarrados, . . . (I, 359).

In this battle, the weapons are not rifles but knives. The
enemy, inches away, is described in detail:

> --¡No me mates, padrecito!--implora el viejo
> sargento a los pies de Demetrio, . . .
>   El viejo levanta su cara indígena llena de
> arrugas y sin una cana. . . .
>   . . . La lámina de acero tropieza con las
> costillas, que hacen crac, crac, y el viejo cae
> de espaldas con los brazos abiertos y los ojos
> espantados (I, 359).

The narrator has taken care to show Demetrio killing a human
being. The sound of his knife and the victim's reaction are
recorded.
    In Chapter 7, Part III, Demetrio and his men are ambushed
by an enemy whom the narrator does not reveal:

> Pero el enemigo, escondido a millaradas, desgrana
> sus ametralladoras, y los hombres de Demetrio caen
> como espigas cortadas por la hoz (I, 417).

Nowhere else in the novel does the narrator dehumanize men to
this extent, describing them botanically.
    When presented individually, human beings in Los de abajo
are many times characterized by their clothing, their voice or
some other immediately recognizable feature. The narrator reveals many subjects as if at first glance, "freezing" them just
as they would be seen if perceived only for an instant. The
technique is not that of the camera's eye view, for a camera
records everything within range. The narrator, in accord with
the impressionistic vision of later Modernism, has duplicated
the visual perception of the human brain, which, incapable of
recording at once all that the eye takes in at a glance, picks
out salient features.
    Such impressionistic imagery would be unconvincing in a
battle scene. There the narrator reveals the participants not
imperfectly perceived but miniaturized by distance or obscured
by dim light. The battle passage least de-personalized describes the hand-to-hand combat on the roof of the garrison.
There the enemy is revealed close up, in great detail. No
longer members of a group, the participants are treated separate-
ly.

Nature

    It might be said that Los de abajo is a novel of the
sierra. The narrative paragraphs describing the Mexican high
country capture its vastness and the frightening element of
its beauty:

> Vanse destacando las cordilleras como monstruos
> alagartados, de angulosa vertebradura; cerros que
> parecen testas de colosales ídolos aztecas, caras
> de gigantes, muecas pavorosas y grotescas, que ora
> hacen sonreír, ora dejan un vago terror, algo como
> presentimiento de misterio (I, 381).

The works of man are presented as insignificant in comparison:

> Cuando atardeció en llamaradas que tiñeron el
> cielo en vivísimos colores, pardearon unas casucas
> en una explanada, entre las montañas azules (I, 329).

The humble appearance of the "casucas" (with a suffix which augments their insignificance, far more than would the word jacal, which the narrator uses in many cases) comes not only from their size, compared to mountains, but to their nondescript brownish hue. The dwellings are the only colorless items in the panorama of sunset, sky, and blue mountains.

In Chapter 2, Part I, the macrocosm and microcosm of Nature are twice juxtaposed. A canyon is described as Demetrio descends its wall:

> . . . El angosto talud de una escarpa era vereda,
> entre el peñascal veteado de enormes resquebrajaduras
> y la vertiente de centenares de metros, cortada como
> de un solo tajo (I, 323).

Nature's grandeur does not eclipse her smaller phenomena. The narrator describes the canyon bottom where Demetrio lies sleeping:

> El río se arrastraba cantando en diminutas
> cascadas; los pajarillos piaban escondidos en los
> pitahayos, y las chicharras monorrítmicas llenaban
> de misterio la soledad de la montaña (I, 323).

Insisting on the small scale of the elements he describes, the narrator reinforces his images with the word "diminutas" and the suffix "-illos."

Demetrio ascends to a plateau, which the narrator reveals first through its hugeness and then fixes upon one small detail:

> . . . Hacia la barranca se veían rocas enormes rebanadas;
> prominencias erizadas como fantásticas cabezas africanas;
> los pitahayos como dedos anquilosados de coloso;
> árboles tendidos hacia el fondo del abismo. Y en
> la aridez de la peñas y de las ramas secas, albeaban
> las frescas rosas de San Juan . . . (I, 323).

Twice in Chapter 3, Part III, the narrator introduces a succession of man-made and natural items which progress from the smallest and closest at hand to the largest and most distant. The first time it is Valderrama who gazes at the items, one by one, as he prepares to sing:

> . . . Vagando su mirada por la plazoleta, por el
> ruinoso quiosco, por el viejo caserío, con la
> sierra al fondo y el cielo incendiado como techo,
> comenzó a cantar (I, 411).

There is more distinction among the items than their relative
size or distance. The works of man are miserable, worn and
old, while the mountains and the sky are splendid.

In the same chapter, the drunken Valderrama begins conversing with a succession of objects, each larger than the one
before:

> Después siguió hablando loco, pero loco del
> todo, con las yerbas empolvadas, con el quiosco
> podrido, con las casas grises, con el cerro altivo
> y con el cielo inconmensurable (I, 412).

In this paragraph, small things are made unattractive, even
the grass, and beauty is reserved for the mountains and the
sky.

In Chapter 6, Part III, describing a thunderstorm, the
narrator traces its effects first upon the small flowers near
the cave where Demetrio and his wife have taken shelter, next
upon the larger trees at the canyon bottom, and finally upon
the huge and endless mountains:

> El aguacero se desató con estruendo y sacudió
> las blancas flores de San Juan, manojos de estrellas
> prendidos en los árboles, en las peñas, entre la
> maleza, en los pitahayos y en toda la serranía.
>   Abajo, en el fondo del cañón y a través de la
> gasa de la lluvia, se miraban las palmas rectas y
> cimbradoras; lentamente se mecían sus cabezas
> angulosas y al soplo del viento se desplegaban en
> abanicos. Y todo era serranía: ondulaciones de
> cerros que suceden a cerros . . . (I, 416).

The narrator does not mention any effect of the storm upon the
mountains, which are stronger than thunder and lightning.

Once the narrator describes Nature as if all her elements
were small and not so much imposing as quieting. The following
paragraph is from Chapter 10, Part II:

> Era un amanecer silencioso y de discreta alegría.
> Un tordo piaba tímidamente en el fresno; los animales
> removían las basuras del rastrojo en el corral;
> gruñía el cerdo su somnolencia. Asomó el tinte
> anaranjado del sol, y la última estrellita se apagó
> (I, 393).

The words "silencioso," "discreta" and "tímidamente" convey
the impression of a very small, unfrightening, consoling
Nature.

The final image of the novel, Demetrio's dead body, seems
insignificant because of the other image in the same paragraph:

> Y al pie de una resquebrajadura enorme y suntuosa
> como pórtico de vieja catedral, Demetrio Macías, con los
> ojos fijos para siempre sigue apuntando con el cañón
> de su fusil . . . (I, 418).

Demetrio's work-like pose, futile because he sustains it in death, seems pathetic when one considers the size of a rifle compared to the cliff.

Man at times is made to seem very small, scaling a mono-lithic canyon wall or silhouetted against the grandiose sier-ra; in such passages, the characters seem rather pathetic. The narrator uses both large and small elements of Nature in a technique of personification in which those elements sometimes stimulate or participate in the jubilation or depression of the characters. Chapter 15, Part I, describes how the spendid natural panorama makes Demetrio and his men delight in return-ing to the open road after many weeks in the village:

> Todos ensanchaban sus pulmones como para respirar
> los horizontes dilatados, la inmensidad del cielo, el
> azul de las montañas y el aire fresco, embalsamado de
> los aromas de la sierra (I, 352).

Nature stimulates a reaction among the men, who seem to grow larger through their participation. A similar phenomenon is recorded in Chapter 7, Part III.

> Fue una verdadera mañana de nupcias. Había
> llovido la víspera toda la noche y el cielo amanecía
> entoldado de blancas nubes. Por la cima de la
> sierra trotaban potrillos brutos de crines alzadas
> y colas tensas, gallardos con la gallardía de los
> picachos que levantan su cabeza hasta besar las nubes.
> Los soldados caminan por el abrupto peñascal
> contagiado de la alegría de la mañana (I, 416).

Here it is not immensity but freedom, symbolized by the wild horses, which enthuses the characters.

In Chapter 14, Part I, Nature responds to a character, joining Camila's grief over losing Luis Cervantes:

> Y rompió a llorar.
> Entre los jarales las ranas cantaban la implacable
> melancolía de la hora.
> Meciéndose en una rama seca, una torcaz lloró
> también (I, 351).

The melancholy of the frogs' croaking is the narrator's sub-jective interpretation; he manipulates Nature to enhance Camila's mood. He then interprets lyrically the song of the bird.

At times the narrator interprets Nature as mocker of man's suffering. In Chapter 4, Part I, the wounded Demetrio is being carried on a makeshift stretcher, his leg causing him great pain. The sound of locusts, always present, takes on a new meaning when accompanied by groans of human suffering:

> Al mediodía, cuando la calina sofocaba y se
> obnubilaba la vista, con el canto incesante de
> las cigarras se oía el quejido acompasado y mono-
> corde del herido (I, 328).

The narrator singles out more specific mockery of Nature in
Chapter 1, Part III:

> La gente ardía de sed. Ni un charco, ni un
> pozo, ni un arroyo con agua por todo el camino.
> . . . Y como una mofa, las flores de los cactos se
> abrían frescas, carnosas y encendidas las unas,
> aceradas y diáfanas las otras (I, 407).

The cactus flowers are described true to life. The only
narrative "management" consists in placing thirsty men there
and in using the word mofa.

Nature mocks the characters in a more general sense, by
going on unchanged despite war, destruction, and death. The
narrator gives examples in Part III. In Chapter 5, the troops
have entered the ravaged city of Juchipila:

> Y en la tristeza y desolación del pueblo, mien-
> tras cantan las mujeres en el templo, los pajarillos
> no cesan de piar en las arboledas, ni el canto de
> las currucas deja de oírse en las ramas secas de los
> naranjos (I, 415).

Though the dry branches of the orange trees may reflect damage
from warfare, the bird life goes on. The narrator, equating
the singing of the women and that of the birds, seems to attach a certain religiosity to Nature. That connotation is repeated in the last paragraph of the novel, with its reference
to the cliff, "as enormous and sumptuous as the doorway of an
ancient cathedral" (I, 418).

In Chapter 7, the sounds of battle have died out and nothing more is heard except Nature:

> El humo de la fusilería no acaba de extinguirse.
> Las cigarras entonan su canto imperturbable y mister-
> ioso; las palomas cantan con dulzura en las rinconadas
> de las rocas; ramonean apaciblemente las vacas (I, 418).

Man has been removed, departing with his guns and leaving behind only the corpses of Demetrio and his comrades. The narrator emphasizes the peacefulness of the scene, choosing the
doves, symbols of peace, and the imperturbable cattle.

The narration reveals an unusual attention to the sight
and sound of Nature; four of the seven above-cited examples
contain auditory images. There is even animal and vegetable
symbolism: the cacti, always associated with aridity; the
doves and the cattle, symbols of peace; and the wild horses
which suggest freedom. The author, inserting narrative paragraphs to complement or summarize character action, manipulates Nature in order to lyricize events which might otherwise seem quite matter-of-fact.

Illumination

Several passages of the novel reveal the use of light or darkness to complement the accompanying incident. Twice in Chapter 1, Part I, the narrator mentions that the opening action takes place at night. So important is the lack of illumination that it is established before the characters are detailed. The first words of the novel suggest uneasiness which is then amplified by the introduction of darkness:

> --Te digo que no es un animal. . . . Oye cómo ladra el Palomo. . . . Debe ser algún cristiano.
> . . .
> La mujer fijaba sus pupilas en la oscuridad de la sierra (I, 320).

A few paragraphs later the narrator, repeating his reference to darkness, reinforces the potential for uneasiness contained in the passage:

> Salió paso a paso, desapareciendo en la oscuridad impenetrable de la noche (I, 320).[3]

It is also night when Luis Cervantes stumbles upon the village where Demetrio lies wounded. The narrator, de-emphasizing the darkness of the hour, avoids creating the fearful expectation of Chapter 1:

> . . . El cielo estaba cuajado de estrellas y la luna ascendía como una fina hoz . . . (I, 330).

Darkness, then, may produce either high or low anxiety. It may also be idyllic when described in chiaroscuro. In Chapter 10, Part II, Demetrio and Camila seek lodging at a ranch composed of:

> . . . tres casitas alineadas que . . . recortaban sus blancos muros sobre la faja púrpura del horizonte . . . (I, 391).

The twilight is insinuated lyrically in mundane activities close at hand:

> A orillas de un arroyuelo, Pifanio estaba tirando rudamente de la soga de un bimbalete. Una olla enorme se volcaba sobre un montón de hierba fresca, y a las postreras luces de la tarde cintilaba el chorro de cristal desparramándose en la pila . . . (I, 392).

The approaching night fills Demetrio not with uneasiness but with desire:

> El valle se perdió en la sombra y las estrellas
> se escondieron.
> Demetrio estrechó a Camila amorosamente por la
> cintura, y quién sabe qué palabras susurró a su oído.
> --Sí--contestó ella débilmente (I, 393).

With concentration on the immediate surroundings and the small
pinpoints of light, the darkness is made less vast and less
absolute.

During the first half of Chapter 2, Part I, where Demetrio flees from his home canyon to the plateau where his
followers await him, several hours are to transpire. Three
references to illumination orient the reader in time:

> Todo era sombra todavía cuando Demetrio Macías
> comenzó a bajar al fondo del barranco.
>
> . . . .
> Y llegó al fondo del barranco cuando comenzaba
> a clarear el alba.
>
> . . . .
> Cuando escaló la cumbre, el sol bañaba la alti-
> planicie en un lago de oro (I, 323).

The same technique can be observed in Chapter 6, Part I,
where Luis Cervantes, guarded by Manteca and Pancracio, has
been sent to the corral. The first sentence of the chapter
reminds the reader that it is still night:

> Luis Cervantes no aprendía aún a discernir
> la forma precisa de los objetos a la vaga tonalidad
> de las noches estrelladas, . . . (I, 333).

Nearly all the rest of the chapter is devoted to a summary of
Luis' past. Near the end, elapsed time is capsulized in the
terse revelation: "Fue de día: . . . " (I, 334).

In Chapter 5, Part II, growing illumination indicates
the passage of time as Demetrio and his troops approach Moyahua.
The hour is fixed at sunrise as the men gallop through the
sierra:

> El paisaje se aclara, el sol asoma en una faja
> escarlata sobre la diafanidad del cielo (I, 381).

It is obviously mid-morning when they enter the city:

> Cuando los rayos del sol bordearon los pretiles del
> caserío, de cuatro en fondo y tocando los clarines
> comenzaron a entrar a Moyahua (I, 381).

There is at one point a carefully-observed distinction
between sunlight as seen outdoors and from inside. A contrast to the "lago de oro" of Chapter 2, Part I (I, 323),
are the beams of sun as Demetrio would observe them from his
bed in Señá Remigia's hut:

    Era de día: los rayos del sol dardeaban entre
los popotes del jacal (I, 334).

    An interesting phenomenon of the settings is the illumi-
nation of each battle. When Demetrio and his men first face
the huertistas, in Chapter 3, Part I, they sight isolated
enemy soldiers by the first light of dawn. Only when the sun
has risen can the federales be seen as an endless file of
adversaries.
    The only description of hand-to-hand combat is found in
Chapter 17, Part I, where the rebels attack a government garrison. That battle, fought at close range with knives, takes
place at night. The dim illumination softens the brutality
of the conflict.
    The aftermath of the rebel victory at Zacatecas, in
Chapter 21, Part I, is disclosed in full daylight. Glaring
light, psychologically associated with truth, complements
Alberto Solís' remarks about the Revolution. The same intense
illumination, disguised by lyric imagery, is used to reveal
Demetrio's death in Chapter 7, Part III.
    As employed in Los de abajo, darkness may promote anxiety
or tenderness. It may also be quite neutral. Its function
is controlled by concentration on blackness, on the semi-
illumination of the moon and the stars, or on earthly objects
as seen by dim light. The progression from dawn to sunrise
to morning light is at times used to suggest the passage of
time. The character of battle scenes is in part governed by
the illumination in which they take place. In summary, Los
de abajo demonstrates an awareness of the imagery of light
and darkness.

Auditory Images

    Sounds function independently or with visual images
throughout the novel, enhancing the effectiveness of some
actions and symbolizing others. In Chapter 1, Part I, for
instance, the narrator establishes from the outset that darkness limits the characters' ability to know from visual in-
spection what is happening. Accordingly, the passage contains
a series of purely auditory descriptions:

        Se oyó un ruido de pesuñas en el pedregal
    cercano, y el Palomo ladró con más rabia.
    . . . .
        El Palomo, enfurecido, había saltado la cerca del
    corral.
        De pronto se oyó un disparo, el perro lanzó un
    gemido sordo y no ladró más.
        Unos hombres a caballo llegaron vociferando y
    maldiciendo (I, 320).

A visual image follows the series of auditory descriptions:

    Dos se apearon y otro quedó cuidando las bestias (I, 320).

The same technique is used in Chapter 5, Part I, to describe
sensorially the nocturnal capture of Luis Cervantes:

> . . . De las casucas salió rumor confuso de
> mujeres asustadas, y se oyó el ruido de armas de
> los hombres que dormían afuera . . .
> --¡Estúpido! . . . Me has destrozado un pie!
> La voz se oyó clara y distinta en las inmediaciones.
> --¿Quién vive?--repitió . . . Anastasio, . . .
> --¡Demetrio Macías!--respondieron cerca.
> --¡Es Pancracio!--dijo la Codorniz regocijado.
> . . .
> Pancracio conducía a un mozalbete cubierto de
> polvo, desde el fieltro hasta los toscos zapatones
> . . . (I, 330).

Pancracio's friend identifies him through an auditory sensation,
recognizing his voice, before Pancracio himself appears.
    In Chapter 3, Part II, the narration offers pure sounds
to symbolize the activity of a banquet: "Siguió un ruido
de bocazas y grandes tragantades" (I, 377). Likewise, in
Chapter 12, Part II, details of Camila's murder are revealed
through auditory phenomena mixed with a vivid visual image:

> Un grito estridente y un cuerpo que se desploma
> arrojando sangre a borbotones (I, 398).

Sound may take precedence over a readily-available visual
sensation, as in Chapter 4, Part II, which relates the aftermath of Demetrio's promotion banquet:

> Al atardecer despertó Luis Cervantes, . . .
> Cerca de él respiraban ruidosamente . . . Anastasio
> Montañés, Pancracio y la Codorniz (I, 379).

The image given priority is the men's labored breathing, not
their prostrate forms.
    In Chapter 16, Part I, the commander of the huertista
garrison has mentally composed a letter to the Minister of War,
detailing the victory he expects to win over the revolutionaries:

> Y luego--siguió pensando--mi ascenso seguro a
> "mayor".
> Y se apretó las manos con regocijo en el mismo
> momento en que un estallido lo dejó con los oídos
> zumbando (I, 357).

The explanation for that sound, suggested by the hand grenades
mentioned twice earlier in the chapter, is confirmed in Chapter
17:

Demetrio contempló un instante el negrear de
los capotes a lo largo del pretil, en todo el frente
y por los lados, en las torres apretadas de gente,
tras la baranda de hierro.
Se sonrió con satisfacción, y volviendo la cara
a los suyos, exclamó:
--¡Hora! ....
Veinte bombas estallaron a un tiempo en medio de
los federales, . . . (I, 358).

In Chapter 7, Part I, a sound immediately precedes the
visual image with which it is associated. Demetrio, awakening,
hears Camila:

Distinta oyó la voz femenina y melodiosa
que en sueños había escuchado ya, . . . (I, 334)

He sees the girl a moment later:

. . . La misma moza que la víspera le había
ofrecido un apastito de agua deliciosamente fría
. . . ahora, igual de dulce y cariñosa, entraba
con una olla de leche . . . (I, 334, 335).

The auditory evocation at times immediately follows a
visual image. An example is in Chapter 6, Part II:

Luis Cervantes . . . tiró luego de un sillón
sin respaldo . . . Chirriaron las patas de la silla
y la yegua prieta de la Pintada bufó, . . . (I,
385).

In the above passage the shrill rasping of the chair legs
must be interpreted as simultaneous with Luis' action; the
mare's snorting is a subsequent reaction to the first sound.
In a similar passage of Chapter 8, Part II, sounds enhance a visual description with which they share a general
simultaneity. It is impossible to attribute a given noise to
a specific source:

. . . Los sombreros galoneados de cóncavas y colosales
faldas se encontraban en vaivén constante; caracolea-
ban las ancas de las bestias, que sin cesar removían
sus finas cabezas de ojazos negros, narices palpitantes
y orejas pequeñas. Y en la infernal alharaca de los
borrachos se oía el resoplar de los caballos, su rudo
golpe de pesuñas en el pavimento y, de vez en vez, un
relincho breve y nervioso (I, 388).

After the establishment of a noiseless image, appropriate
sounds are added.
Chapter 15, Part I, contains an example of simultaneous
visual and auditory impressions from a great distance. The
people of Camila's village catch a last glimpse of the departing revolutionaries:

> A lo lejos . . . se perfilaron en la claridad
> zafirina del cielo y sobre el filo de una cima los
> hombres de Macías en sus escuetos jamelgos. Una
> ráfaga de aire cálida llevó hasta los jacales los
> acentos vagos y entrecortados de La Adelita (I, 352).

The visual image is more precise than the accompanying sound;
the words used to establish each ("perfilaron" and "claridad"
as opposed to "vagos" and "entrecortados") suggest unequal
perceptibility.

In one passage, sounds evoke memories of the past. Chapter 5, Part III, describes the troops' entry into Juchipila.
Their journey has come almost full cycle, for they are very
near Demetrio's home. Their nostalgia is prompted not by familiar landmarks but by the sound of church bells, particular
bells with a sound unmistakable to their ears:

> Entraron a las calles de Juchipila cuando las
> campanas de la iglesia repicaban alegres, ruidosas
> y con aquel su timbre peculiar que hacía palpitar
> de emoción a toda la gente de los cañones (I, 414).

The bells make Anastasio recall happier days:

> --Se me figura, compadre, que estamos allá en
> aquellos tiempos cuando apenas iba comenzando la
> revolución, cuando llegábamos a un pueblito y nos
> repicaban mucho, . . . (I, 414).

When the troops enter Moyahua, in Chapter 5, Part II, they
announce themselves audibly and inspire a noisy reaction in
the city:

> . . . de cuatro en fondo y tocando los clarines
> comenzaron a entrar a Moyahua.
> Cantaban los gallos a ensordecer, ladraban con
> alarma los perros; pero la gente no dio señales de
> vida en parte alguna (I, 381).

The townspeople participate in the troops' welcome to
Tepatitlán, presented with no auditory images:

> Entraron regocijados; a las ventanas asomaban
> rostros sonrosados y bellos ojos negros (I, 395).

In Chapter 7, Part III, faint auditory stimuli first
prefigure the battle and then mark its beginning:

> Los hombres de Macías hacen silencio un momento.
> Parece que han escuchado un ruido conocido: el estal-
> lar lejano de un cohete; pero pasan algunos minutos y
> nada se vuelve a oír (I, 417).

The next sound the troops hear, almost as faint as the detona-
tion of the rocket, provokes a very different reaction:

> Y cuando comienza un tiroteo lejano, donde
> va la vanguardia, ni siquiera se sorprenden ya.
> Los reclutas vuelven grupas en desenfrenada fuga
> buscando la salida del cañón (I, 417).

The nature of the noise, not its remoteness, is what matters
to the soldiers. In this passage a link is observed between
sound stimuli and physical reactions.

In Los de abajo, sounds are sometimes used to underline
the absence of visual imagery or to replace it. In several
passages, preference is given to auditory phenomena over visual descriptions. What is heard may be related immediately
after what is seen, in which case the two images must be
considered simultaneous. Auditory impressions sometimes evoke
reminiscences of the characters; they may also cause an extreme
physical reaction. Sound imagery is not unlike the visual
impressionism evident in the novel.

Manner of Dress

Costume, abundantly detailed in Los de abajo, subtly
conveys new meaning to a number of passages or actions. The
first description of Demetrio, in Chapter 1, Part I, concentrates equally on his clothing and on his physical make-up:

> Demetrio ciñó la cartuchera a su cintura y
> levantó el fusil. Alto, robusto, de faz bermeja,
> sin pelo de barba, vestía camisa y calzón de
> manta, ancho sombrero de soyate y guaraches (I,
> 320).

Except for the cartridge belt and rifle, Demetrio is dressed
like a typical peasant. His clothing is more that of a civilian than of a military man. His costume sets him apart from
the followers whom he summons from their mountain hiding
place:

> En la lejanía, de entre un cónico hacinamiento
> de cañas y paja podrida, salieron, unos tras otros,
> muchos hombres de pechos y piernas desnudos, . . .
> (I, 323-324).

Peasants are typically dressed in rags which barely cover
their bodies. The villager who guides the rebels to the
huertista barracks, in Chapter 16, Part I, appears in clothes
which he may have put on hastily when he was awakened in the
night. For whatever reason, he is "descalzo, con una garra
de jorongo abrigando su pecho desnudo" (I, 355). The deformed
Pifanio, briefly introduced in Chapter 10, Part II, has a
withered foot and clothing which matches his bizarre physical
appearance:

. . . Vestía unas garras de camisa y chaleco, una
piltrafa de pantalón, abierto en dos alas, cuyos
extremos, levantados, pendián de la cintura.
      Anduvo, y su paso marcó un compás grotesco
(I, 392).

The revolutionaries, returning from their initial defeat
at Zacatecas, are caricatured through their clothing. The
passage in Chapter 19, Part I, describes the men's oversized
hats and contains a nickname based on them:

> Volvía la turba desenfrenada de hombres requem-
> ados, mugrientos y casi desnudos, cubierta la cabeza
> con sombreros de palma de alta copa cónica y de
> inmensa falda que les ocultaba medio rostro.
> Les llamaban los gorrudos . . . (I, 363).

Humor at the expense of characters with large hats is found
again in Chapter 1, Part II:

> --Es muy malo eso de comerse uno sólo sus corajes--
> afirma, muy serio, uno de sombrero de petate como
> cobertizo de jacal-- . . . (I, 372).

La Codorniz is twice associated with a humorous costume
or lack of costume. In Chapter 3, Part I, he performs an
amusing but reckless stunt in the heat of battle. Hearing
the enemy soldiers shout for the rebels to show their faces,
if they are brave enough, he obliges them:

> La Codorniz surgió de improviso, en cueros,
> con los calzones tendidos en actitud de torear a
> los federales. Entonces comenzó la lluvia de
> proyectiles sobre la gente de Demetrio (I, 326).

In Chapter 7, Part I, Demetrio pretends to sentence Luis Cervantes to death so that Codorniz, dressed as a priest, can
"hear his confession" and determine whether he is an assassin
sent by the enemy to murder Demetrio. The irrepressible
Codorniz, dressed in a cassock, is presented as a hilarious
figure:

> Cuando después de algunos minutos vino la
> Codorniz ensotanado, todos rieron a echar las
> tripas (I, 336).

The humor no doubt lies in the incongruity of the character's
ecclesiastical garb.
      In Chapter 20, Part I, the insurgents talk in glowing
terms about the splendor of Pancho Villa's Army of the North.
Those troops' luxurious uniforms, which may exist only in
speculation, contrast sharply with the miserable attire of
Natera's and Demetrio's men:

¡Ah, las tropas de Villa! Puros hombres norteños,
muy bien puestos, de sombrero tejano, traje de kaki
nuevecito y calzado de los Estados Unidos de a cuatro
dólares.
    Y cuando esto decían los hombres de Natera, se
miraban entre sí desconsolados, dándose cuenta cabal
de sus sombrerazos de soyate podridos por el sol y
la humedad y de las garras de calzones y camisas que
medio cubrían sus cuerpos sucios y empiojados
(I, 365-366).

Few characters are dressed well. El güero Margarito
seems comfortably attired with his "sombrero galoneado, cotona
de gamuza y mascada solferina al cuello" (I, 370). Upon
arriving in Moyahua, Demetrio is dressed quite elegantly:

    . . . sombrero galoneado, pantalón de gamuza con
    botonadura de plata y chamarra bordada de hilo de
    oro (I, 381).

Men dressed in a coat and tie are shown in disfavor. In Chapter
8, Part II, Pancracio shoots in cold blood the parish sacristan
of Moyahua because the man's clothing has offended him:

    . . . ¿Pues a quién se le ocurre, señor, vestir
    pantalón, chaqueta y gorrita? ¡Pancracio no puede
    ver un catrín enfrente de él! (I, 388).

In Chapter 13, Part II, it is el güero Margarito whose path
is crossed by a short, fat tailor, "correctamente vestido"
(I, 401). Margarito ridicules the man and makes him dance
by firing bullets at his feet. Since Margarito himself is
short and rotund, it is presumably the man's coat and tie
which prompt the ridicule and harrassment.
    Women's attire, not mentioned as frequently as men's,
does have a significant role. Señá Remigia, the kindly old
woman in whose hut Demetrio convalesces from his leg wound,
is dressed in as squalid a fashion as any character of the
novel. She is introduced in Chapter 4, Part I:

    . . . una vieja enchomitada, descalza y con una
    garra de manta al pecho a modo de camisa (I, 329).

Later, in the privacy of her hut, Señá Remigia is "desnuda
arriba de la cintura" (I, 338). Evidently Camila, on one
occasion, ventures outdoors with her chest uncovered. When
Luis Cervantes speaks to her she becomes highly embarrassed
and ducks her head "hasta tocarse el desnudo pecho" (I, 343).
Those two instances are not presented as extraordinary events;
they are probably observaciones costumbristas.
    When a female character is dressed up, she is always
described condescendingly or comically. In Chapter 14, Part
I, just after Luis has rejected her, the broken-hearted Camila
sees her reflection in the creek:

48

. . . se reprodujo con su blusa amarilla de cintas
verdes, sus enaguas blancas sin almidonar, lamida la
cabeza y estiradas las cejas y la frente; tal como
se había ataviado para gustar a Luis (I, 351).

The passage suggests that Camila lacks the means and the
knowledge to compete in beauty with the properly brought-up
criollas of Luis' acquaintance.

The flashily-dressed Pintada is presented humorously,
incongruous with her elegant clothes. Ransacking a wealthy
family's home in Zacatecas, in Chapter 2, Part II, Pintada
models a beautiful silk and lace gown which she has found.
The men's reaction is not admiration but ridicule of her
slovenliness:

      --¡Nomás las medias se te olvidaron!--exclamó
el güero Margarito desternillándose de risa.
· ·
      Pero a la Pintada nada se le dio; hizo una mueca
de indiferencia, se tiró en la alfombra y con los
propios pies hizo saltar las zapatillas de raso
blanco, moviendo muy a gusto los dedos desnudos,
entumecidos por la opresión del calzado . . .
(I, 376).

Far from being a pitiable victim of ridicule, Pintada is made
to conduct herself in such a vulgar manner that she seems
out of place in a fine dress. In Chapter 5, Part II, the
effect of Pintada's lovely dress is marred by her posture
astride a horse, by the unkempt condition of her silk hose
and by the weapons she carries:

      Muy ufana, lucía vestido de seda y grandes
arracadas de oro; . . . Perniabierta, su falda
se remangaba hasta la rodilla y se veían sus
medias deslavadas y con muchos agujeros. Llevaba
revólver al pecho y una cartuchera cruzada sobre
la cabeza de la silla (I, 381).

In all probability the adjective ufana and the verb lucía
convey Pintada's self-image, oblivious to her insuperable
unattractiveness.

In Chapter 4, Part II, the beautiful young girl whom
Luis Cervantes brought to Demetrio's banquet has spent two
nights as virtual prisoner in the bedroom of el güero
Margarito. Seeing Margarito leave the room for a moment,
la Pintada helps the girl escape:

      --¡Criatura de Dios! . . . ¡Anda, vete a tu
casa! . . . ¡Estos hombres son capaces de matarte!
. . . ¡Anda, corre! . . .
      Y sobre la chiquilla de grandes ojos azules
y semblante de virgen, que sólo vestía camisón y
medias, echó la frazada piojosa del Manteca; . . .
(I, 380).

Nowhere is the aristocratic girl described in the clothing
she wore to the banquet. In the above passage, her state
of semi-undress suggests her vulnerability, an impression
strengthened by the reference to a virgen and by Pintada's
solicitous conduct, the novel's sole indication that she
can be compassionate. The vile blanket seems like a sacri-
lege.

In the first two chapters of Los de abajo, costuming
establishes that Demetrio is not a soldier but a civilian
under arms and that he is materially superior to his half-
naked followers. Throughout the novel there are described
poor peasants with scarcely enough rags to cover their bodies.
In the case of the peón Pifanio, tattered clothes seem congruous
with his grotesque deformity. One character, Codorniz, is made
comic through his dress. A stigma is attached to men dressed
in coat and tie; one is shot for daring to appear in that attire, and another is ridiculed and bullied by el güero Margarito.

Though the costume of female villagers is usually presented
without comment, Camila seems ridiculous in her awkward attempt to dress alluringly. La Pintada, always out of place
in her expensive gowns, is regularly made absurd because of her
attire. In only one case is a disheveled appearance inappropriate for a character. Luis Cervantes' unnamed campanion,
whom Pintada regards with awe, seems defiled by the filthy
blanket around her shoulders. Costuming, presented repeatedly but never in minute detail, fulfills multiple functions in
the novel.

Narration

Narrative Passages

The adverbial clauses and narrative phrases which indicate under what circumstances or in what tone of voice a
character's speech is recited, amplify the vividness of count-
less conversations. Although examples may be found in nearly
every chapter, analysis of a few key passages, particularly
rich in explicatory phrases, will illustrate how narration
enhances and expands dialog.

Chapter 3, Part I, describes the insurgents' battle with
the federales. At dawn Pancracio, sounding his horn, wakes
the troops. Their readiness is immediately established:

--¡Hora sí, muchachos, pónganse changos!--dijo
Anastasio Montañés, reconociendo los muelles de su
rifle (I, 325).

The character's gesture, symbolic of preparedness for combat,
lends sincerity to his exhortation. The troops take up hidden
positions and watch the enemy file past across the canyon from
them. Demetrio gives an oral command for all twenty riflemen
to open fire simultaneously: "--¡Hora!--ordenó con voz apagada"
(I, 325). The hushed tone of Demetrio's voice contributes to

the pre-battle tension of the passage.

At the height of the battle, la Codorniz recklessly draws enemy fire by running out nude and waving his trousers in front of him. The reactions of two of his comrades are recorded in the text:

> --¡Huy! ¡Huy! Parece que me echaron un panal
> de moscos en la cabeza--dijo Anastasio Montañés, ya
> tendido entre las rocas y sin atreverse a levantar
> los ojos.
> --¡Codorniz, jijo de un . . . ! ¡Hora adonde les
> dije!--rugió Demetrio (I, 326).

Demetrio's roared epithet and command are more impressive when contrasted with Anastasio's apparent nonchalance. Following Demetrio's instructions, the rebels take up new positions and open fire again. The enemy reacts with an erroneous deduction:

> --¡Ya llegaron más!--clamaban los soldados
> (I, 326).

The verb _clamar_ multiplies the cry, stimulating the mass panic which is described in the next paragraph:

> Y presos de pánico, muchos volvieron grupas
> resueltamente, otros abandonaron las caballerías
> y se encaramaron, buscando refugio, entre las
> peñas . . . (I, 326).

Another passage where the specified delivery of speeches is important, is Luis Cervantes' interrogation in Chapter 7, Part I. Luis, with no food or sleep for two days, is brought into Demetrio's hut. His condition affects his speech: "Habló con lentitud y torpeza" (I, 336). Luis then begins to speak, but stops after two sentences. The text stipulates: "Hubo un prolongado silencio . . ." (I, 336). The silence, observed by the rebels as well as by the prisoner, augments the tension of the passage. In this instance, what is not said at all creates a powerful effect. Summoning all his talents and energy, Cervantes begins to fight for his life:

> Poco a poco iba animándose, y la languidez de su
> mirada desaparecía por instantes (I, 336).

Presumably, this process of re-vitalization takes place while Luis is talking. It renders more urgent his desperate rhetoric about revolutionary ideals.

Chapter 17, Part I, relates the storming of the federal garrison. Narrative comment accompanying the dialog increases the emotion of the incident. Demetrio and his men discharge their hand grenades, killing and wounding several of the garrison's defenders. A villager who has accompanied the attackers becomes concerned for his brother, who was forcibly recruited by the _federales_:

> --¡Tovía no! . . . ¡Tovía no! . . . Tovía
> no veo a mi hermano . . . --imploraba angustiado
> el paisano (I, 359).

Both the verb and the adjective suggest desperation which the repetition and the exclamation points cannot by themselves communicate. The man's concern becomes profound fright when he spies his brother:

> --¡A mi hermano, no! . . . ¡No lo maten, es
> mi hermano!--grita loco de terror el paisano que
> ve a Pancracio arrojarse sobre un federal (I, 359).

The narrative portion of the quote implies extreme alteration of the man's voice, adding appropriate urgency to his speech.

During the battle, Luis Cervantes displays rapidly-changing emotions. Noticing that the men's grenades are spent and their rifles below in the churchyard, he exclaims "alarmadísimo" (I, 359). Luis is apparently concerned for the troops' safety, not realizing that they plan to use their knives and kill every defender.

Cervantes, who several times warned Demetrio that he was attacking recklessly, relying on questionable sources for information on the garrison's strength, has been proven correct in his fears that there are many more defenders than Demetrio first believed. He sees an aged sergeant who is the same innocent-looking "peasant" who told them there were only a dozen huertistas in the garrison and whom he warned Demetrio not to trust:

> --¡El espía!--clama en son de triunfo Luis
> Cervantes-- No se los dije (I, 359).

Luis' triumph is one of vindication, a rather petty delight in having predicted correctly. Apparently he does not see his discovery as an opportunity for revenge, as does Demetrio, who stabs the old man to death.

The text of Los de abajo contains numerous adverbial constructions and more explicit variations of the matter-of-fact decir, declarar, and contestar. Those verbs and expressions bring to life much of the dialog.

More extensive than the brief narrative comments which describe how something is said, are the sentences or entire paragraphs taking the place of dialog which would convey the same message. An example is in Chapter 2, Part I, summarizing in a few words the reaction of Demetrio's followers when he tells them the federales have burned his house: "Hubo imprecaciones, amenazas, insolencias" (I, 324).

In Chapter 9, Part I, a village comadre tells Demetrio, Codorniz, and Anastasio how she hates the federales for having kidnapped her daughter. The narrator summarizes her story in just two sentences:

> . . . Ella le tenía muy buena voluntad a los señores
> de la revolución. Hacía tres meses que los federales
> le robaron su única hija, y eso la tenía inconsolable
> y fuera de sí (I, 340).

A quick summary at that point allows the narrator to stress
the men's humorous reaction to the woman's long, involved
story.

In Chapter 12, Part I, the narrator's summary itself
carries the humor. He describes an argument over a game of
cards:

> En estas corrió Pancracio la baraja, vino la
> sota y se armó un altercado. Jácara, gritos,
> luego injurias. . . . A falta de insolencias
> suficientemente incisivas, acudían a nombrar padres
> y madres en el bordado más rico de indecencias
> (I, 345).

A similarly humorous summary is found in Chapter 12, Part II:

> Y la Pintada insultó a Camila, a Demetrio, a
> Luis Cervantes y a cuantos le vinieron a las mientes,
> con tal energía y novedad, que la tropa oyó injurias
> e insolencias que no había sospechado siquiera (I, 398).

In that chapter the narrator's humor is qualified, so closely
followed by Pintada's gruesome stabbing of Camila. The murder is also summarized, reduced to two piercing sounds and a
hideous vision:

> Un grito estridente y un cuerpo que se desploma
> arrojando sangre a borbotones (I, 398).

The violence of Pintada's act is conveyed by the vocabulary,
with the forceful words estridente, desplomar, arrojar and
(coupled with sangre) borbotones.

On occasion the narrator essayistically intervenes in a
passage, relaying opinions which are his own and not of any
character. He synthesizes in past tense what the characters
say or think, then shifts to present tense to insert his own
observations. An example is in Chapter 20, Part I, where
General Natera's troops discuss Pancho Villa. First come their
ideas, quoted indirectly:

> Pero los hechos vistos y vividos no valían nada.
> Había que oír la narración de sus proezas portentosas,
> . . . (I, 365).

Then the narrator, abandoning the imperfect tense, states
his own ideas:

> Villa es el indomable señor de la sierra, la
> eterna víctima de todos los gobiernos, que lo
> persiguen como una fiera; Villa es la reencarna-
> ción de la vieja leyenda: el bandido-providencia,
> que pasa por el mundo con la antorcha luminosa
> de un ideal: ¡robar a los ricos para hacer ricos
> a los pobres! Y los pobres le forjan una leyenda
> que el tiempo se encargará de embellecer para que
> viva de generación en generación (I, 365).

A similar intervention is used to comment on Villa's defeat,
in Chapter 2, Part III:

> . . . Villa derrotado era un dios caído. Y los
> dioses caídos ni son dioses ni son nada (I, 410).

Once again, the change to a present-tense verb marks the
point where the narrator sets forth his own ideas.

Narration, capsulizing a character's silent thoughts,
sometimes anticipates dialog, as in Chapter 10, Part II,
where Demetrio and Camila have slept overnight as guests of
a hospitable farmer. The surroundings remind Demetrio of his
own farm land, his oxen, and his tender, loving wife. Later
he summarizes verbally his silent nostalgia, telling Anastasio:
" . . . ¡Tengo ganas de ver a mi mujer!" (I, 393).

On one occasion, the narrator subtly confesses a fact
previously withheld or disguised from the reader. In Chapter
5, Part II, describing the troops' entry into Moyahua, the
narrator says:

> Comenzó a oírse el abrir forzado de las puertas.
> Los soldados, diseminados ya por el pueblo, recogían
> armas y monturas por todo el vecindario (I, 381).

In Chapter 11, Part II, the narrator clarifies what is meant
by such a requisitioning of "weapons and horses":

> Después los soldados se desperdigaron, como
> siempre, en busca de "avances," so pretexto de
> recoger armas y caballos (I, 395).

The narrator is intentionally unreliable in Chapter 5, unless
what he suggests in Chapter 11 is a change in the troops'
behavior.

Narration can lend humor to dialog which by itself is not
comic. In Chapter 3, Part II, Anastasio proposes a toast in
honor of Demetrio's promotion to general:

> --Compadre--pronunció trémulo y en pie Anastasio
> Montañés--, yo no tengo que decirle . . .
> Transcurrieron minutos enteros; las malditas
> palabras no querían acudir al llamado del compadre
> Anastasio. Su cara enrojecida perlaba el sudor en
> su frente, costrosa de mugre. Por fin se resolvió
> a terminar su brindis:

> --Pos yo no tengo que decirle ₀ . . . sino
> que ya sabe que soy su compadre . . .
> Y como todos habían aplaudido a Luis Cer-
> vantes, el propio Anastasio, al acabar, dio la
> señal, palmoteando con mucha gravedad (I, 377).

The hilarity of the passage is due totally to the narration.
Humor lies in the character's trembling and perspiring, and
in the narrator's absurd shift of blame from the speaker to
the words. The comment "costrosa de mugre" makes Anastasio
seem more ridiculous. The crowning touch of humor is the
applause initiated by the speaker himself.

Narration frequently summarizes what would be a longer
passage of dialog, sometimes for the sake of brevity and
sometimes to emphasize an adjacent passage. Occasionally summary replaces distasteful dialog with a humorous allusion.

At times the narrator is made to intervene in an incident,
making comments which do not belong to any character. A shift
from past tense to present usually heralds such an intervention.
Narration is also used to anticipate or enhance dialog.

Dialog

Chapter 1, Part I, opens with a speech by Demetrio's wife:

> --Te digo que no es un animal . . . Oye cómo ladra
> el Palomo . . . (I, 320)₀

Her words allude to the sound which in truth sets in motion
the action of the novel: the dog's barking, which the narrator does not reveal directly to the reader.

A similar indirect reference to a noise is in Chapter 5,
Part I, where la Codorniz sits up in bed and shouts, "¡Un
balazo!" (I, 330). In the ensuing conversation, Codorniz
and Anastasio use the word balazo four times, underlining what
the reader has no other way of knowing.

In Chapter 12, Part I, dialog calls attention to a visual
stimulus which the narrator never mentions. Anastasio interrupts himself to tell Luis Cervantes:

> . . . Oiga, curro--prosiguió Anastasio, cambiando el
> acento de su voz, poniéndose una mano sobre la frente
> y de pie--, ¿qué polvareda se levanta allá, detrás de
> aquel cerrito? . . . ¡Caramba! ¡A poco son los mochos!
> ₀ ₒ . (I, 345).

The character not only reveals the existence of the cloud of
dust but also interprets it, though only tentatively. The
narrator then identifies correctly the source of the dust:

> Pero el enemigo se redujo a un hatajo de burros y
> dos arrieros (I, 345).

It is possible to trace the ever-increasing role of dialog
as a substitute for narration in Part I. The huertista
intruders of Chapter 1 reveal their own drunkenness, in a

passage which contains no other allusion to their condition:

> --¡Maldita sierra! ¡Sólo el diablo no se
> perdería!
> --Se perdería, mi sargento, si viniera de
> borracho como tú . . . (I, 321).

Later in the same chapter, the federalista sergeant identifies
the "silueta blanca" which the narrator has just mentioned:
"--¡Demetrio Macías!--exclamó el sargento despavorido, . . ."
(I, 322).

In Chapter 3, the narrator never says directly that
Demetrio has been wounded, but only that the enemy has begun
firing from the flank. He merely describes two reactions, one
of pain and one of swooning. Coupled with Demetrio's words,
they convey an unmistakable message:

> --¡Ya me quemaron!--gritó Demetrio, y rechinó
> los dientes--. ¡Hijos de . . . !
> Y con prontitud se dejó resbalar hacia un bar-
> ranco (I, 327).

In Chapter 7, a conversation reveals the outcome of Luis
Cervantes' "confession" by la Codorniz, disguised as a priest,
the scheme which Demetrio invented to decide justly whether
or not to have the prisoner executed:

> Cuando después de algunos minutos vino la Codorniz
> ensotanado, todos rieron a echar las tripas.
> --¡Hum, este curro es repicolargo!--exclamó--.
> Hasta se me figura que se rio de mí cuando comenzó
> a hacerle preguntas.
> --Pero, ¿no cantó nada?
> --No dijo más de lo de anoche . . .
> --Me late que no viene a eso que usté teme,
> compadre--notó Anastasio.
> --Bueno, pues denle de comer y ténganlo a una
> vista (I, 336).

The author has, in his imagination, placed himself as a bystander in Demetrio's hut. The narrator has recorded without
comment exactly what such a bystander would see and hear.

The most extensive replacement of narration by dialog
is found in Chapter 21, Part I, where Alberto Solís describes
an entire skirmish during which Demetrio and his men commit
an act of great heroism:

> . . . El caballo de Macías, cual si en vez de pesuñas
> hubiese tenido garras de águila, trepó sobre estos
> peñascos. "¡Arriba, arriba!," gritaron sus hombres,
> siguiendo tras él, como venados, sobre las rocas,
> hombres y bestias hechos uno. . . . aparecieron en
> breves instantes en la cumbre, derribando trincheras
> y acuchillando soldados. Demetrio lazaba las
> ametralladoras, tirando de ellas cual si fuesen toros
> bravos. . . . Ah, qué bonito soldado es su jefe"
> (I, 368).

Addressing his comments to Luis Cervantes, the only other
character present, Solís is also made to reveal new material
to the reader. Indirect narration of Demetrio's brave deeds
contributes to his mythification, gradually undermined during
Part I but re-emphasized in Chapter 1, Part II.

In Parts II and III there is less substitution of dialog
for narration. The best example is in Chapter 12, Part II.
At the close of Chapter 11, the narrator has described an
humble peasant's request that Demetrio order restitution of
his corn which the troops took from him. At Camila's insistence, Demetrio issues such a command (I, 396). In the
first speech of Chapter 12, Anastasio tells Demetrio how el
güero Margarito disobeyed the order and beat the man with
his sword (I, 396-397). Here the sequel to a narrated incident is supplied, after it has occurred, by an eyewitness
other than the narrator. The intervention of a new chapter
might reinforce the altered point of view.

In Chapter 2, Part II, remarks by la Pintada suggest unrecorded comments by Demetrio's newly-arrived men:

>   --¡Qué brutos!--exclamó la Pintada riendo a carcajadas.
>   --¿Pos de dónde son ustedes? Si eso de que los
>   soldados vayan a parar a los mesones es cosa que
>   ya no se usa. ¿De dónde vienen? Llega uno a
>   cualquier parte y no tiene más que escoger la casa
>   que le cuadre y ésa agarra sin pedirle licencia a
>   naiden . . . (I, 373).

Half the conversation contributes as much information as the
whole. Though the narrator never specifically says that the
characters are pillaging the abandoned home of a prominent
zacatecano, Pintada's remarks and subsequent narration make
that fact quite clear.

Part I contains an interesting contrast between narration
and dialog. In Chapter 7, Camila has brought the convalescing
Demetrio some goat's milk. Never taking his eyes from the
girl, he compliments her on her melodious voice:

>   Camila se cubrió de rubor, y como él intentara
>   asirla por un puño, asustada, tomó la vasija vacía y
>   se escapó más que de prisa (I, 335).

In Chapter 11, Camila relates a much more exciting incident
to Luis Cervantes:

>   . . . pos l'otro día entré con el champurrao, y
>   ¿qué te parece que hizo el viejo e porra? Pos
>   que me pepena de la mano y me la agarra juerte,
>   juerte; luego comienza a pellizcarme las corvas
>   . . . ¡Ah, pero qué pliegue tan güeno le he echao!
>   . . . Y que me doy el reculón y me le zafo, y que
>   ai voy pa juera a toa carrera . . . (I, 343).

The dialog is an elaborate embellishment of the simple actions
revealed in Chapter 7. Whether the reader understands the
quotes as referring to the same incident or to two different

ones, the technique is the same. Dialog has enhanced a skeletal action set down by the narrator.

Chapter 14, Part II, contains perhaps the novel's finest example of narration and dialog combined to create a humorous effect. The characters' words are highly comic, as demonstrated by the passage describing the woman, infant in her arms, who goes begging from car to car on the train:

> --Caballeros, un señor decente me ha robado mi petaca . . . Los ahorros de toda mi vida de trabajo. No tengo para darle de comer a mi niño.
> ° . . . .
> --¿Qué dice esa vieja?--preguntó el güero Margarito entrando en busca de un asiento.
> --Que una petaca . . . que un niño decente . . .
> --respondió Pancracio,. . . (I, 402).

The humor is augmented by the narrator, who takes his place among the passengers. Though in quoted form, the following paragraph can be attributed only to the narrator:

> --¡Un señor decente! ¡Un señor decente que se roba una petaca! ¡Eso es incalificable! Eso despierta un sentimiento de indignación general. ¡Oh, es lástima que ese señor decente no esté a la mano para que lo fusilen siquiera cada uno de los generales que van allí! (I, 402).

The repetition, the abundant use of exclamation points and the interjection "Oh" contribute to the humor of the passage.

At times, a character's speech refers to something heard or seen which the narrator has not mentioned. The author sometimes imagines himself a witness to events, recording without narrative comment just what he would observe. The technique is used to reveal Demetrio's wound and the result of Luis Cervantes' "trial."

In Chapter 21, Part I, Alberto Solís takes the place of the narrator, telling in dialog form Demetrio's exploits during the Battle of Zacatecas. Anastasio Montañés is made to do the same in Chapter 12, Part II, where he reveals how el güero Margarito repudiated Demetrio's written order.

Dialog can synthesize a previous comment, not presented in the text, or embellish a simple action described by the narrator. That dialog and narration are inseparable is manifest in Chapter 14, Part II, where neither is dispensable to the rich humor of the cuadro costumbrista.

Elliptical Conversations

On occasion the narrator becomes briefly effaced and the reader is allowed to use his imagination freely. In each case, the author presents one character's side of a conversation, with ellipses replacing the other participant's words or actions, more or less specifically inferred by the text. The effect is sometimes duplicated in theater, when a character's replies during a telephone conversation convey what has been said by the hypothetical person to whom he is talking.

The first elliptical conversation is spoken by the huertista lieutenant, in Chapter 1, Part I:

> --Sargento, tráeme una botella de tequila; he decidido pasar la noche en amable compañía con esta morenita . . . ¿El coronel? . . . ¿Qué me hablas tú del coronel a estas horas? . . . ¡Que vaya mucho a . . . ! . . . Oye, chatita, deja a mi sargento que fría los blanquillos y caliente las gordas; tú ven acá conmigo. . . . Sargento, mi botella, mi botella de tequila. Chata, estás muy lejos; arrímate a echar un trago . . . ¿Cómo que no? . . . (I, 321-322).

A potential source of humor is that the lieutenant's speeches are directed sometimes at the sergeant and sometimes at Demetrio's wife. Insofar as that technique makes him seem pressed or confused, it renders him comic.

The lieutenant is assigned another one-sided speech after Demetrio has suddenly appeared:

> --¡Ah, dispense, amigo! . . . Yo no sabía . . . Pero yo respeto a los valientes de veras.
> Demetrio se quedó mirándolos y una sonrisa insolente y despreciativa plegó sus líneas.
> --Y no sólo los respeto, sino que también los quiero . . . Aquí tiene la mano de un amigo . . . Está bueno, Demetrio Macías, usted me desaira . . . Es porque no me conoce, . . . (I, 322).

Here, the ellipses mean that the other character says nothing at all. Demetrio's staid silence makes the garrulous lieutenant seem absurd in contrast. Since the narrator suggests that Demetrio never moves, the lieutenant's words probably indicate only his own actions. He presumably extends his hand to Demetrio and, achieving no reaction, withdraws it. His effusiveness, contrasted with Demetrio's disdain, contributes to the ridiculous position in which the lieutenant is placed.

There is another case where a speaker is made ridiculous by another character's apparent reluctance to participate in a dialog. In Chapter 8, Part I, Camila attempts to sustain a conversation with the reticent Luis Cervantes:

> --Oiga, ¿y quién lo insiñó a curar? . . . ¿Y pa qué jirvió la agua? . . . ¿Y los trapos, pa qué los coció? . . . ¡Mire, mire, cuánta curiosidá pa todo! . . . ¿Y eso que se echó en las manos? . . . ¡Pior! . . . ¿Aguardiente de veras? . . . ¡Ande, pos si yo creiba que el aguardiente no más

pal cólico era güeno! ₒ ₒ ₒ ¡Ah! ¿De moo es que
usté iba a ser dotor? ₒ ₒ ₒ ¡Ja, ja, ja! ₒ ₒ ₒ
¡Cosa de morirse uno de risa! ₒ ₒ ₒ ¿Y por qué no
regüelve mejor agua fría? ₒ ₒ ₒ ¡Mi' qué cuentos!
ₒ ₒ ₒ ¡Quesque animales en la agua sin jervir!
ₒ ₒ ₒ ¡Fuchi! ₒ ₒ ₒ ¡Pos cuando ni yo miro nada!
ₒ ₒ ₒ (I, 337)ₒ

The rustic dialog, colorful interjections and repetitions
contribute to an impression that Camila is lovestruck and
giddy. Such a long elliptical conversation strongly suggests that Cervantes has contributed little to it.

In Chapter 1, Part II, the recently-arrived Margarito
has a disagreement with a waiter:

> --Oye, mozo--gritó el güero Margarito--,
> te he pedido agua con hielo ₒ ₒ ₒ Entiende que
> no te pido limosna. ₒ ₒ ₒ No me importa saber
> si se acabó, ni por qué se acabó. ₒ ₒ ₒ Te digo
> que no quiero explicaciones, sino agua con
> hielo ₒ ₒ ₒ ¿Me la traes o no me la traes?
> ₒ ₒ ₒ ¿Ah, no? ₒ ₒ ₒ Pues toma ₒ ₒ ₒ
> El mesero cae al golpe de una sonora
> bofetada (I, 372)ₒ

The effect of having omitted the waiter is that he is highly
depersonalized. The only action assigned to him is to fall
down from Margarito's punchₒ The reader, unable to identify
with or feel sympathy for the waiter, will react positively
to the potential humor of el güero's words. The same technique is used for the same purpose in Chapter 13, Part IIₒ
The drunken Margarito spies a short, fat, correctly-dressed
tailor on the sidewalk:

> --Oiga, amigo, ¡qué chiquito y qué bonito es
> usted! ₒ ₒ ₒ ¿Cómo que no? ₒ ₒ ₒ ¿Entonces yo soy
> mentiroso? ₒ ₒ ₒ Bueno, así me gusta ₒ ₒ ₒ ¿Usted
> sabe bailar los enanos? ₒ ₒ ₒ ¿Que no sabe? ₒ ₒ ₒ
> ¡Resabe! ₒ ₒ ₒ ¡Yo lo conocí a usted en un circo!
> ¡Le juro que sí sabe y muy rebién! ₒ ₒ ₒ ¡Ahora
> lo verá! ₒ ₒ ₒ
> El güero saca su pistola y comienza a disparar
> hacia los pies del sastre, que ₒ ₒ ₒ a cada tiro
> da un saltito (I, 401)ₒ

In this instance the narrator turns el güero's victim into
a caricature, a transformation useful for the comic effect,
which resides equally in Margarito's words and the man's
reaction. Assigning no speeches to the victim confines him
to the role of caricature, literarily incapable of arousing
the reader's sympathy or his indignation at Margaritoₒ

The elliptical conversations are all potentially humorous, subjecting to ridicule either the speaker who is presented or the other participant, who is conjecturedₒ

Establishing the illusion of another character, whose con-
tributions are suggested, they allow the reader's imagination to reconstruct that character's part. They are passages open to the various interpretations of the readers.

In this section, devoted to Azuela's techniques of
narrative description, it has been demonstrated that although
the author does not manipulate his characters, their adventures are those which best develop their personalities or
move them closer to a goal. For that reason, the episodes
which the narrator describes do not account for all of the
nearly two years which elapse during Demetrio's absence from
home. The reader might under-estimate how many months have
gone by, did not the narrator mention from time to time
historical events which have just taken place.

The narrator, singling out one or two physical traits of
several of the characters, makes them appear grotesque. They
may be distorted directly or through the vision of another
character, as is the case of Camila, whom Luis sees as a "mono
enchomitado." At times a physical trait indicates a moral
defect; an example is the wild look in la Codorniz' "ojos
de serpiente."

The predominant bizarre feature in Part III is a con-
spicuous scar. An old villista veteran has one, as does the
hag who operates a fonda in Juchipila. Those scars symbolize
the ravages of war.

Many characters not rendered grotesque are de-personalized,
made identifiable only by their clothing, voice or some other
secondary trait. Faces are infrequently described in detail.
The technique of observation is inspired by the impressionism
of the late Modernists.

In battle, where adversaries are seen long enough for
one to aim and fire, facial detail must be obscured by distance
or camouflage. During the rebels' first battle, the federales
are so far away that they are dehumanized targets, identifiable
only by the horses they are riding. When Demetrio's men storm
the garrison, however, they are killing not with long-range
rifles but with knives. The narrator reveals the faces of the
enemy and their reactions as they die. The third battle is
highly impersonal; the enemy, armed with machine guns, is not
described at all. They do not appear, for they simply lay
down a barrage and kill men whom they do not necessarily see.

Man, sometimes rendered anonymous by the narrator, may
seem even more insignificant when set against the background
of a monumental Nature. Houses, cradled in the sierra, seem
not just tiny but colorless in comparison with the mountains
and the sky. Nature also is made to affect men psychologically
or to be subtly colored by their moods. In Part III, amid
widespread destruction of buildings and human suffering, Nature
continues unchanged and exuberant.

Narrative passages frequently replace dialog. They may
be matter-of-fact summaries or contribute humor to an incident.
On occasion, the narrator expresses an unmediated opinion
about the event being described.

Dialog may also replace narration, referring to a sound which the narrator has not revealed to the reader or to a past event which one of the characters describes. In many cases, the author is like an observer, present with the characters, who learns only the minimum of facts, no more than those revealed by the character who is speaking.

The novel makes use of elliptical conversations where the second participant's words and actions are unrecorded and must be inferred by what the first participant says. The effect is usually humorous, ridiculing either the revealed speaker or the inferred partner.

The narrator in Los de abajo, rarely effaced or absent during even a brief passage, appears omniscient but does on occasion conceal his foreknowledge of events. He sometimes allows a character to reveal past events which he never reconstructs for the reader. In a few passages the narrator expresses an idea which is obviously unmediated; it cannot be attributed to any character. The undramatized narrator restricts himself to third-person verbs, never using I, we or you. He never specifically addresses the reader.

Dramatized Narrators

The characters of Los de abajo are not limited to performing their respective acts and discussing those acts with other characters. As was indicated in the section covering dialog as a substitute for narration, a character may on occasion summarize a past event which the undramatized narrator did not reveal as it took place. Characters may also fill in details which orient the reader. In Chapter 2, Part I, quotation marks are used to set off Demetrio's silent thoughts as he descends a canyon wall:

> "Seguramente ahora sí van a dar con nuestro
> rastro los federales, y se nos vienen encima como
> perros. La fortuna es que no saben veredas, en-
> tradas ni salidas. Sólo que alguno de Moyahua
> anduviera con ellos de guía, . . . En Moyahua está
> el cacique que me trae corriendo por los cerros, y
> éste tendría mucho gusto en verme colgado de un
> poste del telégrafo con tamaña lengua de fuera
> . . . " (I, 323).

Demetrio, whose speeches and actions are nearly always inextricable from the plot and are not usually philosophical in nature, is only an occasional narrator. Other characters too are from time to time given that role. In Chapter 11, Part I, Camila's point of view becomes that of the undramatized narrator as she describes Luis Cervantes' " . . . ojos glaucos de tierna expresión, sus carrillos frescos y rosados como los de un muñeco de porcelana" (I, 344), features which might seem bizarre to anyone but Camila, who gazes on Cervantes "con embeleso" (I, 344). Conversely, the narrator calls Camila a "mono enchomitado" (I, 337), reflecting Luis' prejudiced vision. Under such circumstances, Camila and Luis become what might be called semi-independent narrators.

Four characters, however, orient or influence the reader by their comments on passing events. They are Alberto Solís, the disillusioned intellectual; Luis Cervantes, the self-seeking charlatan; el güero Margarito, the revolutionary par excellence; and Valderrama, the mad prophet.

Alberto Solís

Solís, introduced in Chapter 18, Part I, is removed by death in Chapter 21. Though his presence is brief and his actions do not affect the plot, he has an important role. If his words have no effect on Luis Cervantes, the only character who hears them, they still are a prelude to Part II:

> . . . Hay que esperar un poco. A que no haya
> combatientes, a que no se oigan más disparos que
> los de las turbas entregadas a las delicias del
> saqueo; a que resplandezca diáfana, como una
> gota de agua, la psicología de nuestra raza, con-
> densada en dos palabras: ¡robar, matar! . . .
> (I, 368).

The chapters of Part II, which describe no battles, are filled with examples of the pillage and cruelty which Solís predicts. He, in his role as the predictor of those events fulfilled, does not appear in those chapters which bear him out.

He seems to be a type, the idealistic young liberal who, having fallen in love with the gallantry of the Revolution, becomes indignant at his comrades, who he believes have betrayed it and made it ugly. He tells Cervantes:

> . . . hay hechos y hay hombres que no son sino pura
> hiel . . . Y esa hiel va cayendo gota a gota en el
> alma, y todo lo amarga, todo lo envenena. Entusiasmo,
> esperanzas, ideales, alegrías . . . , ¡nada! . . .
> (I 361).

He says in Chapter 21:

> . . . ¡Qué chasco, amigo mío, si los que venimos a
> ofrecer todo nuestro entusiasmo, nuestra misma vida
> por derribar a un miserable asesino, resultásemos
> los obreros de un enorme pedestal donde pudieran
> levantarse cien o doscientos mil monstruos de la
> misma especie! . . . ¡Pueblo sin ideales, pueblo
> de tiranos! . . . (I, 368).

One speech assigned to Solís, ostensibly to explain his continued adherence to the Revolution, also sheds light upon Demetrio's refusal to stop fighting even when there is nothing left to do but face the carrancistas, erstwhile allies who are now tracking him down. Solís' philosophy is as follows:

> --Me preguntará que por qué sigo entonces en
> la revolución. La revolución es el huracán, y el
> hombre que se entrega a ella no es ya el hombre,
> es la miserable hoja seca arrebatada por el venda-
> val (I, 362).

In Chapter 6, Part III, Demetrio's wife asks him why he remains a revolutionary after defeating the Federación. Demetrio's answer is much like Solís':

> . . . toma distraído una piedrecita y la arroja
> al fondo del cañón. Se mantiene pensativo viendo
> el desfiladero, y dice:
> --Mira esa piedra cómo ya no se para . . .
> (I, 416).

The two analogies, both based on Nature, emphasize man's insignificance. With no more stature than a dead leaf or a
small stone, he is swept along by the blind force of the
Revolution. In Solís' speech the conflict is compared to a
strong wind, and in Demetrio's, to the pull of gravity.
Solís, not developed like the helpless revolutionary
drifter which he insinuates that he is, twice expresses his
love for the conflict. After describing Demetrio's heroics
during the Battle of Zacatecas, he exclaims: "¡Ah, qué bonito
soldado es su jefe!" (I, 368). Later, seeing the lovely, sun-
lit city of Zacatecas, shrouded with the white smoke of rifles
and stained here and there by the black smoke of burning buildings, he senses an esthetic value in the contrasts: "--¡Qué
hermosa es la Revolución, aun en su misma barbarie!--pronunció
Solís conmovido" (I, 368).
Solís, whose ideals have turned to cynicism, laughs at
his own past enthusiasm for an ideological cause. Speaking of
Pancho Villa, Solís calls him:

> de . . . "el águila azteca, que ha clavado su pico
> de acero sobre la cabeza de la víbora Victoriano
> Huerta" . . . Así dije en un discurso . . . --habló
> en tono un tanto irónico Alberto Solís, . . . (I, 365).

Solís' death is described in Chapter 21, Part I:

> Sintió un golpecito seco en la vientre, y como
> si las piernas se le hubiesen vuelto de trapo, res-
> baló de la piedra. Luego le zumbaron los oídos
> . . . Después, oscuridad y silencio eternos . . .
> (I, 369).

The silence of his death is nearly unviolated. With the battle
drawing to a close, no sound reaches Solís on his hilltop
except that of a bullet which "pasó silbando" (I, 369). So
insulated from noise is the vantage point that the narrator

mentions no sounds to accompany visual images. The "humareda blanca de la fusilería y los negros borbotones de los edificios incendiados" (I, 368) are purely visual. Also without sound is the "golpecito seco" which kills Solís.

As a dramatized narrator, Alberto Solís is granted an elevated vantage point which other characters do not share. From the hilltop he can perceive symbols in the smoke which, below him, hovers over the city:

> Su sonrisa volvió a vagar siguiendo las espirales
> de humo de los rifles y la polvareda de cada casa
> derribada y de cada techo que se hundía. Y creyó
> haber descubierto un símbolo de la revolución en
> aquellas nubes de humo y en aquellas nubes de polvo
> que fraternalmente ascendían, se abrazaban, se
> confundían y se borraban en la nada (I, 369).

The dust from the caved-in roofs, ambiguous at this point in the novel, becomes a clear symbol when seen in the light of Part II. Undoubtedly the victorious rebels are sacking and plundering throughout the city. If the rifle smoke reminds Solís of the heroism which he loves, the billowing dust makes him think of the greed which he despises.

Solís sees yet a third source of smoke, with its own meaning:

> Y su mano tendida señaló la estación de los
> ferrocarriles. Los trenes resoplando furiosos,
> arrojando espesas columnas de humo, los carros
> colmados de gente que escapaba a todo vapor (I, 369).

The smoke from the locomotives might symbolize to Solís the cruelty and injustice of the Revolution. Words like "furiosos" and "arrojando" make this a forceful passage.

Alberto Solís apparently dies accidentally and unintentionally. His killer may be an enemy or an ally. It is even possible that no one has taken aim at him, that he dies from a stray bullet. His death is peaceful, without struggle or pain. His legs simply go limp and he slides off the rock where he has been sitting. His non-violent death climaxes Part I, which is quite low in violence. Half the twenty-one chapters take place in the peaceful village where Demetrio convalesces.

Solís, the only major character who appears just in Part I, is the character who best sets forth the message of that part. As the struggle against Huerta comes to a successful end and the revolutionaries achieve what they set out to do, Solís predicts that they will begin to rob and kill for their own benefit. He points out that maderista idealism has already been betrayed and that the struggle will not make Mexico free, merely exchange the old oppressors for new. Much of what Solís predicts comes true in Part II. Thus, Solís' function as a dramatized narrator is to set forth a point of view which the undramatized narrator, in the interest of objectivity, does not present. Solís' removal as soon as he has made his prediction, preserves his pure quality of dramatized narrator, a character who does little except to elaborate a philosophical posture.

Luis Cervantes

The character who proclaims the doctrine of self-gain through revolution, who advocates what Solís would call "betrayal of the movement," is Luis Cervantes. Luis is not a pure narrator, for his words and actions affect the plot. He is what Booth would call a narrator/agent.[4]

Cervantes, who originally enlisted with the federales, deserts because they have treated him with indignity. Why he has joined the revolutionaries instead of going home, he explains during a paragraph describing his silent thoughts:

> . . . los parientes y favoritos de Huerta abandonaban la capital rumbo a los puertos, . . . Por tanto, revolucionarios, bandidos o como quisiera llamárseles, ellos iban a derrocar al gobierno; el mañana les pertenecía; había que estar, pues, con ellos, sólo con ellos (I, 337).

These words express pure opportunism. Cervantes cares not who is morally right, only which side will win.

Pleading for his life in Chapter 7, Part I, Cervantes conceals his private reasons for changing sides:

> --Creí que ustedes aceptarían con gusto al que viene a ofrecerles ayuda, pobre ayuda la mía, pero que sólo a ustedes mismos beneficia . . . ¿Yo qué me gano con que la revolución truinfe o no?
>
> . . . .
> --La revolución beneficia al pobre, al ignorante, al que toda su vida ha sido esclavo, a los infelices que ni siquiera saben que si lo son es porque el rico convierte en oro las lágrimas, el sudor y la sangre de los pobres . . .
>
> . . . .
> --Yo he querido pelear por la santa causa de los desventurados . . . (I, 336).

His reference to sweat, blood and gold is stylized rhetoric, as is "la santa causa de los desventurados." To his question "¿qué me gano?" Cervantes himself supplies an answer, in Chapter 6, Part II. He brings Demetrio a bag bulging with gold, explaining:

> . . . al buen sol hay que abrirle la ventana . . . Hoy nos está dando de cara; pero ¿mañana? . . . Hay que ver siempre adelante (I, 385).

Later, Luis adds:

> --Mire, mi general; si, como parece, esta
> bola va a seguir, si la Revolución no se acaba,
> nosotros tenemos ya lo suficiente para irnos a
> brillarla una temporada fuera del país . . .
> (I, 386).

It becomes evident, in Part II, that Cervantes has gained a
great deal from the Revolution.

His remarks in Chapter 13, Part I, reveal a dual philosophy of patriotic sacrifice and personal gain:

> . . . ¿es de justicia privar a su mujer y a sus
> hijos de la fortuna que la Divina Providencia le
> pone ahora en sus manos? ¿Será justo abandonar
> a la patria en estos momentos solemnes en que va
> a necesitar de toda la abnegación de sus hijos,
> los humildes para que la salven, para que no
> la dejen caer de nuevo en manos de sus eternos
> detentadores y verdugos, los caciques? . . .
> (I, 348).

The first sentence urges lining one's own pockets, and the
rest of the exhortation, sacrifice for one's country. Luis'
sophistry seems to equate those contradictory values. The
allusion to patriotism has a hollow ring in this novel where
no character is shown in an act of self-abnegation for Mexico.

Luis' statements are sometimes direct contradictions of
what he has previously said or thought. In Chapter 13, Part
I, he tells Demetrio:

> --Mi jefe-- . . . usted me ha simpatizado desde
> que lo conocí, y lo quiero cada vez más, porque sé
> todo lo que vale (I, 348).

In Chapter 8, his thoughts run just the opposite:

> . . . ¡Bah! Una veintena de encuerados y piojosos,
> . . . (I, 337).

Luis Cervantes, whose words do not always reflect his
thoughts, once makes a statement rendered ironic by the undramatized narrator's subsequent comment. In the closing
argument of his effort to proselytize Demetrio, Luis declares:

> . . . No peleamos por derrocar a un asesino miserable,
> sino contra la tiranía misma. Eso es lo que se llama
> luchar por principios, tener ideales. Por ellos
> luchan Villa, Natera, Carranza; por ellos estamos
> luchando nosotros (I, 348).

In Chapter 20, Part I, the undramatized narrator states the
ideals for which Villa fights:

. . . ¡robar a los ricos para hacer ricos a los
pobres! . . . (I, 365).

That notion corresponds closely with what Luis intends to
do, but not with what he says.

Cervantes, who does not die during the novel, is removed
from the plot in two steps. His last direct appearance is in
Chapter 13, Part II, where he explains that Demetrio must go
to Aguascalientes to vote for provisional president (I, 400).
In Chapter 1, Part III, Venancio reads a letter from Luis,
mailed to him from El Paso, Texas. The letter has two functions: it summarizes conjectured events which are to have
occurred between Parts II and III, and provides an interme-
diate step for Cervantes' removal from the novel.

In the first paragraph, the letter discloses that Pancracio and el Manteca have stabbed each other to death, in
a dispute over a game of cards, and that el güero Margarito
has committed suicide (I, 406). Those incidents are revealed
nowhere else.

Cervantes does not die, nor is his departure detailed;
he simply fails to appear after Part II. The letter makes
his disappearance more gradual. Physically present in Chapter 13, Part II, Luis becomes abstracted into words on a
sheet of paper, in Chapter 1, Part III. Thereafter he is not
mentioned again.

Luis Cervantes' role is appropriate to Part I, where his
words help to clarify the still-nebulous philosophy of revolution. Alberto Solís expresses a doctrine of self-sacrifice,
while Demetrio sees the conflict as an opportunity for personal revenge. Luis rejects Demetrio's notions as too near-
sighted:

> . . . Mentira que usted ande por aquí por don Mónico,
> el cacique; usted se ha levantado contra el
> caciquismo que asola toda la nación (I, 348).

He combines Solís' idea with his own philosophy of opportunism:

> Hubo vino y cervezas. . . . Luis Cervantes
> brindó "por el triunfo de nuestra causa, que es
> el triunfo sublime de la Justicia; porque pronto
> veamos realizados los ideales de redención de
> este nuestro pueblo sufrido y noble, y sean
> ahora los mismos hombres que han regado con
> su propia sangre la tierra los que cosechan
> los frutos que legítimamente les pertenecen"
> (I, 360).

Cervantes consistently asserts the right of Mexico's liberators
to a substantial reward for their patriotic services.

Cervantes is a narrator/agent whose twofold philosophy
has a strong influence on Demetrio's fate. His gospel of
revolution for personal gain persuades Demetrio to ally himself with General Natera and to accept large numbers of

ex-huertista recruits. His advice that Demetrio leave Mexico,
before the Revolution degenerates into a fratricidal struggle,
has a literary bearing on the events of Part III. Demetrio,
refusing to take that advice, exposes himself to the vengeance
of the carrancistas. Luis Cervantes' words, a synthesis of
Alberto Solís' ideas and Demetrio's, cast light on the events
of Part II while helping to shape those events.

El Güero Margarito

The character who exemplifies pursuit of pleasure and
gratification of every impulse is el güero Margarito. Many
of his actions are comic, some cruel. His words sometimes
explain what he has done. In Chapter 1, Part II, he knocks
a waiter to the ground because the man did not bring him ice
water. To explain his action, he tells Demetrio:

> --Así soy yo, mi general Macías; mire cómo ya
> no me queda pelo de barba en la cara. ¿Sabe por
> qué? Pues porque soy muy corajudo, y cuando no
> tengo en quién descansar, me arranco los pelos
> hasta que se me baja el coraje. ¡ Palabra de honor,
> mi general; si no lo hiciera así, me moriría del
> puro berrinche! (I, 372).

His speech, humorous in its extravagance, reveals a rationale
underlying the acts of other revolutionaries. In Chapter 8,
Part II, Pancracio shoots a sacristan who has committed no
offense except that of appearing on the street with a coat
and tie (I, 388). Though no explanation is offered for what
Pancracio has done, it seems likely that he detests middle-
and upper-class Mexicans, becomes enraged upon seeing one,
and shoots him to avoid suffocation from "puro berrinche."
In Chapter 9, Part II, el güero captures a federalista
straggler and decides to keep him as a prisoner.

> --¿Saben por qué? Porque nunca he visto bien
> la cara que pone un prójimo cuando se le aprieta
> una reata en el pescuezo (I, 390).

While his words suggest mere curiosity, his actions reveal
a more profound motivation. Drawing his revolver, he threatens
to kill the prisoner. Holding the weapon against the man's
chest, Margarito watches his reaction of fear:

> . . . Y sus ojos brillaron de un modo extraño, y
> su cara regordeta, de inflados carrillos, se
> encendía en una sensación de suprema voluptuosidad
> (I, 391).

Whether or not Margarito is cruel, is not as important as the
way in which other characters react to him. Camila, having
seen his treatment of the prisoner, reacts violently. She
reports to Demetrio:

--¡Ah, qué malo es el hombre ese Margarito!
. . . ¡Si viera lo que viene haciendo con un preso!
(I, 391).

Demetrio raises his eyebrows but says nothing, and la Pintada
shouts to Camila:

--Oye, tú, ¿qué chismes le trais a Demetrio?
. . . El güero Margarito es mi mero amor . . .
¡Pa que te lo sepas! . . . Y ya sabes . . . Lo
que haiga con él, hay conmigo. ¡Ya te lo aviso!
. . . (I, 391).

Margarito is a catalyst in the rivalry between the two women.
Camila consistently condemns el güero's cruelty, while Pintada
always defends him. The situation is repeated in Chapter 12,
Part II, where el güero disobeys Demetrio's order, not only
refusing to return the citizen's corn but beating him with
his sword (I, 397). Pintada causes Camila to fall from her
horse, so upsetting her that Camila tells Demetrio he must
leave her behind or send Pintada away. When Demetrio chooses
the latter course, Pintada murders Camila out of revenge. That
incident is caused indirectly by el güero's cruel pranks.
  Margarito is the voice of unemotional reaction. When his
huertista prisoner dies, in Chapter 11, Part II, he laughs
heartily and says:

--¡Qué bruto soy! . . . ¡Ahora que lo tenía
enseñado a no comer! . . . (I, 395).

Further evidence of Margarito's aplomb in the presence of
death is his reaction to Camila's murder. Changing the subject, he celebrates la Pintada's departure:

--¡Ah, qué bueno! . . . ¡Hasta que se me despegó
esta chinche! . . . (I, 399).

He is not necessarily more unfeeling than other revolutionaries but perhaps more articulate. Demetrio expresses a similar
under-reaction to death in Chapter 18, Part I, where Anastasio
tells him two of his new recruits have been killed in brawls
the previous night:

--¡Psch! . . . Pos que los entierren . . . (I, 363).

When el güero compares murder with theft, in Chapter 14,
Part II, he declares that to kill is more honorable than to steal:

. . . no creo que sea malo matar, porque cuando uno
mata lo hace siempre con coraje; ¿pero robar? . . .
(I, 403).

Margarito, in his defense of killing in the heat of
anger, takes a stand against premeditated murder. His philosophy of life is summarized in that speech and in one other:

> --¡Bueno! ¡A qué negarlo, pues! Yo también
> he robado--asintió el güero Margarito--; pero aquí
> están mis compañeros que digan cuánto he hecho
> de capital. Eso sí, mi gusto es gastarlo todo
> con las amistades. Para mí es más contento
> ponerme una papilina con todos los amigos que
> mandarles un centavo a las viejas de mi casa
> . . . (I, 403).

He advocates the pursuit of pleasure, to him the only goal
worth pursuing. In Chapter 13, apparently moved by
Demetrio's depression over Camila's death, he attempts to
instill his own outlook on life:

> --Ya verá cómo llegando a Lagos le quito esa
> murria, mi general. Allí hay muchachas bonitas
> para darnos gusto-- . . . (I, 399).

Margarito is the most exuberant character of the novel,
the one who most frequently laughs. His physical appearance
is testimony to his disposition:

> El güero Margarito era un hombrecillo redondo,
> de bigotes retorcidos, ojos azules muy malignos que
> se le perdían entre los carrillos y la frente cuando
> se reía (I, 375).

Margarito is a "type," personification of all the qualities which make up a revolutionary. He is boisterous, irresponsible and irrepressible. His primary function is to
summarize the rebel personality, which without him would be
dispersed among a number of minor characters. He is confined
to Part II because that is the only part which shows the
Revolution in all its glory. He does not appear in Part I,
the examination of men's motives for joining the struggle, or
in Part III, the study of their lives as affected by that
conflict as it grinds to an agonizing halt. Margarito per-
sonifies the revolutionary type who flourishes only while the
conflict is at full force.

Valderrama

The mad, drunken troubadour Valderrama, who appears exclusively in Part III, is the only dramatized narrator who
comments upon events which occur after Villa's repudiation
of Carranza. Valderrama emphasizes, in Chapter 3, Part III,
that there is no longer joy in revolution. He sings a melancholy song which brings tears to Demetrio's eyes. He embraces
his general, then comments:

> --¡Y he ahí cómo los grandes placeres de la
> Revolución se resolvían en una lágrima! . . .
> (I, 412).

Valderrama is the first character to pinpoint the vile condition to which the rebels have sunk. Later, in Chapter 5,
Part III, Demetrio and his men discuss the vanished "placeres
de la Revolución." As they enter Juchipila, they hear ringing
church bells. Anastasio recalls the early days of the struggle, when ringing bells, orchestras and waving flags welcomed
them at every town:

> --Ahora ya no nos quieren--repuso Demetrio.
> --Sí, como vamos ya de "rota batida" --obser-
> vó la Codorniz.
> --No es por eso . . . A los otros tampoco
> los pueden ver ni en estampa.
> --Pero ¿cómo nos han de querer, compadre?
> Y no dijeron más (I, 414).

Elaborating on Valderrama's statement, the speaker refers not
just to the rebels' changed fortunes but to the fruits of their
past abuses.

The historic event around which the action of Part III
revolves is Pancho Villa's defeat at Celaya. Valderrama's
response to the news expresses neither the disbelief of some
of his comrades nor the profound discouragement of others:

> --¿Villa? . . . ¿Obregón? . . . ¿Carranza?
> . . . ¡X . . . Y . . . Z . . . ! ¿Qué se me da
> a mí? . . . ¡Amo la Revolución como amo al volcán
> que irrumpe! ¡Al volcán porque es volcán; a la
> Revolución porque es Revolución! . . . Pero las
> piedras que quedan arriba o abajo, después del
> cataclismo, ¿qué me importan a mí? . . . (I, 409-
> 410).

His disdain toward individual chieftains is sincere; to him
they are like the stones hurled from a volcano. Valderrama
proclaims the Revolution as a compelling force behind men,
refusing to recognize that they may in fact guide and shape
it. He is a pure revolutionary, caught up in the conflict for
its own sake, with no political or ideological loyalties to
anyone.

At times Valderrama waxes rhetorical, pronouncing eloquent eulogies. He praises the serranos in an effort to defend them against Demetrio, who has ordered the capture of
any villagers caught fleeing from the troops. Indignantly
Valderrama exclaims:

> . . . ¿A los serranos? ¿A estos valerosos que no
> han imitado a las gallinas que ahora anidan en
> Zacatecas y Aguascalientes? ¿A los hermanos nuestros
> que desafían las tempestades adheridos a sus rocas
> como la madrepeña? ¡Protesto! . . . ¡Protesto! . . .
> . . . .
> --Los serranos-- . . . son carne de nuestra carne
> y huesos de nuestros huesos . . . (I, 407-408).

When Valderrama emphasizes his words by striking Demetrio on
the chest with his fist, Demetrio smiles benevolently. He
later explains why he does not become angry at Valderrama:

> --Le tengo voluntá a ese loco-- . . . porque
> a veces dice unas cosas que lo ponen a uno a
> pensar (I, 410).

But it is not Valderrama's truthfulness which protects him, so
much as his apparent madness or drunken irresponsibility.
The text suggests several times that Valderrama is not responsible for what he says. In Chapter 1, Part III, the undramatized narrator summarizes a question which might be attributed to several of the insurgents:

> ¿Valderrama, vagabundo, loco y un poco poeta,
> sabía lo que decía? (I, 408).

After his speech equating Villa, Obregón and Carranza,
spoken with a pose "solemn as an emperor," Valderrama quickly
forgets what he was saying:

> Y como al brillo del sol . . . reluciera sobre
> su frente el reflejo de una blanca botella de tequila,
> volvió grupas y con el alma henchida de regocijo se
> lanzó hacia el portador de tamaña maravilla (I, 410).

While he sings his song which causes Demetrio to weep,
Valderrama's eyes gleam "como esos ojos donde resplandece el
brillo de la locura" (I, 411).
     Just as Valderrama's madness protects him from the wrath
of others, he of his own account avoids all potential conflict.
At his first sight of Juchipila, he drops to one knee and kisses
the ground. The soldiers passing by laugh at him or make in-
sulting remarks, but he hears no one (I, 412). He eulogizes
the city:

> --¡Juchipila, cuna de la Revolución de 1910,
> tierra bendita, tierra regada con sangre de mártires,
> con sangre de soñadores . . . de los únicos buenos!
> . . . (I, 412).

An officer, passing by, interrupts him with a brutal retort:
"Porque no tuvieron tiempo de ser malos" (I, 412). Valderrama furrows his brow, laughs very loud and runs after his
detractor to ask him for a drink. He has an impermeable shield
which protects him from being insulted or hurt. His refuge
seems to be either insanity or advanced alcoholism. With no
loyalties, fears or ambitions, with every passion under control except his appetite for tequila, Valderrama is a free man.
     His freedom makes him the most forthright of the drama-
tized narrators. He is a soothsayer or prophet whose infirm-
ity gives him a vision which no other character has. His type
is the "loco cuerdo" or "ciego vidente." His prophecy seems
biblical in one passage, where he watches the sunset and
declaims:

--"¡Señor, Señor, bueno es que nos estemos aquí!
. . . Levantaré tres tiendas, una para ti, otra
para Moisés y otra para Elías" (I, 411).

Valderrama is a "flat," unidimensional character, only
one side of whose personality is revealed. In that respect
he is unique among the dramatized narrators. He does not
both love and hate the Revolution, like Alberto Solís, nor
preach a dual gospel of patriotic sacrifice and self gain, like
Luis Cervantes. He is not both comic and cruel, like el güero
Margarito. Valderrama is more stylized, more literarily "shal-
low" than any other character and has little in common with
any other.
Valderrama, the dramatized narrator who proclaims his love
for the Revolution as a blind force, does not love it for its
violence. On the contrary, he detests bloodshed. When it appears that Demetrio might order the execution of the four fugitives who turn out to be villista deserters, he rides off
alone:

Porque Valderrama, poeta romántico, siempre que
de fusilar se hablaba, sabía perderse lejos y durante
todo el día (I, 409).

Witnessing a cockfight, he reacts with "un gesto de violenta
indignación" (I, 411). The text states that the struggle was
particularly fierce, "de una ferocidad casi humana" (I, 411).
Valderrama's indignation, in a symbolic sense, represents a
protest against the violence of men against men.
Valderrama is surrounded by mystery, introduced without
explanation in Chapter 1, Part III. His origins are revealed
in the same paragraph with his disappearance. In Chapter 4,
Part III, Demetrio has mentioned an imminent encounter with
the carrancistas, a revelation which spurs Valderrama to
action:

Valderrama, el vagabundo de los caminos reales,
que se incorporó a la tropa un día, sin que nadie
supiera a punto fijo cuándo ni en dónde, pescó algo
de las palabras de Demetrio, y como no hay loco
que coma lumbre, ese mismo día desapareció como
había llegado (I, 413).

Valderrama's function is to enhance the other characters'
communication of despair in Part III. His madness runs parallel
to the illogical events which affect them. It is illogical,
after defeating one's enemies, to be pursued by one's allies;
to carry a wallet bulging with paper money, but find it impossible to buy even a little food, when indeed there is any
food to buy. It is illogical to come home after nearly two
years' absence, only to leave the next day. Valderrama is a
character ideally suited to Part III.
Each of the dramatized narrators has a distinct relationship with mortality. Alberto Solís' death is described with a

few details while el güero Margarito's is revealed second hand,
after it has occurred. Although Luis Cervantes does not die,
the reader knows that he has fled to the United States; but
when Valderrama leaves Demetrio's brigade, he has no destination. Continuing to exist in an unidentified place, Valderrama seems more nearly immortal than does Cervantes.

Solís' death, at the close of Part I, symbolizes the death
of idealism. Presented vividly, it marks the transition to the
very different Part II. Margarito's death, revealed subtly,
perhaps delimits the eclipse of humor. There are no comic incidents in Part III. Luis Cervantes' fate is presented with
verisimilitude. Always a realistically-portrayed character,
he passes from active participation in the novel to passive
existence in a geographically authentic place. Valderrama,
surrounded by an aura of the supernatural, presumably lives
on in some inaccessible sphere beyond the scope of the novel.
Never realistic, he is a symbolic character with an undefined
beginning and end.

In Los de abajo there are several degrees of literary
distance between the author and the reader. Distance is greatest when a character reveals something about another character,
one step greater than when he talks about himself. Both techniques involve direct quoting of a dialog or a monolog. The
next most distant level, that of narrative description of a
character's actions, is followed by the narration of events.
Less authorial distance is involved in the comments of a
dramatized narrator, though more than if the observation comes
unmediated at the closest possible level: the undramatized
narrator. The use of several dramatized narrators, therefore, adds increased flexibility to authorial distance.

Temporal Progression

In the broadest terms, all the characters who appear in
several different chapters show the effect of passing time.
Demetrio's wounded leg heals, as does Luis Cervantes' foot;
el güero Margarito's prisoner dies from mistreatment. Time
affects some characters in groups and others individually.
It works through gradual process or sudden alteration.

Hardship and suffering cause Demetrio's wife to age rapidly in two years:

> Demetrio, pasmado, veía a su mujer envejecida,
> como si diez o veinte años hubieran transcurrido ya
> (I, 415).

Without giving details, the narrator reveals that the wife
has changed a great deal. Demetrio's extreme reaction is testimony that she has aged astonishingly. She is the only
character upon whom time works vast physical changes.

Anastasio Montañés is a character whose experiences
change his philosophical viewpoint. In Chapter 2, Part I,
the narrator presents him as a foolhardy braggart who makes a
fetish of bravery in battle. Eager for a skirmish, he exclaims:

--Yo sólo les sé decir--agregó--que dejo
de llamarme Anastasio Montañés si mañana no soy
dueño de un máuser, cartuchera, pantalones y
zapatos. . . . Yo traigo media docena de plomos
adentro de mi cuerpo . . . Pero a mí me dan
tanto miedo las balas, como una bolita de cara-
melo (I, 324).

Anastasio's bravado is typical of the revolutionaries. In
Chapter 16, Part I, prior to the storming of the huertista
garrison, Luis Cervantes suggests that they take a guide
who knows the topography of the town. Demetrio answers
disdainfully:

. . . ¿Ha visto cómo sacan la cabeza las ardillas
por la boca del tusero cuando uno se los llena de
agua? Pues igual de aturdidos van a salir estos
mochitos infelices luego que oigan los primeros
disparos. No salen más que a servirnos de blanco
(I, 354).

In Chapter 1, Part III, Anastasio has become a spokesman
for prudence:

-- . . . lo que yo no podré hacerme entrar en
la cabeza . . . es eso de que tengamos que seguir
peleando . . . ¿Pos no acabamos ya con la Federación?
(I, 407).

When he goes from group to group, telling his comrades how he
feels, they laugh at his naïveté:

. . . Porque si uno trae un fusil en las manos y
las cartucheras llenas de tiros, seguramente que
es para pelear. ¿Contra quién? ¿En favor de
quiénes? ¡Eso nunca le ha importado a nadie! (I,
407).

Anastasio, who once expressed the reckless, exuberant confidence of the others, has now become spokesman of an un-
popular stand against conflict for the joy of conflict.
    The individual who changes most is Camila. The stereo-
type of an innocent country adolescent in Part I, she is
presented as a tormented woman in Part II. In Chapter 11,
Part I, she tells Luis Cervantes that she must say something
important to him. His challenge that she proceed with her
message embarrasses her to inarticulateness:

Camila sintió entonces la lengua hecha un
trapo y nada pudo pronunciar; su rostro se encendió
como un madroño, alzó los hombres y encogió la
cabeza hasta tocarse el desnudo pecho. Después,
sin moverse y fijando, con obstinación de idiota,
sus ojos en la herida, pronunció con debilísima voz:

--¡Mira qué bonito viene encarnando ya!. . .
Parece botón de rosa de Castilla。
    Luis Cervantes plegó el ceño con enojo
manifiesto y se puso de nuevo a curarse sin
hacer más caso de ella.
    Cuando terminó, Camila había desaparecido
(I, 342-343)。

When first presented, Camila is in the role of a child, incapable of influencing another character or affecting the
plot. The beginnings of her maturation are revealed in Chapter 14, Part I, where Luis counsels her to take advantage of
Demetrio's interest in her, thus qualifying to share in the
wealth and prestige which will be his. Crushed by Luis'
advice, Camila answers him more straightforwardly than ever
before:

        --¡Ay, curro . . . si vieras qué feo siento
que tú me digas eso! . 。 . Si yo a ti es al que
quero . . 。 pero a ti no más . . 。 Vete, curro,
vete, que no sé por qué me da tanta vergüenza . . 。
¡Vete, vete! 。 . . (I, 350-351).

Because her speech reveals the confession of a woman, Camila
is seen as a less ineffective character. Her evolution is
complete in Part II, where her continued defiance of Pintada
is the principal moving force of the plot. Camila's growth
from girlhood to womanhood is traced to its completion.
    A principal theme of Part III is time, run full cycle.
As action returns to where it began, the narrator begins to
mention reminders of the past。 In Chapter 5, the troops hear
church bells as they enter Juchipila. Anastasio recalls how
they used to be welcomed in every town by church bells, music
and skyrockets (I, 414). Seeing an old woman scurrying toward
the church, Venancio asks her what feast day is being celebrated:

        --¡Sagrado Corazón de Jesús!--repuso la beata
medio ahogándose.
    Se acordaron de que hacía un año ya de la toma
de Zacatecas. Y todos se pusieron más tristes
todavía (I, 414).

In Chapter 7, Part III, the narrator re-creates the
exuberant confidence which the rebels felt in Part I:

        Los soldados caminan por el abrupto peñascal
contagiado de la alegría de la mañana. Nadie
piensa en la artera bala que puede estarlo esperando
más adelante. La gran alegría de la partida estriba
cabalmente en lo imprevisto. Y por eso los soldados
cantan, ríen y charlan locamente. En su alma rebulle
el alma de las viejas tribus nómadas. Nada importa
saber adónde van y de dónde vienen; lo necesario es

caminar, caminar siempre, no estacionarse jamás;
ser dueños del valle, de las planicies, de la
sierra y de todo lo que la vista abarca (I, 416-
417).

The unwritten inference is that their enthusiasm is hollow,
so much has their world changed.

Demetrio comments that he and twenty men once inflicted
over five hundred casualties on the huertistas, in the very
place which they are now approaching (I, 417). His remark
closes the cycle in time and place. The characters are back
where their adventures began. Reference has been made to the
first skirmish recorded in the novel. With a link established
between Chapter 3, Part I, and Chapter 7, Part III, time has
at last retraced itself and action ceases.

Conclusions

The plot deals with the odyssey of Demetrio Macías. It
is cyclical, returning him to his home and his wife just prior
to his death. Demetrio, at first endowed with a mythlike
quality, is gradually humanized, his vices and weaknesses
revealed in stylistic preparation for his death.

Demetrio falls in love with Camila, a girl of the village
where he recovers from a wound. At first in love with Luis
Cervantes, she is rejected by him and at last becomes Demetrio's
companion. She is soon murdered by la Pintada, jealous over
Demetrio's attentions to her. Demetrio's depression after her
death provides a transition from the euphoria of Part II to
the despondency of Part III.

The novel is composed of forty-two chapters, each quite
brief, containing one or two complete actions. The typical
chapter introduces few characters and describes an action
concluded in a rather short period of time. The chapters are
divided into three parts of twenty-one, fourteen and seven
chapters. Part I contains the development of the key figures'
personalities and complications of the basic plot. Part II
details the characters' development in public, while Part III
contains Demetrio's homecoming and death. The pace of action
accelerates in each succeeding part.

The incidents occur in specific places, sometimes detailed and sometimes generalized. Outdoor locations are usually
described metaphorically or lyrically. When action takes place
indoors, the site is frequently unattractive. The characters'
movement from place to place accelerates as the novel progresses.
Usually, episodes high in dramatic tension take place in a
rather confined setting which augments the illusion of
urgency.

Since the narrator relates only incidents which develop
the personalities of characters, a reader might receive the
mistaken impression that only a few months transpire during
the course of plot development and resolution. To convey the
impression that nearly two years go by, the narrator periodi-
cally refers to historic events of 1913-15.

The narrator views some minor characters as through a distorting lens, concentrating on one or two grotesque facial features. Most characters remain faceless, identifiable by a non-facial feature. The narrator's impressionistic technique imitates human vision, recording one most quickly observable feature of a character, as if he were seen for only a fraction of a second. The anonymity of combatants is crucial to the description of Demetrio's first and last battles. The enemy is not seen fleetingly but rather from a great distance or hidden by camouflage. Only during the storming of the garrison are enemy forces observed close up.

Nature is depicted on an enormous scale, dwarfing man and his works, which are not only small but colorless. Nature also echoes or mocks the moods of the characters. She may stimulate moods or reflect them.

Illumination sometimes suggests the passage of time, as when an episode begins at dawn and ends in mid-morning light. Illumination or the lack of it is a factor in the relationship between combatants in each battle. Auditory phenomena sometimes accentuate the absence of visual images, when darkness limits the latter. Sounds may also evoke the characters' nostalgia or stimulate an emotional reaction. Since Demetrio's men are so shabbily and scantily dressed throughout the novel, his more substantial attire subtly identifies him as their superior. Prestigious male characters, however, never wear a coat and black tie; the minor characters who do so are made to suffer for their ostentation. Female characters, however, are placed in ridicule whenever they attempt to wear urban fashions or to entice a man. Only one woman seems out of place in tattered clothes: the young girl, presumably of aristocratic birth, whom Luis brings to Demetrio's banquet.

Narration sometimes replaces dialog, usually in the form of a summary. On occasion, the narrator intervenes to insert his own observations. Dialog may replace narration, especially when the author becomes a conjectured observer, not omniscient, knowing only what a character reveals about some event. Occasionally there appears in the dialog an elliptical conversation where the author presents only one character's part of an exchange. The statements infer what the unrevealed participant has done or said.

Philosophical content is at times conveyed by one of the four dramatized narrators. Alberto Solís, who appears in Part I, is a typical revolutionary idealist. Luis Cervantes, intervening in Parts I and II, is a narrator/agent whose words influence the plot. He proclaims self gain through insurrection. El güero Margarito, confined to Part II, exemplifies pursuit of pleasure. He is also the catalyst in the crucial dispute between Camila and Pintada. The mad, drunken troubadour Valderrama, a "flat" character with no origins or destination, is a prophetic "loco cuerdo." He exemplifies the pure revolutionary, in love with the movement, unfettered by politics or ideology.

Time, progressing during the course of the novel, affects some characters. Most altered by time is Camila, who grows

from a girl to a woman. In Part III, time has run full cycle.
Demetrio, returning to the canyon where he won his first
battle, loses his last.

In the dramatic novel, according to Muir, time develops
in a progression of causality.[5] Los de abajo, according to
Muir's definition, is a dramatic novel. It fulfills a number
of criteria, such as action which works upon the characters
and in turn is determined by them.[6] Demetrio Macías, whose
decision to ally himself with General Natera influences the
events of Part II, receives a bullet wound which immobilizes
him so that Luis Cervantes' path crosses his. Luis then persuades him to seek out Natera. Conversely, political vicissi-
tudes beyond Demetrio's control propel him toward his situation of Part III, where he and the remnants of his army must
face the carrancistas who will annihilate them. Demetrio un-
wittingly incurs Carranza's wrath by casting his lot with Natera, an ally of Villa, who subsequently rebels against Carranza.
Los de abajo demonstrates classic cause and effect.

Muir insists that the action be a logical outgrowth of
the characters' personalities, that future events be predictable
on the basis of the past, and that such events not be contradictions of pre-established personal characteristics.[7] That
Pintada will murder Camila is foreseeable, given Pintada's
aggressive personality and the build-up of enmity between the
two women. So carefully is the reader prepared for the homicide, that it is not a surprise; neither is it inconsistent
with what one already knows about Pintada.

Muir says the following about the plot of the dramatic
novel:

> . . . It may contain antithesis, but no mere contra-
> dictions. It will be logical in so far as the
> characters have something unchangeable in them
> which determines their responses to one another
> and to the situation. It will have a progression
> which is at once spontaneous and logical inasmuch
> as the characters will change, and the change will
> create new possibilities.[8]

Camila's change of heart makes her murder unavoidable. Rejected and then deceived by Luis Cervantes, she feels her
infatuation for him turn to hate. Originally afraid of
Demetrio, she spends enough time with him to be at ease
in his presence and finally to care for him. Given Camila's
new affections and Pintada's unswaying determination to win
the general's attentions, the clash between them becomes at
once natural and logical.

According to Muir, the dramatic novel moves in time.
Time is essential to it, because it describes a progression
and resolution of an action. Figures move from a beginning
to an end.[9] Not only must time be taken into consideration;
the rhythm, the rapidity or graduality of its flow, works upon
the action:

> In the beginning of a dramatic novel . . . we
> see Time gradually gathering itself up; then
> beginning to move, its end still unknown to us;
> then as its goal becomes clearer, marching with a
> steady acceleration; and finally fate is there and
> all is finished.[10]

Demetrio's fate becomes clear before the last chapter. Unable or unwilling to avoid it, he is sped toward it. When death does overtake him, it seems neither unjust nor surprising. In a dramatic novel such as <u>Los de abajo</u>, the climax is tragic but logical.

81

Footnotes

[1]Leal, Mariano Azuela, p. 125.

[2]One reason for the illusion of accelerated action in Part III is the concision of the units. Only Chapter 1, the transition from Part II, can be considered lengthy. It encompasses 90 lines of type in the Obras completas. Chapter 2 is only 60 lines long; Chapter 3, 60 lines; Chapter 4, 65; Chapter 5, 50 lines. The last chapter of the three leading up to Demetrio's homecoming is so brief that it propels the action forward. The crucial Chapters 6 and 7 contain, respectively, 50 and 60 lines.

[3]The subject of salió is Demetrio.

[4]Wayne C. Booth, The Rhetoric of Fiction (Chicago, 1961), pp. 153-154.

[5]Edwin Muir, The Structure of the Novel (New York, 1929), p. 45.

[6]Ibid., p. 41.

[7]Ibid., pp. 45-46.

[8]Ibid., pp. 47-48.

[9]Ibid., pp. 62-63.

[10]Ibid., p. 72.

CHAPTER II

LOS DE ABAJO, THE PLAY

Azuela's theatrical adaptation of his novel consists of
six cuadros or long scenes, not internally subdivided, portrayed in six settings, no two of which are alike. They represent varied material: political and personal crises, exuberant love and love so deep that it seems almost sad, philosophical expositions, raucous celebrations, and violent deaths.

Incidents, performed by characters typically Mexican in
their speech and dress, take place in a specifically Mexican
milieu. Time progresses as in life: during the approximately fifteen months which elapse in the course of represented
events, the characters evolve emotionally.

The play portrays the military period of Demetrio Macías'
life, during the Mexican Revolution. The plot is in progress
before representation begins, for he has already assembled a
make-shift army of serranos who, like him, are fugitives from
the law. When two federal soldiers chance upon his hut in the
night, discovering his whereabouts, he sends his wife to his
parents' home and escapes to join his men.

Demetrio is next revealed lying wounded in a hut in a
small village. It is later disclosed that he was injured in
a battle with the huertistas. During the rebels' extended
stay in the village, two new characters indispensable to the
plot are introduced: Luis Cervantes, a government deserter
who wins Demetrio's confidence by healing his leg; and Camila,
a girl of the village who will become Demetrio's mistress.

Demetrio, his leg again sound, is next shown with his
friends in a cantina, possibly in Zacatecas, where he performed a feat of heroism in the victory over Huerta's last
supporters. In the restaurant Demetrio meets la Pintada, a
saloon girl who so resents his affection for Camila that she
kills her.

After the murder of Camila, Demetrio and his followers
are next revealed dressed poorly, in ramshackle surroundings.
Their conversation attests to the ill fortune and hardships
which have befallen them. Awaiting an inevitable clash with
the carrancistas who pursue them, the revolutionaries seem
very depressed.

Demetrio is briefly reunited with his wife, before going
out to the battle in which he is killed. His off-stage death
is revealed indirectly through his wife.

Patterns of Action

The Hero: Mythified and Humanized

Cuadro I establishes Demetrio as a civilian forced by the
politics of his day to take up arms. It is evident that he is
not at home all the time, but always in the area. His wife's
concern that he and his men eat heartily suggests that they
sleep many nights under the stars: " . . . Esto no es cosa
que comen ustedes todos los días. ¡Las hambres y miserias que
habrán pasado en la vida que llevan!" (III, 10). It is the
wife who introduces the enemy, the federales. She calls them
"perros del mal" (III, 11) and recites a brief list of their
abuses. Speaking in the first person plural, she is made a
representative of oppressed Mexicans.
Anastasio, boasting that the revolutionaries have had
some success against the federales, inflicting on them a
"cueriada" (III, 11), introduces Demetrio, who speaks for the
first time. His question about the two latest recruits evokes
an answer which establishes in what part of Mexico they are:

> ANASTASIO
> Los conoce tan bien como yo. ¿Quién, pues,
> tocaba los platillos en la música de viento de
> Juchipila? (III, 11).

Demetrio places on the cacique of nearby Moyahua the blame for
his having to hide out in the area. In his next speech he
specifically names don Mónico (III, 12).
When Anastasio and Codorniz have left, Demetrio tells his
wife that the federación seems about to attack. He orders her
to go to his parents' home for safety. His instructions about
the disposition of his property (III, 13-14) establish him as
head of a family first, who is only secondarily an insurgent
leader.
Of the character traits with which the playwright endows
Demetrio, one of the most essential is his fearlessness. He
makes no statement like Anastasio's ("Traigo adentro de mi
cuerpo media docena de plomos. ¡Ahi que diga mi compadre si
yo les tengo miedo!" (III, 13)). Demetrio's actions, never-
theless, are more convincing than anything he could say. When
the dog begins barking, Demetrio's wife begs him to hide outside the hut in case the huertistas are approaching. His calm
actions convey a refusal to be afraid:

> (Demetrio, parsimoniosamente, coge a dos manos
> el cántaro de agua y bebe a borbotones; . . . levanta
> su rifle y paso a paso sale del jacal, . . .) (III,
> 15).

Taking the time for a prolonged drink and going out slowly,
Demetrio proves that danger does not alter his measured actions.

The enemy intruders' remarks prove that Demetrio is quite famous in the region. They instantly associate his name with that of his village. The huertistas' bravado when they mention Demetrio's name demonstrates that they fear and respect him:

SARGENTO
. . . Oiga, señora, ¿cómo se llama este ranchito?

LA MUJER
Pos Limón, ¿cómo quiere que se llame?

SARGENTO
¿Lo oyó, mi teniente? Estamos en Limón, en la mera tierra del famoso Demetrio Macías.

TENIENTE
. . . ¿Conque aquí es Limón? . . . Pos pa mí, ¡plim! ¿Demetrio Macías? ¡Plim! Y si he de irme al infierno nunca mejor que ahora que voy en buen caballo. (Señalando con el gesto a la mujer.) (III, 16).

The most significant of the lieutenant's remarks is his allusion to hell. Apparently he would expect to come off second best in an encounter with Demetrio.

Toward the end of Cuadro I, the lieutenant tries to embrace Demetrio's wife. When she pushes him down, he throws himself upon her. At that moment, Demetrio appears in the doorway. The huertista sergeant steps back, horrified, and pronounces the famous rebel's name. The lieutenant stops as if he were a statue. Standing at attention, he becomes effusive in polite phrases directed at Demetrio. He calls him "amigo" twice and alludes three times to his courage (III, 18). During this incident Demetrio assumes the stature of a legend. He is to appear in the door "como una sombra" (III, 18). The actor, dressed in white or pale grey pajamas, is framed by the blackness which envelops all the stage except the interior of the hut. The enemy sergeant, retreating, pronounces Demetrio's name with awe, as if it were a magical formula. Demetrio, never saying a word, watches the aggressors with an insolent stare. His silence, showing the powerful effect of his mere presence, also contributes to the irreality which surrounds him during the incident.

In Cuadro IV is presented the spectacle of Demetrio, sitting in a cantina, hearing his heroic exploits as they are recounted by someone else at his table. Demetrio's presence adds vividness to Valderrama's account of his deeds at Zacatecas. That effect is increased when Anastasio, who accompanied Demetrio in his brave acts, intervenes in the narration (III, 48-49). Concluding his story, Valderrama recites Demetrio's name, contributing to his image as a living legend. Pintada reinforces that image, saying: "¿Entonces usted es el famoso Demetrio Macías que tanto se lució en Zacatecas?" (III, 49). His name, repeated in his presence, becomes like a fixed formula. His first and last names are frequently pronounced together.

When Pintada asks if he is the one who so distinguished
himself at Zacatecas, Demetrio's bearing and reply are haughtily reserved:

DEMETRIO
(Volviendo su rostro adusto. . . .)
Al orden (III, 49).

He does not relate his own heroics, but instead listens to
them in silence. When congratulated, he shows no pleasure
nor even interest. If the playwright assigned to him long
speeches in praise of himself, Demetrio might be a less convincing folk hero. His emotional distance or detachment enhances his larger-than-life characterization.

A brief incident of Cuadro II augments the irreality surrounding Demetrio, showing his icy calm as contrasted to the
emotional outbursts of his disciples. The dispute begins when
Anastasio suggests that Demetrio call in Luis Cervantes to
treat his leg. When Venancio, the company medic, protests
vigorously, Pancracio retorts:

¡Pero qué dotor ni qué nada eres tu! ¡Voy
que ya hasta se te olvidó por qué veniste a dar
aquí!

VENANCIO
(Exaltado.)
Sí, ya me acuerdo que andas con nosotros porque
te robaste un reloj de oro y unos brillantes.

PANCRACIO
Peor tú que envenenaste a tu novia con cantáridas
pa . . .

VENANCIO
(Sacando un cuchillo.)
¡Mientes!

DEMETRIO
(Con el revólver en las manos que ha tomado de
su almohada de yerbas.)
Se callan o . . . los acuesto (III, 36).

The dialog and stage directions seem to suggest that Demetrio
shares none of his comrades' agitation. The incident is
truncated, not concluding with a threat carried out, an apology,
a cooling of tempers nor a sheathing of weapons. Its effect
is to maintain Demetrio's aura of inner strength and self-
control.

Scattered throughout Cuadros II-IV are subtle examples of
Demetrio's humanization. In Cuadro II, when Camila enters the
hut to bring him a bowl of milk, Demetrio reacts to her as any
man might:

(Muy reanimado.)

¿Cómo dices que te llamas? ¿Camila? Tienes
una vocecita como campanita de plata。
(Al devolverle la vasija, Demetrio coge por
un brazo a Camila y ésta pugna por deshacerse de
él.) (III, 34-35).

For the first time in the play, Demetrio is affected normally
by an emotional situation. That human reaction is closely
followed by the scene where Demetrio coldly threatens to
shoot Pancracio and Venancio if they do not halt their violent
quarrel。 No sooner does his humanity emerge than his emotional
superiority is re-established.

A major element contributing to Demetrio's mythlike quality
is his relative silence early in the play. He has only fourteen short speeches in Cuadro I and only eighteen in the much
longer Cuadro II. Demetrio becomes suddenly loquacious in
Cuadro III, telling Cervantes at great length how he became a
revolutionary. Breaking his silence, he seems more nearly
mortal than before.

Demetrio first shows emotional agitation at the close of
Cuadro IV, when Pintada stabs Camila to death. His speech
is "demudado" (III, 63) as he orders his men to kill Pintada
instantly。 Defiantly she offers him the bloody dagger, which
he siezes from her but is then afflicted again by his emotions.
He raises the dagger; then his hand begins to tremble and he
cannot execute Pintada. His voice is "apagada y ronca" (III,
63) as he orders her away. The process of Demetrio's humanization is quite advanced; his fierce emotions have for the
first time in the play prevented him from doing what he
intended.

In Cuadro V, Demetrio no longer seems like a gigantic,
legendary figure of immortal fame. Nowhere is he called by
both his names; old doña Nica, who knows him well, addresses
him as "don Demetrio" (III, 65); to Anastasio, he is "compadre
Demetrio" (III, 69, 71). To María Antonia and Valderrama,
who are not old acquaintances, he is "mi general" (III, 66,
67, 70)。 The familiar address renders Demetrio more a vulnerable man than an immortal legend. The playwright, manipulating
Demetrio's image, prepares the spectator for his death in
Cuadro VI.

In the last incident of Cuadro V, Demetrio displays lack
of emotion upon receiving news of a grave peril:

PANCRACIO
(Entra alarmado.)
Traigo malas noticias; tenemos muy cerca a los
carranclanes.

DEMETRIO
(Oyéndolo con indiferencia.)
A ver, doña Nica, una copa para Pancracio. . . .

DEMETRIO
(Incorporándose perezosamente.)
Muchachos, mientras doña Nica nos hace de
almorzar, vamos a traernos unos músicos para
acabarnos de alegrar, antes de entrarle a los
tecolotazos (III, 71-72).

The incident cannot be compared to Demetrio's leisurely drink
of water, in Cuadro I, as he hears the federales outside his
hut. The words indiferencia and perezosamente, in the stage
directions, suggest not extraordinary courage but physical
exhaustion or a psychological defense which shelters Demetrio
from the truth. The "eat, drink and be merry" philosophy,
insinuated by Demetrio's words and actions, suggests a fatal-
ism which is evident in other speeches. Instances are found
early and late in the play. In Cuadro I, when his wife asks
him why he did not kill the huertista lieutenant and his sergeant, Demetrio replies: "Asiguro que todavía no les tocaba
. . ." (III, 19). In Cuadro VI she asks him why he continues
to fight, despite the overthrow of the federación. Demetrio
makes no attempt at political or moral justification but
simply expresses his acquiescence:

(Sin levantar los ojos, melancólicamente, toma
una piedrecilla y la arroja al barranco. . . .)
Mira esa piedra cómo ya no se para . . . (III, 77).

Taking leave of his family, Demetrio points to his young son
and tells his wife: "Cuídalo y rézale a Dios por mí" (III,
78). That request and his metaphor of the carroming stone
constitute Demetrio's public acceptance of his forthcoming
death and the dispelling of the illusion of his immortality.

In summary, an important element of the plot is the
creation of Demetrio as a semi-legendary hero and the gradual
exposition of his humanity. The incident of the abusive
federales and the recitation of his exploits, in Cuadro IV,
show Demetrio more as a myth than as a man. The enemy intruders, pronouncing his name as if in awe, freeze with fear
when he enters the room. When they first see Demetrio in the
doorway, he seems like an incorporeal shadow. He says nothing
to them, the ironic smile on his face never changing. His
silence and immutability contribute to his image as a living
legend. In Cuadro II Demetrio remains icily calm amid a heated
debate between two of his followers. In Cuadro IV he listens
without comment as Valderrama tells of his heroic attack on
huertista positions at Zacatecas. His presence in silence
contributes to the aura of supernaturality which surrounds
him. A key factor in the mythical quality which Demetrio possesses in Cuadro I and IV is the frequent formula-like repetition of his name, first and last, by other characters.

The first index of Demetrio's gradual humanization is his
lustful grabbing of Camila's wrist, in Cuadro II. In Cuadro
III he delivers several long speeches, telling frankly about
his past. He seems for the first time loquacious, violating

the norm of speaking very little. The extended speeches
make him seem much more open and, consequently, human. In
Cuadro IV Demetrio's emotions render him nearly helpless to
avenge Camila, who has just been murdered by Pintada. That
incident shows him vulnerable like other men.

In Cuadro V, the characters who surround Demetrio treat
him as an esteemed friend or respected leader, never as an
awesome legend. He is not addressed by both of his names, as
in a mystic formula, but simply as "Demetrio," "compadre" or
"mi general." That warm, intimate treatment completes
Demetrio's mortalization, a stylistic prelude to his death in
Cuadro VI.

The Hero and Women: Camila

Demetrio, who is with his wife very little in the play,
develops another love interest in Camila, the girl who period-
ically brings him water or milk during his convalescence in
the village. She does not meet Demetrio until after having
fallen in love with Luis Cervantes. Her comments as she
watches Luis treat his injured foot reveal her concern for
his safety and suggest that she is infatuated with him. She
asks if he is really a government soldier, and he says that he
was forced to become one. Though no stage directions call for
a display of relief, Camila's words suggest a keen interest
in Luis' welfare. She assumes that if he did not intentionally
join with the enemy, his life will be spared:

¡Ah, qué bueno! Porque entonces no lo fusilan a usted
(III, 26).

Cervantes, muttering half to himself, vows revenge on his
commanding officer, who discovered him hiding from the battle.
Camila's colloquial expression of enthusiasm (újule) and the
liberal use of exclamation points portray her relief quite
vividly:

¡Ujule, pos si usted tampoco los puede ver!
¡Qué gusto me da que no sea usted de esos condenados
federales! . . . (III, 26).

Camila's keen interest in Luis becomes a fight to save
his life. When she brings Demetrio a drink of water, she
hears him ask about "el mocho" (III, 29), an expression the revolutionaries use to refer to the enemy. Camila boldly defends
Cervantes, pointing out how useful he might be to Demetrio:

No es mocho, a mí me lo dijo. ¡Y si viera qué
bien sabe curar! Cómo no lo llama (III, 30).

Seeing Luis escorted into Demetrio's hut, Camila "se levanta
al punto para acercarse a fisgonear por las rendijas" (III,
32). She slips away as Cervantes is led out, presumably to
be executed. At that point another character, María Antonia,

declares Camila's love for the young prisoner:

> ¡Ya te mueres por el curro! Pero sólo por
> eso que ya lo van a fusilar (III, 34).

Though she has no reason to doubt María Antonia's prediction,
Camila continues to press for commutation of Luis' sentence.
Fetching a bowl of milk, she brings it to Demetrio and once
again states her case. She pleads for mercy, then reminds
Demetrio that Cervantes' might help him:

> Oiga, ¿que izque siempre van a jusilar al
> hombre? . . . No sea malo, don Demetrio. . . .
> Le digo de de veras que no es de los federales.
> Mire, ¡si viera qué bien sabe curar! Yo que
> usté mejor me ponía en sus manos (III, 34).

Camila's bravery and determination, well established in Cuadro
II, make plausible her defiance of la Pintada in Cuadro IV.
Pintada gives her a warning and an opportunity to return home
in peace. Camila, defending her prerogative as tenaciously as
she defended Cervantes' life, not only refuses to go but persuades Demetrio to send Pintada away. Her resolute spirit,
strong enough to overcome fear of death, is a direct cause of
her murder.
    Camila, profoundly infatuated with Luis Cervantes in Cuadros
II-III, appears equally committed to Demetrio in Cuadro IV;
her fatal defiance of Pintada does not seem artistically weak.
She does not undergo an unexplained transferral of capricious
affection but rather a transformation of love into shattering
disillusion to love re-directed. At the close of Cuadro III,
Cervantes advises Camila to accept Demetrio's attentions, because he can give her wealth and prestige. Camila, devastated
by Luis' rejection of her love, orders him to leave her alone.
    In Cuadro IV, Camila tells Pintada that Luis lied to her,
bringing her to Zacatecas from her village under the pretext of
claiming her for himself. The text makes it clear that she
has suffered a great deal because of Luis. She has, however,
accepted her role as Demetrio's mistress. She has already
decided not to return home:

> LA PINTADA
> ¡Pobrecita de ti! Oye, ¿quieres volverte a
> tu casa?
>
> CAMILA
> ¡Ni lo mande Dios! A palos acababa conmigo mi
> mamá (III, 55).

Pintada contrives an elaborate scheme to return Camila to her
home, but Camila again rejects the idea, adding a half-hearted
declaration for Demetrio: " . . . Más segura estoy con él"
Pintada then asks a direct question:

Entonces, ¿es que ya lo quieres, pues?

CAMILA
¡Pos si viera que es tan güeno que ya le voy
cobrando voluntá! (III, 56).

Camila's conversation synthesizes the four steps which have
in order led her from strong feelings for Luis to equally
strong feelings for Demetrio: desolation at Luis' lies
when he took her from her village; fear of her mother's
wrath if she should return home; a feeling of safety at Demetrio's side; and at last an appreciation of his good qualities.

Camila's murder, at the close of Cuadro IV, is a prelude
to Demetrio's arrangements to return home. In Cuadro V, he
and his troops arrive in Juchipila, not far from his home,
where he is greeted by an acquaintance, old doña Nica, to
whose kiosk they have come for lunch:

¡Don Demetrio! ¡Alma mía de usted! ¡Pos qué
esperanzas tenía ya de volverlo a ver! . . . ¡Cuánto
gusto va a darle a su siñora! . . . (III, 65).

Demetrio's reunion with his wife is a result of his having
traveled through space and time from the place of Camila's
death to Juchipila, during the interval between Cuadros IV
and V. Logically, then, the murder of Camila did not nec-
cessarily cause Demetrio to return to his wife. Structurally,
though, the adjacency of the two events affirms an emotional
link if not causality.

In no scene of the play are Demetrio and Camila alone.
They are together on a stage full of characters throughout
Cuadro IV; in Cuadro II, when Demetrio seizes her wrist, there
is a witness in the hut:

(Camila logra deshacerse de él en un reculón y
sale. Demetrio repara entonces en su compadre
Anastasio, que llegó sin ser advertido y ha estado
contemplando la escena, . . .) (III, 35).

The stage directions make it clear that Demetrio thinks he is
alone with the girl and is startled to see Anastasio. The
absence of private moments between Demetrio and Camila keeps
their relationship distinct from and inferior to that which
Demetrio shares with his wife, to whom Camila is, therefore,
never a true rival.

Camila's words and actions reveal a deep concern for Luis
Cervantes' safety. Infatuated from the first moment she sees
him, she boldly works to save his wife. Saved through his own
cleverness, Luis rejects her and tries to win her over to
Demetrio. When at last he tricks her into joining the revolutionaries, she finds that she is intended not for Cervantes but
for Demetrio. Desolate at Luis' deception, she so fears going
back to face her mother's wrath that she elects to remain with
Demetrio. She feels safe at his side and begins to appreciate

his good qualities. Once having chosen loyalty to Demetrio, Camila remains steadfast despite Pintada's threat on her life. Camila's refusal to back down leads directly to her murder. That violent deed is a structural prelude to Demetrio's homecoming and reunion with his wife, although her loss is not necessarily what prompts him to go home. Demetrio and Camila, never sharing an intimate moment, have a relationship which is emotionally inferior to the love he feels for his wife. Camila, not presented as the object of Demetrio's passion, has another function in the play. A key participant in two of the most important subplots of the play (her fight for Cervantes' life and her rivalry with la Pintada), she is also a principal comic figure in Cuadro II. Her rustic dialect and naïveté render her ludicrous despite her admirable boldness.

Heroic Purpose and Political Insophistication

Demetrio, seeing the Revolution on a narrow scale, never understands the implied consequences of his participation in the conflict. Early in Cuadro I, Demetrio reveals that he sees the war basically as a local phenomenon:

> En Moyahua está cabalmente el cacique que
> me trae corriendo por acá . . . (III, 12).

In Cuadro III Demetrio expands on his conception of why he must fight the federales:

> . . . antes de la revolución yo tenía ya mis
> tierras hasta volteadas para las siembras, y si
> no hubiera sido por el choque con don Mónico,
> el cacique de Moyahua, a estas horas andaría
> yo jalando con mi yunta . . . (III, 39).

Demetrio, conversing with Luis Cervantes, explains that he once spit in don Mónico's face, so enraging the local political chief that he accused Demetrio as a maderista and asked for government troops to hunt him down. That Demetrio has only a sketchy notion of the crucial events of February, 1913, is manifest:

> . . . Usted ha de haber oído hablar de ese chisme
> de México donde resultó muerto el señor Madero y
> un tal Félix o Felipe Díaz . . . (III, 39).

Luis Cervantes impresses the illiterate Demetrio and his followers with what to them is his vast erudition. After he persuades the rebels to cast their lot with General Natera, they discuss the decision they have made:

> ANASTASIO
> ¡Qué bien explica las cosas este curro!

> DEMETRIO
> ¡Lo que es saber leer y escribir!

> ANASTASIO
> Pero lo que a mí no se me alcanza es eso de
> que usted se presente con ese señor Natera, con los
> poquitos que semos.

> DEMETRIO
> Y que nos hagan algún mal modo.

> ANASTASIO
> Tan mugrosos y tan desgarrados como andemos.
> Dicen que toda la gente de Villa viene con sus
> trenes apretados de bueyes, vacas y carneros;
> furgones llenos de ropa y de bastimento . . .
> (III, 43).

Anastasio's words underline the peasants' vague notions about
the key figures of the Revolution. To them, Pancho Villa
is little more than an opulent legend. It is Pancracio who
displays the most complete ignorance, in Cuadro II, when he
does not recognize Cervantes' password sufficiently even to
repeat it correctly: "Yo no sé quién es ese Carranzo" (III,
21).

The play contains so few references to political events
that it is unclear whether the revolutionaries, in Cuadro V,
understand why Carranza's partisans are pursuing them. Demetrio makes just one allusion to the feud which so vitally
affects him:

> . . . nosotros estamos por despachar a Villa y a
> Carranza a que se diviertan solitos . . . (III,
> 71).

No reference is made to the historical event which gained
Carranza his ascendancy over Villa: the Battle of Celaya.
Demetrio's continuation in the conflict, despite his
desperate situation, appears to be a function of his belief
in machismo. In Cuadro V Anastasio complains bitterly about
the morale of the troops. Demetrio agrees with his evaluation but not with his candor:

> Lo sé, compadre, lo sé. Los soldados no quieren
> a las clases, las clases hablan mal de mos oficiales,
> los oficiales de nosotros, . . . Pero esto no hay que
> decirlo, compadre.

> ANASTASIO
> ¿Por qué no, si es el puro credo?

> DEMETRIO
> No sé por qué; pero yo siento que no es cosa de
> hombres . . . (III, 71).

Demetrio, somewhat like Camila, seals his own doom through stubborn determination. He does not seem any more enlightened about his purpose in Cuadro VI, casting the symbolic stone into the chasm to explain to his wife why he must continue to fight, than in Cuadro I where he first lays the entire blame upon Don Mónico. The drama does not record a process by which Demetrio becomes more aware of why he is participating in the Revolution. He may in fact be less certain than at the outset; begging Anastasio not to voice his complaints, Demetrio offers no concrete reasons of even local scope. Evidently neither man is any longer concerned about defending himself from law officers. The rationale for their revolutionary activities, most articulately expressed in Cuadro III, thereafter declines in validity.

Demetrio Macías, early in the play, has a mythlike quality which submerges his humanity. A more nearly normal personality is gradually revealed as he reacts to a series of situations as an average person might. The process of de-mythification is a stylistic preparation for Demetrio's death.

Wounded in battle, Demetrio convalesces in a tiny village where he meets Luis Cervantes, the medical student whose counsel will lead him to fleeting wealth and ultimately to his death. Luis' decisive intervention casts Camila with Demetrio and indirectly causes her death at the hand of the jealous Pintada.

Demetrio and his followers, originally believing they have taken up arms because of the injustices which local officials have done them, lose all rationale for fighting and persevere because of tenacity and pride. It is unclear whether they realize why the carrancistas have hunted them down. To the extent that they do not know the consequences of each of their acts, Demetrio and the others are innocent victims of an internecine struggle.

Scenario Organization

Cuadro

The six cuadros, the only divisions of Los de abajo, vary considerably in length. Cuadros I and III each constitute approximately one-sixth of the entire play; II and IV are each half again as long, while Cuadros V and VI are considerably shorter.

Every cuadro except V and VI contains one complete major incident. Cuadros II and III each contain a whole incident plus part of another, begun in II and concluded in III. Cuadros V and VI share one major incident.

The number of characters who participate in each cuadro varies from six to nine; the principal incidents, however, involve fewer characters. No more than five characters and as few as two take part in the major incidents.

The action in each cuadro is continuous, with no transitions which represent elapsed time. Therefore each cuadro accounts for less than an hour's progression. Since a year or more is to go by during the enactment of the play, the illusion of long periods of elapsed time is achieved in the transitions from cuadro to cuadro.

Structure

The six-cuadro structure seems based on a single rhythmic cycle governed by Demetrio Macías' career. He is a private person in Cuadro I, public figure in Cuadros II-IV, and a private man again in Cuadros V and VI, surrounded by friends rather than allies and principally concerned about domestic matters. He is a private figure in three cuadros and a celebrity in three. The presence or absence of Camila and Luis Cervantes seems governed by that cyclic structure; each appears only in Cuadros II-IV. Emphasis upon Demetrio's private life in the last two cuadros affects the tone of the drama, which is in part an exposition of the effect of war upon individuals. The psychological aspect of the work, concentrated at the end, is in a structurally strong position to impress the audience.

The structure of each cuadro is based on an individual rhythm or cycle. The rhythm may be based on proportion, alternation, interruption, tempo or time. Proportion is the basis of the structure of Cuadro I, which is divided quite equally between an introductory scene and the first episode of the play: the arrival of the huertista intruders. The introduction orients the spectator concerning Demetrio the man, in the circumstance of the Revolution, which affects him in a specific way. The cuadro closes with the departure of Demetrio and his wife, linking it with Cuadro VI, which portrays their reunion.

The structure of Cuadro II consists of the alternate presentation of three subplots: the fate of Luis Cervantes, Camila's relations with him and Demetrio's relations with Camila. The first two themes are introduced in long scenes, and the third, in a very short episode. There follows a return to the disposition of Cervantes' future, the principal theme of the cuadro. It is re-introduced three times, and the other subplots, only once. After the first re-introduction of the problem of Luis' fate comes an interlude, costumbrista in nature, during which Señá Remigia attempts to cure Demetrio's leg. The interlude provides a structural release before action returns to each of the three subplots in order. There follows the fourth segment dealing with Cervantes' fate, which contains the resolution of the theme. Camila's romantic interest in Luis is not resolved in Cuadro II, nor is Demetrio's interest in her. The cuadro closes with Demetrio's decision to call in Cervantes for treatment of his leg. That incident, representing the leader's confidence in his prisoner, is a bridge to Cuadro III, where that confidence bears serious consequences.

Cuadro III is structured temporally. The first half deals with the present: Cervantes demonstrates the favor he has won with his new allies. He expounds upon his doctrine of personal gain through revolution. Following is a brief future-oriented recapitulation during which Demetrio and his followers discuss the probable results of following Luis' advice. The cuadro closes with the return to two past themes: Camila's infatuation with Luis and Demetrio's interest in her. The former is terminated, truncated by Cervantes' abrupt rejection of the girl, while the latter theme is left to be resolved later.

The structure of Cuadro IV is based on the repeated interruption of the principal incident: Pintada's jealousy toward Camila, leading to violent revenge. The cuadro opens with Valderrama's description of Demetrio's heroics in battle. The scene is a transition between unrepresented past events and the incidents soon to occur on stage. Next is the introduction of Pintada and el güero Margarito, the new characters indispensable to the cuadro. The principal theme is then presented for the first time, as several characters discuss Camila's recent arrival. Their conversation is interrupted by the first comic interlude, Margarito's assault of the waiter who fails to bring him ice water. Following that incident and a brief humorous exchange between Anastasio and Codorniz, the main theme is presented for the second time. Pintada tries to persuade Camila to return home, at first offering help and then threatening the girl. Their hostile exchange is followed by a second comic interlude, shorter than the first, during which Luis, Codorniz and la Pintada discuss the booty they have plundered. In a very brief return to the principal action, Camila asks Demetrio to send her home and he promises to send Pintada away instead. Before he makes good his vow, there intervenes the banquet scene, the third and longest interlude. The jealousy between the two women is climaxed in a rather lengthy scene at the close of the cuadro, where Pintada murders Camila. The last unresolved subplot from Cuadro II, Demetrio's interest in Camila, is thereby resolved. Only one problem remains: Demetrio's absence from home.

Cuadro V, like Cuadro III, has a structure built upon the examination of past, present and future events. The cuadro begins with Valderrama's lament about the crosses, a transition between unrepresented past events and the on-stage present. Following is the introduction of doña Nica, an important auxiliary character. There is a reference to the future, to events of Cuadro VI, as María Antonia leaves to contact Demetrio's wife. There follow two equally long series of scenes, the first dealing with the past (Cervantes' letter and reminiscences of the characters) and the second, with the present (complaints about troop morale and Pancracio's announcement that the enemy is approaching).

Cuadro VI is structured around a tempo of acceleration and deceleration of events. The build-up consists of Demetrio's slow arrival, described by María Antonia and the wife. Animation reaches its maximum tempo as the women see Demetrio arrive and he at last appears on stage. After his departure, the pace of animation slows until Demetrio's wife stands alone, grieving over his death. Her gradual collapse slows movement to a halt. The pace of animation is controlled by the characters' activity and by the number of figures on stage. That number varies from three (the women and the small child) to a maximum of five (when they are joined by Demetrio and Pancracio) to just Demetrio's wife and son, alone on stage when the curtain descends.

Los de abajo is structured upon an over-all cycle of six cuadros governed by the events of Demetrio's life. Within the larger framework are the individual structures of the cuadros. No two are constructed alike and only two are based upon the same principle. Though the structure of the play is complex, control of the themes keeps the work from becoming confused. The subplots are few in number, involving simple incidents and only a few characters who overlap; each major character plays a role in more than one subplot. Resolving all minor themes before turning to the central problem, Demetrio's separation from his wife, the playwright further avoids confusion and maintains the thematic unity of the individual cuadros.

The Settings

Place

Each cuadro takes place in a single set which remains unchanged throughout. There are in the play, then, six settings, no two of which are alike. Some are exclusively interior or exterior while others are a combination.

That the action takes place in a certain region of Mexico is made evident in the set directions for Cuadro I. On the wall of Demetrio's hut, hanging from manguey thorns, are "ollas, jarros, cazuelas, tazas de barro de Guadalajara" (III, 9). Also on the wall is a typical Mexicon icon, a picture of the Virgin of Jalpa.

Demetrio, in Cuadro I, is more a family man than a political figure. The crockery on the wall of his hut contributes to that image, as do the plow and other farming implements in the corner. The most domestic article of all, a cradle, is suspended from the ceiling. A rifle with cartridge belts, the symbol of Demetrio's public life, is hidden under a blanket.

The set of Cuadro II is an indoor-outdoor combination. Stage front and at the right is a straw hut, its interior exposed. On the left and at the rear of the stage is the extended roof and an outside wall of a second hut. Painted in the scenery is a mountain, part of which extends onto the stage between the two buildings. It is represented by simulated rocks. The split set provides a physical separation of the actions which comprise Cuadro II. In the interior of the hut on the right, Cervantes is brought before Demetrio and later interrogated. There it is decided whether he shall live or die. Outside the hut on the left, Camila converses with Luis as he treats his foot. In practice, half the set is used for portrayal of political incidents, and the other half, for actions with a personal content.

The hut on the right is bare of furnishing except for the cot where Demetrio lies. Certain aspects of everyday life are, then, suspended within that hut. Food is neither prepared nor eaten there; family-type activities do not take place. Demetrio, while confined to the hut, is not portrayed as a private citizen with normal activities. Only a few roles are open to him: commander, convalescent, and rather impersonal pursuer of Camila.

The set of Cuadro III binds it to Cuadro II, using as its painted background the huts of the previous unit. The action is to take place in an unpopulated area represented by two large simulated rocks. The set, though it is not dual, divides in space the two types of action of which the cuadro is composed. When the characters are seated on the rocks or standing near them, they discuss their future or that of the Revolution. When one of them enters or exits through the hut area, he establishes a link with the present or past: Demetrio's preparations for leaving the village or Luis' termination of his relationship with Camila. Position in or movement around the set determines the viewpoint (looking backward or forward) of each act.

The set of Cuadro IV is completely interior, representing the dining room of a restaurant. It contains a bar at one end of the stage, several tables with chairs, and mirrors on the walls. The set, not typically Mexican, could represent a restaurant anywhere. No element belonging exclusively to the set, such as utensils or thatched huts, establishes a Mexican-ness independent from costumes or dialog.

The set of Cuadro V is the most intricate, most carefully detailed of the six. Stage front and at the right is "el ruinoso portalón de una fonda" (III, 63). Rarely does the author use a qualifying term like "ruinoso." Through the door is to be seen "un sucio trastero" (III, 63)--another of the playwright's very specific adjectives. Hanging across the doorway is "una cortina de manta desteñida y arrugada" (III, 63). The scene is designed to connote a decrepitude which is transferrable to the characters.

The prescribed staging for Cuadro VI, extremely brief, allows considerable latitude to the viewers' imagination. It says only the following:

En la cima de un cerro y al pie de una roca enorme cortada a pico por el frente. Fondo de montañas y cielo azul (III, 72).

Apparently the only property is to be a large simulated rock. The playwright is, for the first time, rather inspecific. The purpose of the boulder is to serve as a vantage point for observation of conjectured offstage events which, when they take place, are more important than what transpires in the view of the audience.

In summary, the sets are composed with economy of elements. Demetrio's hut, in Cuadro I, is furnished only with the bare essentials for the mood the playwright wishes to convey.

Demetrio and his comrades are "sentados en cuclillas" (III,
10) awaiting the food which the wife is preparing. Chairs
or benches, which would serve no specific purpose, are
omitted. In Cuadros IV and V, on the other hand, tables and
chairs are essential to the action and are included. In
Cuadro II, where it is necessary to show the interior of one
hut and the exterior of another, the cooking utensils are
not placed inside the first hut but outside the second. That
distribution avoids cluttering of the stage and allows for a
shifting center of action. It also eliminates duplication of
properties. The sets of Los de abajo are austere, functional
and specific rather than generalized or symbolic. The sets
of Cuadros I, IV and V, more detailed than the others, might
be called cuadros vivos.

Space

An interesting feature of the settings of the six cuadros
is their varying potential for confining or unfettering the
movement of the actors. One factor in the degree of confinement inherent to a set is the ratio of space available to space
suggested. In a wholly interior set like that of Cuadro IV the
two are equal, with no expandability save indirect representation of offset events, a technique which the author does in
fact employ. At the opposite extreme, a set may represent the
mere foreground of a vast outdoor panorama which includes a
high proportion of sky. In that instance, of which the set
of Cuadro VI is an example, the ratio of space available to
space suggested is virtually one to infinity.
The other factor which restricts or frees characters movement is the illusion created by exits. If a doorway is understood to lead from one room to another, the exit of an actor
suggests passage from the area given to another, implied, of
approximately equal dimensions. If the door is understood to
lead outside, the area suggested is indefinite but rather vast.
In a setting like that of Cuadro VI, suggesting the foreground
of a totally outdoor panorama, an exit is effectively a passage into infinite space. Finally, a set might represent a
clearing, patio or courtyard with the fronts of buildings in
the background, as is the case in Cuadro III. An actor
leaving the stage to enter a fictitious building passes into
an area more restricted than that represented on stage. An
examination of the settings of Los de abajo will demonstrate
alternating expansion and contraction of the space in which
the actors move and that into which they may pass.
The action of Cuadro I takes place in a set which at the
same time confines the actors and suggests an enormous area
into which they may exit. In the foreground and on the right
is Demetrio's one-room hut, its interior exposed. Outside
the door, intense darkness represents the vast sierra into which
Demetrio and his wife will go at the close of the cuadro.
The dim light, rendering the actors nearly invisible when they
walk outside the hut, augments the illusion of vastness.
Cuadro II, like Cuadro I, has a dual indoor/outdoor set,

but with a more narrowly confined area. Half the stage represents the interior of Señá Remigia's hut, and the other half, the front of a neighboring hut. Between the buildings are simulated rocks representing the base of a mountain which is painted in the background. The mountain does not govern the actors, whose movements are confined to the area of the two huts. It is between the rocks, however, that Pancracio leads in his prisoner, Luis Cervantes. They enter from a theoretically broad sphere into the restricted on-stage area.

Cuadro III is less confining than Cuadro II but more than Cuadro I. The set represents a small clearing with the two huts of the previous cuadro in the immediate background. Several large rocks form the center around which the actors move. The background suggests an area more limited than that in which the actors are. Their exits do not, like the departure of Demetrio at the end of Cuadro I, visually suggest passage into greater spatial freedom.

The set of Cuadro IV, representing a large saloon, is completely indoors. There the actors, spatially confined, are symbolic prisoners of events. It is appropriate that the action of the cuadro take place indoors; no one can escape the violence and death which restrict the characters in just as real a way as do the walls of the cantina.

Cuadro V is spatially less restrictive than any previous cuadro. It represents a clearing in front of a half-destroyed quiosco, even less confining than the flimsy peasant huts of Cuadros I and II. The background represents a whole town, suggesting freedom of movement. While the characters are on stage, there is little illusion of their being surrounded or held in.

Cuadro VI has the most expansive set of the six, with no evidence of buildings and a background which consists largely of endless blue sky. The painted backdrop of the boundless sierra, seen by morning light, suggests spatial freedom.

To summarize the six settings: while the set of Cuadro I is quite expansive, that of Cuadro II is restricted. Cuadro III, in turn, is somewhat less confining. Cuadro IV, an interior, is the most limiting set of the six. Cuadro V is spatially very free, but not as free as Cuadro VI. Throughout the play, space begins quite ample, then becomes more limited and expands again, only to contract dramatically in Camila's murder scene. Space then expands rapidly in the final two cuadros. The climax occurs in limitless space.

Both the confining and the liberating elements of Cuadro I are well employed. The cramped interior of Demetrio's hut serves well as the site for the tension-packed intrusion of the federales. Also, when the respective characters walk out from the hut into darkness, their exits represent a release from danger or tension. Demetrio leaves at the approach of the enemy, as does his wife, who does not become involved in the difficult situation until she returns to the hut. The federales, going outside, escape Demetrio's wrath. The exit of Demetrio and his wife, at the end of the cuadro, bears qualification. Escaping the immediate danger of capture by the federales, they expose themselves to unknown dangers, which will accompany their presence in other places touched by the Revolution.

In Cuadro II, entry into the set constitutes a liability to dramatic tension. Luis Cervantes, coming in between the rocks which represent the sierra, faces a life-and-death situation. Being out of doors in the set does not, as in Cuadro I, constitute freedom from danger. Still, entry into an exit from Demetrio's hut does affect tension within the cuadro. Luis enters to plead for his life, and Camila, to face Demetrio's first romantic overtures. Camila, taking the lead in her romance with Cervantes, meets him outside; but when she becomes the passive recipient of Demetrio's attentions, she is confined to the hut, which makes her a symbolic prisoner.

All action in Cuadro III takes place outdoors but with a backdrop which suggests the confinement of a village. The characters, about to return to the military campaigns, move about in an appropriate middle ground, half village and half sierra. Entries and exits do not greatly affect tension, which remains quite constant throughout the cuadro. The background huts are not used for symbolic intensification or relaxation of dramatic tension, for no action takes place within them. Movement toward the group of huts does, however, symbolize the revolutionaries' ties with their past sedentary life. Cervantes exits in that direction to honor María Antonia's request that he dance with her (III, 43). That action stands in sharp contrast to what he has been doing. Dancing with a village girl, the act of a non-military man, links Luis with the civilian past which he has decided to abandon.

All the characters of Cuadro IV are confined in a saloon, prisoners of the momentous events that will occur there. Spatial tension remains quite high throughout the cuadro, with few entrances or exits to relieve it. The set, with its groups of tables and chairs at opposite ends of the stage, provides for internal fluctuation of tension. The action, divided between Pintada and Camila's growing rivalry and the colorful or humorous interludes, shifts from one table to another. As the climax of jealousy between the two women grows or is temporarily relieved, the spectator can see a physical movement toward or away from the spot where Camila and Pintada would be thrust together. That visualization of crisis applies only to the first half of the cuadro. In the second half, where action centers around the banquet table at stage center, tension is carried by action and dialog. Cuadro IV is the only set altered while in progress, when the small tables are removed and the long table is set up.

The set of Cuadro V is only semi-outdoors. Though there are no walls to confine the table and benches where all the action takes place, the background suggests a limited area in which the characters may move. Focus of attention is usually drawn to a narrow area, the tumble-down doorway which represents the kitchen of the open-air restaurant. Painted on the backdrop are houses and a church, representing the town of Juchipila. With no movement to or from the town, there is no specific place to which the characters go out. Spatial tension is, therefore,

unconcentrated. Likewise, action moves toward no specific
climax. The final mass exit of all characters except Doña
Nica does not release any great built-up tension, nor does
it indicate movement in a specific direction.

Cuadro VI has no properties, save the backdrop, except
for a huge simulated rock. The principal function of the rock
is as a lookout for the characters, who when they scale it
have removed all obstacles between themselves and the endless blue sky. Exits toward the unbounded horizon, representing a complete release of spatial tension, stand in contrast
to the action, which moves toward increasing dramatic tension.
Ironically, Demetrio goes out into the unfettering world, only
to meet his death. The final result, however, is qualified by
the uplifting rock. Demetrio's wife, who has climbed up to
hear the news of his death, reacts by collapsing upon the rock.
Her gesture of defeat or despair, upon that pinnacle, seems
less total than if she were sprawled upon the stage. The unspoken suggestion is that she will rise again, go on, and perhaps triumph.

The over-all progression of dramatic tension, as dictated
by the degree of confinement in each set, demonstrates no unbroken direction. The exterior of Demetrio's hut, in Cuadro I,
is used so extensively as a release that tension is quite low.
It mounts in Cuadro II, where the characters leave one hut
only to enter the confines of the front yard of the other.
Spatial tension is momentarily relaxed in Cuadro III, where
the characters remain outside in an area which represents a
small clearing at the edge of the village. The sole exclusively interior set, that of Cuadro IV, is the most confining of
the six. Camila's murder, the principal event of the cuadro,
is more impressive than if it took place outdoors, in a set
which could not bind the characters like prisoners. Dramatic
tension, at its peak, does not decrease at the end of the
cuadro, for no one exits except Pintada. In Cuadro V, spatial
tension is once again relieved, for the characters move in a
semi-exterior setting. Cuadro VI is somewhat paradoxical,
for the set allows the greatest freedom from restriction while
the action moves Demetrio and his followers inexorably toward
death. The expansive scenery, a background to the momentous
events, precludes a mood of despair to accompany the tragedy.

In summary, a minor flux of spatial tension occurs in
Cuadro II and a major flux in Cuadro IV. The flux which might
be expected in Cuadro VI, coincident with Demetrio's death,
is countered by the very open set.

Chronology

The intervals between cuadros, which represent long
periods of elapsed time, create an illusion which is encouraged
by references to unrepresented events, near the beginning of
certain cuadros.

Cuadro II, with no detailed description of how Demetrio
received his wound, gives only one vague index as to how much
time has elapsed since the close of Cuadro I. Explaining to

Venancio who Luis Cervantes is, Anastasio calls him "Uno de los federales que ayer hirieron a Demetrio . . . " (III, 23). Several speeches of Cuadro I convey the idea that a clash with the <u>federales</u> is imminent; if it is that skirmish in which Demetrio was wounded, it logically follows that the time interval between Cuadros I and II is only a few days. Since it is also possible that the revolutionaries have engaged the enemy in a series of battles, there is no certain measure of the days, weeks or months which are to have transpired between cuadros.

Cuadro III completes a theme introduced in Cuadro II: Camila's love for Luis Cervantes. Temporally, therefore, it is a continuation of the preceding cuadro. The different settings of the two cuadros suggest that time does elapse during the interval between them--a short period, in all probability.

Cuadro IV opens with Valderrama's narration of Demetrio's heroics during a battle which is to have occurred between cuadros. There is no indication as to how much time is to have gone by, or how long the men have been gone from the village where Demetrio recuperated. The reintroduction of Camila, in a subplot continued from Cuadro III, suggests that the amount of time transpired may be moderately short.

Cuadro V begins with a speech by Valderrama, attesting to a journey which accounts for an extended period of elapsed time: "¡Lo mismo que en todas partes, muerte y desolación! . . . " (III, 64). Later, Venancio reads aloud the reply he has received to a letter he wrote to Luis Cervantes. Luis' letter opens with an apology for not having answered more promptly:

. . . hasta ahora puedo darme el gusto de contestarle, porque mis atenciones profesionales no me lo habían permitido (III, 67).

During the long interval between Cuadros IV and V, Cervantes has left Demetrio's command, establishing himself in El Paso, Texas. Venancio has written to him there, and Luis has answered him quite a long time after receiving his letter.

The only interval of a length which can be exactly ascertained is that which intervenes between Cuadros V and VI. In Cuadro V Demetrio instructs María Antonia, who has volunteered to take a message to his wife:

. . . Llévale, pues, estos centavos y dile que pasado mañana hemos de pasar por el potrero de Las Hormigas, a más tardar al mediodía; que suba al mero picacho del Zopilote y allí me aguarde (III, 66).

As Cuadro VI opens, Demetrio's wife is with María Antonia, presumably atop Zopilote Peak, awaiting her husband's arrival. The hour is dawn, the second day after the events of Cuadro V. That interval is probably the shortest of the play.

With the list of characters, before the opening stage

directions for Cuadro I, the text specifies: "la acción
tiene lugar en el año de 1915" (III, 9). That detail is in-
accurate, for the first three cuadros contain events ostensibly
occurring before June, 1914, the date of the capture of
Zacatecas and the resignation of Victoriano Huerta. In Cuadro
III, urging Demetrio to ally himself with General Natera, Luis
Cervantes anticipates the final victory over Huerta:

> . . . Natera se prepara a tomar Zacatecas y si
> nosotros tomáramos parte en la acción . . . (III,
> 40).

In Cuadro IV, after Valderrama describes Demetrio's heroics
in an unnamed battle, Pintada asks Demetrio:

> ¿Entonces usted es el famoso Demetrio Macías
> que tanto se lució en Zacatecas? (III, 49).

In all probability, only Cuadros V and VI represent events
which are to be taking place in 1915. Cervantes' letter,
which Vanancio reads aloud in Cuadro V, bears the date "16
de mayo de 1915" (III, 67).[1] The incidents of Cuadros V and
VI probably take place in the summer of 1915, allowing time
for Venancio to receive a letter mailed in May and carried
slowly through the unpacified northern states of Mexico.
Throughout the play are references to los federales
and la federación; Madero, Villa, Carranza and Zapata;
villistas and carrancistas, names and words which give the
spectator a very general orientation in time. There are few
points at which a spectator can so precisely orient on-stage
events as to know how many weeks or months have gone by. The
last reference to a historical occurrence is typically ambiguous.
Demetrio's wife, seeing him approach at long last, states
vaguely and indirectly how long he has been gone:

> ¿Pos qué diré yo, que no lo veo desde antes de
> la toma de Zacatecas? . . . (III, 75).

Stage Techniques

Visual Effects

Though the lighting for much of Los de abajo is left to
the director's discretion, the playwright does from time to
time specify the effect he desires. In Cuadro I, darkness is
essential in the area surrounding the hut. The author intends
that it be dark enough to "swallow up" all characters outside
the hut. Demetrio, hearing the approach of the enemy, is to
slip out of the hut, "perdiéndose en la oscuridad impenetrable
de la sierra" (III, 15). A few minutes later his wife does
the same, "perdiéndose al instante en la oscuridad" (III, 15).
Lighting is crucial for the return of Demetrio, interrupting

the huertista lieutenant's abuse of his wife. He appears
"like a shadow" (III, 18) in the doorway. Just before the
curtain descends, Demetrio and his wife file off stage and
"se pierden en la oscuridad de la sierra" (III, 19). Obviously, there must be no source of light behind the actors.
The illumination, its source in the set itself, is confined to
the hut:

> Una mecha de sebo en una cazuela enhollinada y rota
> y las llamas del fogón al ras alumbran la escena (III,
> 9).

The dim, flickering light will make the actors appear smaller,
illuminating only a part of each figure. Those farthest from
the light may be mere silhouettes. The cuadro presents a
visual impression of the characters' anonymity or mysteriousness.

In Cuadro II, the playwright gives only the broadest
outline for lighting. As the curtain rises, the time of day
is to be dawn (III, 19); the dim light of early morning apparently is to continue until the end of Luis Cervantes' introduction to Demetrio. Only then do the stage directions dictate:
"se aclara la mañana" (III, 24). The lighting, tied to the
structure of the cuadro, is not brightened until the preliminary
action is concluded. While the stage lights are dimmed, Luis
Cervantes is brought on stage and presented to Demetrio. That
opening action contains neither the romantic interaction between
Luis and Camila nor Luis' efforts to have his life spared.
The dawn effect is employed only while Cervantes' personality
is being established.

Since no lighting effects are specified for Cuadros III,
IV or V, it must be assumed that they will be staged with full
illumination. There is no structural or logical motive for
varying the lights in these cuadros, which take place in
broad daylight or indoors. In Cuadro III, the philosophical
discussion between Luis and Demetrio, facing each other like
debaters, seems to suggest normal illumination. The unemotional exposition of clear-cut ideas might be weakened by vague
lighting. Luis' good-by to Camila, presented in direct light,
is less stylized than it might be with special illumination.
By his decision not to fade the lighting as Camila stands
alone weeping, the playwright presents without authorial
"management" the action just as it would naturally occur.
Dimming the illumination would color the incident with a lyric
interpretation which the playwright chooses not to employ.

Lighting, constant throughout Cuadro IV, is enhanced by a
visual illusion. The playwright, calling for mirrors on the
walls of the cantina (III, 48), intensifies the brightness and
creates spots of dazzling light, a background which increases
the impact of the highly visual events presented. No slight
movement is veiled in shadows in this, the most spectacular
of the six cuadros.

In Cuadro V, where emotions are minimized, the constant
illumination contributes to a sense of sameness throughout.

The lighting of the cuadro is designed to leave the audience
with a reaction of indifference, matching the mood of the
characters.

In Cuadro VI, two of the three allusions to lighting are
spoken aloud by María Antonia, who refers first to the "nub-
linazo" (III, 72), then to its dissipation: "El sol viene
abriendo ya la nublina" (III, 73). One might presume that
the light, dimmed as the curtain rises, is brightened as María
Antonia mentions the sun. Illumination then remains constant
until the end of the cuadro. The varied lighting, representing
dawn, also might symbolize the rising spirits of Demetrio's
wife. Illumination reaches its peak as María Antonia first
discerns "unos bultitos" (III, 73) and facts begin to dispel
any doubts lingering in the wife's mind. Evidence in support
of the symbolic interpretation of lighting in Cuadro VI might
be found in the stage directions at the close of the unit.
After the revelation of Demetrio's death, the woman's white
silhouette is to stand out against "el fondo azuloso y oscuro
del cielo" (III, 80). The words "azuloso y oscuro" might mean
that lighting is to be decreased during the last moments of
action. If that interpretation be accepted, there is a stylized
"sunset" which symbolizes the dashed hopes of the grieving wife.
Should a director choose not specifically to lower the lights
just before the curtain, he seems nonetheless bound to close
with soft lighting. Just as Camila's death was presented under
glaring floodlights, Demetrio's is to be depicted in a less
harsh environment.

Seen from the viewpoint of light and shadow, the six
cuadros of Los de abajo take place within a "day." Cuadro I
is at night, and Cuadro II, at dawn. Cuadros III, IV and V
are enacted in full light. Cuadro VI, with its uncertain illumination, might be seen as occurring at "dusk." That interpretation is in keeping with the "dawn," "noon," "twilight"
and "night" of Demetrio's career.

Auditory Effects

Sound effects are employed throughout the play, some
auxiliary to the action and some essential. Most are naturalistic, few symbolic. The first sound used, in Cuadro I, is
the barking of a dog outside Demetrio's hut. It is sufficient
warning so that he slips outside to hide, in case the dog has
sensed the approach of the huertistas. Their arrival is presented audially, with no on-stage action: intensified barking,
a gunshot and the dog's yelp of pain, finally men's voices and
approaching horses' hooves. The audience, seeing no source
for the sounds, might share more fully the apprehension of
Demetrio's wife, who is alone on stage. When the intruding
federales ride off, action is stopped until their horses are
no longer heard:

(Salen y Demetrio, inmóvil, los sigue con
insolente mirada, hasta que desaparecen y deja
de oírse el tropel de sus caballos.) (III, 18).

Not until the sound is gone does Demetrio's wife react to her frightening ordeal, embracing him ardently. The suspended animation and the absolute background silence which follows, intensify the pathos of the man and wife's separation.

As Cuadro II opens, the barking of dogs is heard, followed by a gunshot which wakes the characters and signals a beginning of the action. The circumstances of the shot are revealed later, when Luis Cervantes comes on stage with blood stains on one leg. The sound and the visual image are linked, after a lapse of time.

Sound effects are used structurally in Cuadro III, to clear the stage for Luis Cervantes' farewell to Camila. Loud voices are heard off stage, then shouts and gunfire. Demetrio exits to re-establish order, leaving Cervantes alone on stage. Camila then appears for their last meeting. The sound effects provide a smooth transition into her entry.

In Cuadro IV, sound effects are essential to two incidents inconvenient to present visually. The first is el güero Margarito's opening prank, in which he shoots a full goblet from the head of the waiter. The actor is to stand at extreme stage right, hidden from the view of the spectators. When Margarito aims and fires, the audience sees only his pantomine. They hear a shot and the sound of breaking glass (III, 59-60). The second incident is Pintada's murder of Camila. Dagger in hand, she hurls herself at her terrified victim, pursuing her off stage. Immediately there is a strident scream and the sound of a falling body (III, 62). In each case the realistic sounds, aided by the audience's imagination, communicate the off-stage action.

Cuadro V opens with the muted sound of voices, which grows steadily louder until Demetrio and his followers enter (III, 63-64). When the curtain rises, only Doña Nica is on stage, collecting glasses, bottles and plates. The noise frightens her away, providing a smooth transition into Demetrio's entry. Furthermore, the audience, hearing unidentified voices, might share Doña Nica's puzzlement, perhaps a bit of her apprehension, until it is established that it is Demetrio who has arrived. Later in the cuadro, as Valderrama sings a melancholy song, a far-off tolling of bells is heard. Anastasio and Demetrio remember happier days, when the church bells were rung in welcome in each town which they entered. The sound effect lends motivation for the men's pessimism and nostalgia, an essential preparation for the closing events of the cuadro.

As with the directions for lighting, it is María Antonia, in Cuadro VI, who announces certain sound effects. Just before Demetrio and Pancracio enter, she says to Demetrio's wife: "Oigalos, ya están aquí" (III, 75). Her comment might be accompanied by footsteps from off stage or might conceivably take their place. As soon as the other characters have left Demetrio's wife alone with her child, in order to participate in the battle, gunfire is heard off stage (III, 78). Sound effects and the reports of messengers constitute the spectators' only contact with the fierce off-stage battle, which must be made convincing if Demetrio's death is to have any dramatic impact.

Venancio, who comes on stage to hide his medicine kit, scales the rock to observe the battle. He announces that the carrancistas have hidden machine guns and are slaughtering Demetrio's troops (III, 79). His words might suggest the specifically identifiable sounds of machine guns in the background, so that what he says is not an announcement but merely a confirmation. That addition would give the audience the pleasure of making independent judgments of the situation. After Venancio leaves, increased gunfire is heard in the background (III, 79). As before his arrival, it justifies the wife's agitated words and actions. Demetrio's wife announces the end of the gunfire: "Ya no se oyen más tiros . . . Sólo se miran las humaredas" (III, 80). All is silent as she receives the news that Demetrio is dead. When the curtain falls there are no more sounds of violence. The end of gunfire perhaps allows the spectators to anticipate Demetrio's death; it certainly creates a feeling of tense expectation.

Distinguished from sound effects is the background music heard throughout Cuadro III and at the very end of Cuadro VI. In the stage directions for Cuadro III, the author calls for "sones de Jalisco o de Zacatecas, con arpa, violín y bajo sexto. A veces son bailables rancheros; a veces, canciones" (III, 36-37). The music is to be heard from curtain to curtain, always very soft. Several times a character's speech draws the attention to the music. Demetrio mentions that the troops will leave the following day and that he has arranged a farewell dance (III, 40). Later, Pancracio enters to tell Luis that María Antonia wants to dance with him (III, 43). Here, for the first time, represented events are tied to the music. Cervantes returns after a brief absence, to announce that "se está armando una trifulca porque ya muchos muchachos quieren cargar con sus viejas" (III, 44). The celebration, the source of the music, is thereby revealed in some detail. When shouts and gunfire are heard with the music (III, 45), the audience may imagine more fully what is taking place during the fiesta which they are allowed only to hear. Finally, Luis mentions the dance to Camila, while they are talking alone (III, 46). Here the muted music, which the spectator already associates with the troops' imminent departure, adds to the pathetic quality of Luis' rejection and leave-taking. The background melodies play a steadily-growing part in the action of Cuadro III; only at the beginning are they free from connotation.

Background music is again heard at the close of Cuadro VI, after Demetrio's widow has prostrated herself on the rock. The song "La Adelita" is played softly on a mouth organ, as if very far away (III, 80). Symbolizing Demetrio and the other revolutionaries, it could be a sign that one of Demetrio's disciples has survived. The song could also come from the departing carrancistas, whom circumstances forced to kill men who are basically like them. If a metaphysical interpretation be given the song of the mouth organ, it might be considered as a sign of eternal life for Demetrio and his fallen comrades. He asked his wife to pray for him, which she did. In her last long speech she uttered two supplications:

. . . ¡Madre mía de Jalpa, ampáranos en este
trance! ¡Las cinco llagas de Cristo Crucificado!
(III, 80).

A religious interpretation of the distant music, therefore,
is not incongruous with the tone of Cuadro VI.
    At times, music forms an organic part of the action. It
is integrated with varying degrees of elaborateness. The
first direct use of a song in the drama occurs in Cuadro I, when
the drunken enemy lieutenant sings without accompaniment his
lust for Demetrio's wife:

> No me mires airada ﹒ ﹒ ﹒
> no más enojos . . .
> Mírame cariñosa,
> Luz de mis ojos ﹒ . ﹒ (III, 16).

According to previous stage directions, he is to act intoxi-
cated (III, 15); the romantic ballad, sung with the slurred
intonation of a drunkard, might produce in the audience the
revulsion it presumably causes Demetrio's wife.
    Music is extensively woven into the action of Cuadro IV.
As Demetrio's banquet begins, there enters on stage an
orchestra:

> (. . . trombón, pistón, clarinete, tambora y
> platillos, tocando la "Adelita".) (III, 58).

That song fixes the action specifically in Mexico and specifically during the Revolution. The orchestra contributes to the
mood of jubilation, playing dianas after Valderrama's eloquent
toast to the newly-promoted general (III, 59). Music also contributes to the hilarity of one of el güero Margarito's pranks.
Singling out the shortest of the bystanders, he orders the man
to dance "Los enanos" to the rhythm of bullets fired at his
feet. At Margarito's command, the band plays the appropriate
music (III, 60). The accompaniment lends to the cruel joke the
humor of a circus act. Without the music and the exuberant
shouts of the celebrators, the incident might be merely an
exhibition of bad taste rather than the rollicking interlude
which it was.
    In Cuadro V, at Demetrio's request, Valderrama sings and
plays on the guiltar "La pajarera" (III, 69). His sad song and
the distant tolling of bells cause Demetrio and Anastasio to
reminisce about the happier days they have known. That mood,
in part caused by the song, is necessary to explain Demetrio's
listless reaction when Pancracio bursts on stage to announce
that the carrancistas are near (III, 71).
    The function of music and sound effects in Los de abajo
is sometimes to elicit a response from the audience, sometimes
to relate by totally auditory means an incident which is not
visually portrayed, and sometimes to anticipate through the ears
what the eyes will later verify. The author makes highly effective use of sounds in the play, particularly in Cuadros I,
III, IV and VI.

Costuming

The most immediately noticeable quality of the costumes
in Los de abajo is their Mexican-ness. The following detailed
instructions for dress appear in the stage directions for
Cuadro I:

> La mujer viste camisa de manta trigueña . . .
> y chomite colorado de cenefa verde. . . . Demetrio
> lleva saco y pantalón de gamuza . . . sombrero de
> palma de ancha falda y zapatones amarillos de oreja.
> Anastasio y Codorniz, camisa y calzones de manta muy
> holgados, guaraches, sombrero de soyate . . . y
> frazada musga terciada al hombro (III, 10).

The attire indicates not only that the characters are Mexicans,
but also that they are peasants. Demetrio's dress in Cuadro IV,
indicative of the good fortune which has apparently befallen
him, contrasts sharply with his appearance in Cuadros I-III:

> . . . Demetrio lleva chaqueta y pantalonera de gamuza,
> nuevas, con muchos alamares y botonadura de plata, som-
> brero galoneado y al cuello una mascada de seda
> solferina . . . (III, 48).

Anastasio, Codorniz and Pancracio seem not to have fared so well
as Demetrio. Their clothing is little changed:

> . . . camisa de manta, ancho pantalón de pana,
> mitasas, burdos zapatones amarillos, paliacate
> rojo al cuello y sombreros de palma, de enormes
> faldas . . . (III, 48).

Manner of dress, since it has become differentiated, segregates
Demetrio and those clad like him (Venancio, el güero Margarito,
Valderrama and Cervantes) from the comrades first associated
with Demetrio (Anastasio, Codorniz, Pancracio). For the first
time, the spectator can identify a tangible difference between
the two groups, whose respective costumes indicate prosperity
and penury.

Three women play a role in Cuadro IV: Camila, María
Antonia and la Pintada. The two girls who were first introduced
as villagers are dressed alike:

> . . . visten sencillos trajes de percal floreado muy
> claros, rebozo cruzado sobre el pecho, sombreros de
> soyate con barboquejos; largas trenzas caen sobre
> sus espaldas (III, 48).

Pintada's costume, indicating neither greater affluence nor
less, does suggest that she is morally inferior:

> . . . un vestido de seda de vivísimos colores,
> pésimamente adjustado a su cuerpo, medias azules
> y zapatillas de raso blanco. Muchas cuentas y
> avalorios relumbrosos adornan su traje. Se cubre
> con un gran sombrero galoneado y muestra carrilleras
> ajustadas a la cintura y cruzadas sobre el pecho
> (III, 48).

Camila and María Antonia's feminine appearance is documented
by their actions in Cuadro IV, in sharp contrast to Pintada's
mannish deeds. In the cuadro, male attire seems to indicate
relative economic status, while female dress denotes position
on a scale of femininity.

Costuming in Cuadro V creates the instant impression
that the characters have undergone prolonged misfortune. The
stage directions merely state that Demetrio and his companions
are to enter "vistiendo tan pobremente como en los actos primero
y segundo" (III, 64). The opening speeches, alluding specifically to the hardships they have suffered, confirm the impression conveyed by their drastic change in dress.

Costumes in Los de abajo locate the characters geographically and sociologically. Manner of dress may divide the
characters into opposing groups, later erasing all distinctions
among them. It establishes the individuals' economic ranking,
in Cuadro IV, and shows the effect of events which have occurred during the unrepresented interlude between Cuadros IV and
V. The playwright repeatedly shows his awareness of the function
of costumes.

Stage Directions

Frequently, the text of the play calls for specific actions
or gestures which are to accompany a character's speech and
which give a narrowed interpretation to his words. An example
is found in Cuadro I, when the federales arrive. The lieutenant
and the sergeant are to be "bien borrachos" (III, 15), a condition which makes more objectionable everything they do. It
also demonstrates that not even aguardiente makes them brave
enough to remain calm when Demetrio enters the hut. The lieutenant is to stand at attention as he apologizes to Demetrio,
effusively praising his reputation for valor (III, 18). His
pose, as much as his words, shows respect for the semi-legendary
insurgent leader.

Cuadro II opens in a humorous vein, accentuated by the
actions which accompany Codorniz' and Anastasio's words. A
rifle shot is heard, and Codorniz sits straight up in bed.
He calls Anastasio who, in a sleepy voice, answers him with
an insult: "¡Ya estás moliendo otra vez!" (III, 20).
The humor lies in the contrast between Codorniz' fright and
Anastasio's laziness. That juxtaposition is reinforced when
Codorniz shakes Anastasio to wake him, and Anastasio sits up
"con infinita pereza, estira brazos y piernas y bosteza"
(III, 20).

When Codorniz finds out that it is Pancracio who is
approaching the hut, he lets the butt of his rifle rest on
the ground and exclaims happily: "Es Pancracio" (III, 21).
His relief is communicated by his action and by the inflection he gives his words, which of themselves are neutral.

Another source of humor in Cuadro II is Camila's varied
reactions as she chats with Luis Cervantes and watches him
treat his injured foot. When he cuts his handkerchief into
pieces and tells her to put them in the water she has boiled,
Camila responds with exaggerated surprise:

> (Pasmada.)
> ¡Peor! ¿Qué visión es ésa? (III, 27).

Luis explains that there are microbes, tiny animals, which
exist in water and are killed by boiling. Camila, unbelieving,
stares intently into the pot and claims that she sees nothing
(III, 27). Her actions, contrasted to Luis' apathetic reserve,
are as humorous as her colorful peasant dialect, juxtaposed
with Luis' correct metropolitan Spanish.

Late in Cuadro II, it is Anastasio who performs a comic
act. Demetrio, planning to have Cervantes "confess" to Codorniz,
who will be disguised as a priest, orders the prisoner led away
to be "shot." Anastasio takes Luis gently by the arm and says
cordially: "Véngase por acá, curro" (III, 33). His gesture
is humorous because it is out of place. Ordered to perform an
execution, Anastasio issues a pleasant invitation, as if to
dinner.

In Cuadro III, when Demetrio first appears on stage,
Cervantes asks how his leg is mending. Demetrio shakes it
vigorously and replies that it is "peor que nuevo" (III,
38). His action expresses satisfaction, almost pride, which
his words alone might not easily convey.

When Cervantes begins explaining his doctrine of personal
gain through revolution, Venancio is first to become enthused
with his ideas:

> (Aplaudiendo con entusiasmo.)
> ¡Luisito ha dicho una verdad del tamaño de la parroquia!
> (III, 41).

His action demonstrates a conviction difficult to communicate
with tone of voice alone.

Though Venancio and Pancracio convince Demetrio that he
should follow the advice, Luis continues to expound his doctrinal rhetoric. Pancracio grows tired of the flow of words:

> (Hablando para sí y alejándose hasta desaparecer.)
> ¡Cómo le cuadran los sermones! . . . Este curro
> va a acabar diciendo misa . . . (III, 42).

His speech, humorous in itself, is much funnier when combined
with his slow exit.

During the opening action of Cuadro IV, the stage

directions call for extras, dressed as soldiers, to enter and
exit "en bullicioso y constante ajetreo" (III, 48). Their
raucous movements add to the confused spectacle presented before the audience. The playwright does not specify for how
long the soldiers are to continue their movements; such activity, if carried on throughout the cuadro, would distract
attention from the murder of Camila. A good place to dis-
continue the background movement might be the beginning of
Demetrio's celebration banquet, where action is for the first
time fixed as stage center. Up to that moment, attention has
swung from stage left to stage right and back again. Noisy
entries and exits in the background might soften any artificiality
of that pendulum-like structure. They might also enhance the
impression that conversations are heard only by the figures
sitting at a specific table.

Gestures in the opening incidents of Cuadro IV shows
the characters' contrasting personalities. La Pintada,
introducing herself to Demetrio, is sitting on the bar. She
gets his attention by stretching her legs until they graze
his back (III, 49). That bawdy posture, coupled with her
saloon-girl dress, bespeaks Pintada's character as eloquently
as do her words.

Demetrio's reaction, contrasting sharply with Pintada's
behavior, complements the terseness of his speech to show his
great reserve:

> (Volviendo su rostro adusto y encontrándose con la
> mirada lujuriosa de La Pintada.)
> Al orden (III, 49).

When the focus of action shifts from Demetrio's table to
the one where Venancio, Pancracio, María Antonia and Codorniz
are sitting, the figures at the first table are to simulate
continued conversation throughout the new exchange (III, 52).
That device, like the noisy entries and exits of the soldiers,
contributes to the illusion that a character can be heard only
by the others at his table.

During the banquet to honor Demetrio's promotion, el
güero Margarito "toasts" his general with more-or-less harmless pranks at the expense of innocent townspeople. As his
last joke, he seizes a very short man and makes him dance,
firing at his feet as the orchestra plays. The victim jumps
in rhythm with the shots (III, 60), contributing hilarity to
what might otherwise be merely a cruel abuse, in bad taste.
The victim's comic reaction is displayed "en medio de una
gritería ensordecedora" (III, 60) which increases and general-
izes the jubilation.

In Cuadro V, Venancio reads aloud a letter he has received
from Luis Cervantes. There is a humorous contrast between
Venancio's seriousness and the mirthful taunts of his audience.
When Venancio reads that Cervantes wants to enlist him in the
Salvation Army, Valderrama breaks into hearty laughter: "Ese
es choteo, compañero . . . " (III, 69). Venancio, unaffected,
reads the last sentence, with Luis' promise that they will become rich. Codorniz, shaking with laughter, exclaims that
Venancio has been a dupe (III, 69). The remarks, funny in

themselves, become more humorous when recited with laughter
which contrasts to Venancio's unbroken deadpan.

In the closing incident of Cuadro V, Pancracio "entra
alarmado" (III, 71) to announce that the carrancistas are
near. Demetrio, in contrast to his agitation, listens to
him with calm indifference. When he finally reacts, Demetrio
stands up lazily (III, 71-72). His underreaction, not born
in a vacuum, is a result of the foregoing nostalgia and pessimism.

As the curtain rises for Cuadro VI, Demetrio's wife and
María Antonia strain to see if the troops are arriving. In
order to see farther, María Antonia scales the huge rock at
stage center. On top, she smiles and peers in all directions
(III, 73). Her elevated position and triumphant countenance
symbolize the optimism with which she will report the arrival
of Demetrio and the others. When she sees them, she pulls off
her coat and waves it over her head (III, 74), to attract
their attention. That gesture accentuates further the exuberance which María Antonia conveys.

When la Codorniz bursts on stage to announce that the
enemy has opened fire, Demetrio grabs his rifle and says he
will join his men immediately. His wife, desperate over his
departure after so brief a reunion, begs him with her posture
and words not to leave:

> (Abrazando estrechamente su cintura.)
> No te vayas, Demetrio. ¡Por Dios, no te vayas,
> que mi corazón me avisa que ahora sí te va a suceder
> algo! (III, 77).

The wife might most easily clasp Demetrio's waist if she drops
to her knees. That classic pose of supplication would lend
force to her words.

Dialog versus Animation

Stage directions frequently enhance or lend a particular
interpretation to dialog. In other cases, they may take the
place of words. Likewise, description through dialog may
replace animated representation. In Cuadro I, Demetrio's
wife relates past abuses of the huertistas, telling how they
forcibly enlist young men, steal livestock and requisition
grain for their horses (III, 11). Later in the cuadro,
government excesses are represented directly. Two enemy
soldiers invade the hut while Demetrio's wife is alone; they
demand food. The lieutenant makes crude overtures to Demetrio's
wife and is about to assault her when the famous rebel intervenes (III, 15-18). The episode shows the huertistas as drunken,
undisciplined bullies and cowards.

In Cuadro II, when Luis is brought on stage at gunpoint,
he wears torn, soiled trousers and has a blood stain near one
foot (III, 21). If the blood were the only evidence of Luis'
injury (coupled with the rifle shot heard at the beginning of
the cuadro) some spectators might fail to notice it, were they
not reminded by Cervantes' words, spoken while he is still in

the wings: "Me has destrozado un pie, bárbaro" (III, 21).
When Luis comes on stage and Anastasio asks what has happened,
Pancracio explains with pride: " . . . Le metí un plomo en
la pata . . . " (III, 21). The effectiveness of Luis' speech
and Pancracio's are dependent upon careful costuming. Dialog
and representation together fill in the background of the
prisoner's arrival.

A little farther on in Cuadro II, Demetrio's wounded leg
is presented with simultaneous words and movements from the
same character. Demetrio, interrupting the questioning of
Luis, stifles a groan and exclaims: "¡Ya me está fregando otra
vez esta pata! . . . " (III, 24).

On occasion, action unaccompanied by dialog relays an
emotion or personality trait. When Demetrio first meets
Camila and compliments her on her melodious voice, she lowers
her head, leaves quickly and enters the other hut (III, 30).
Camila's reaction expresses without words her modesty or fear
of Demetrio.

Camila's personality is well developed through representation and dialog. In Cuadro II, when Pancracio and Anastasio
bring Luis Cervantes into Demetrio's hut for his supposed
"trial" and "sentencing," Camila waits outside to watch through
the cracks in the wall (III, 32). Her stealthy presence throughout Luis' interrogation demonstrates how bold her infatuation
has made her, as does her verbal intervention on his behalf (III,
29-30).

Camila is proud in her grief. At the close of Cuadro III,
when Cervantes advises her to become the mistress of Demetrio,
who will soon attain wealth and prestige, she covers her face
with the point of her rebozo and tells him to leave her. Only
when Camila is alone does she burst into tears (III, 47). The
playwright's emptying the stage of all characters except the
grief-stricken girl, accentuates her anguish. Her motionlessness, apparently what the playwright intends, suggests a sorrow
of despair. Agitated movement might give the impression of
forthcoming revenge, which has no part in Camila's role.

Another wordless expression of grief, more profound because
it is the sorrow of a widow rather than that of a lover, is
assigned to Demetrio's wife at the close of Cuadro VI. Having
heard from María Antonia that Demetrio is dead in battle, the
wife:

(Levanta sus manos al cielo, . . . van doblándose
poco a poco su cuello, su cintura, sus rodillas
hasta quedar como aplastada sobre la roca.) (III,
80).

The wife's first reaction, raising her arms high, is her
only forceful motion. Her gradual collapse connotes defeat
or despair.

In Cuadro IV there is a study of feminine personality
in the juxtaposition of Pintada and Camila, whose actions
at times bespeak their respective psychologies, and who on
several occasions react oppositely to the same stimulus.

El güero Margarito, noting Pintada's lewd overtures toward
Demetrio, observes:

> Pero ahora quieres estrenar general, ¿no?.
> (La Pintada lanza una mirada fulminante a
> Demetrio, y Camila, muy cohibida, baja los ojos.)
> (III, 51).

Pintada's glance expresses vulgar brashness, and Camila's,
modesty perhaps mixed with unhappiness.
 Also in Cuadro IV, Pintada offers to help Camila return
to her village. Camila explains that, despite Cervantes'
trickery, she wants to remain with Demetrio because she is
beginning to esteem him. Pintada's brash reply and Camila's
reaction to it compromise a study in comparative feminine
psychology:

> LA PINTADA
> ¿Conque ya le vas cobrando voluntá? Pos por
> la buena o por la mala, tú te me largas de aquí,
> mustia infeliz. ¡Mira! (Le muestra una daga que
> lleva entre la liga y la media. Camila se queda
> aterrada y La Pintada se aleja, . . . Después de
> un momento de estupor, Camila se levanta y va a
> sentarse a la mesa de Demetrio. . . .) (III, 56).

The dagger is made a symbol of Pintada's violent personality.
Camila's moment of indecision, sitting as if in shock after
Pintada walks away, demonstrates how frightened she is. On
the other hand, her subsequent move to Demetrio's table not
only provides her with protection but also constitutes defiance
of Pintada.
 Frequently humor is carried by pantomine. In Cuadro III,
Pancracio calls Luis Cervantes to say that María Antonia wants
to dance with him. Luis, without saying a word, exits "son-
riente y resignado" (III, 43) accompanied by Venancio, who
puts an arm around his shoulder. Cervantes' expression and
Venancio's gesture of mock sympathy make a tacit, unspecific
comment about María Antonia. She is seen very briefly in
Cuadro II, where the playwright describes her as a "muchacha
flacucha y tuerta" (III, 24). Luis and Venancio's attitudes
seem to be good-natured condemnations of the girl's physical
unattractiveness.
 One of the play's most delightful bits of pantomine is
the reunion between Anastasio and el güero Margarito, two old
friends who, seeing each other, embrace with all their might
and take turns lifting each other from the floor:

> ANASTASIO
> (Reparando en el güero Margarito que acaba de
> entrar y busca asiento, se levanta y va a mirarle
> la cara; luego que lo reconoce lanza un grito y
> abre sus brazos.)
> ¡Güero Margarito!

EL GUERO

(Reconociéndolo a su vez.)
Anastasio Montañés!

(Se abrazan fuertemente, levantándose alterna-
tivamente en peso.) (III, 50).

The banquet to celebrate Demetrio's promotion, in Cuadro
IV, is like a tour de force of the techniques of humor. A
comic reaction may be purely verbal, like Demetrio's "acceptance speech" when Cervantes presents him a black, cloth-
covered shield embroidered with a gold eagle, the symbol of
Demetrio's new general's insignia: "¿Y qué voy yo a hacer
ahora con este zopilote? o . . " (III, 58).
The humor of Anastasio's toast lies not just in what he
says but in how he says it:

ANASTASIO
(De pie y con mucha gravedad.)
Compadre Demetrio (abre mucho los ojos y traga
saliva, sin encontrar las palabras). Compadre
Demetrio . . . yo no tengo que decirle . . . (muy
afligido) sino que ya sabe que soy su compadre.
(Deja la copa sobre la mesa y con sus propias manos
inicia el aplauso.) (III, 59).

El güero Margarito toasts Demetrio not with words but with
deeds. Placing a full goblet on the head of a waiter, he es-
corts his victim to extreme stage right, then returns to the
opposite end and takes out his pistol. The waiter, hidden from
the spectators' view, apparently tries to run away:

EL GUERO

. . . ¿A dónde corres, desgraciado? (Corre a detenerlo
y a colocarlo de nuevo en su sitio. Luego vuelve a la
izquierda.) No te buigas . . . que te voy a retratar.
(Gira sobre los talones, da media vuelta y dispara . . .)
(III, 59-60).

As with Anastasio's clumsy toast, Margarito's cruel joke is
humorous both because of what he says and because of his actions. The new meaning given "retratar" is as comical as el
güero's seemingly purposeless dash across the stage, to perform
a task which the audience does not witness, and his about-face
before firing.
At times, Margarito's extreme actions cease to be funny
in themselves, and the humor is carried by his victims. During
his test of marksmanship at the expense of the waiter, several
townspeople try to leave the saloon without being detected.
When el güero stops them, they bow effusively before Demetrio,
provoking the mirth of his friends (III, 60). Though the
amount of humor contained in the townspeople's "solemne

reverencia" (III, 60) depends on the interpretation of the
director and the actors, there is an intrinsic comic quality
in any demeaning act performed in unison. Moreover, the
laughter on stage might provoke a like reaction among the
spectators.

The little man forced to dance "Los enanos" is so subordinated to Margarito that he never speaks. El güero's
words suggest his victim's gestures or grimaces, none of
which is specified in the stage directions:

> . . . Oiga, amigo, ¡qué chiquito y qué bonito es
> usted! ¿Cómo no? ¿Entonces, yo soy mentiroso?
> Usted sabe bailar "Los enanos." Sí, sí, yo ahora
> me estoy acordando que ya lo conozco. Lo conocí
> en un circo y usted bailaba "Los enanos". Le
> juro que requetesabe . . . (III, 60).

The victim's demeaning silence de-personalizes him, assuring
the undiminished humor of the incident by precluding sympathy
for him.

The last comic dialog before Pintada's murder of Camila
is provided by Pancracio and María Antonia, who exchange
lovers' jests. When Demetrio announces his orders to sally
forth against a troop of orozquistas, the men interpret that
mission as involving a trip into Jalisco. Pancracio waves
his hat in the air and shouts:
"Aprevénganse, tapatías de mi alma, que ai voy con mi hacha"
(III, 61). María Antonia begins to pinch him and the two exit
laughing merrily.[2] In this exchange of rather lewd humor,
words and gestures bear equal weight.

The predominant mood of Cuadro V is pessimism, broken only
by the humorous reading of Cervantes' letter to Venancio. The
opening stage directions dictate that Demetrio and all his companions except Valderrama sit down dejectedly (III, 64). Their
disheartened demeanor and humble clothing, so sharply contrasted
to Cuadro IV, establish from the beginning of the cuadro a mood
of melancholy.

In Cuadro VI, the tone is not so much nostalgia as quiet
grief, which the playwright portrays several times. When Demetrio enters and embraces his wife, she is to stay for quite
a long time in his arms, "ahogando su llanto en silencio"
(III, 75). The effect of that extended posture is to show
that her joy is so deep that it borders on sorrow. Soon the
wife notices that her small son, who does not remember his
father, has hidden in the folds of her skirt. Demetrio takes
the boy by the hand and gazes at him "con emoción contenida"
(III, 76). The effect of this action is to re-establish
Demetrio as a family man, in a role which he has not played
since Cuadro I.

Pantomine alone is perhaps insufficient to convey the
emotion of a father who sees his son, grown from an infant
during his absence. Dialog helps create the illusion that there
is more than just a nameless man looking at an unspecific
small boy. Introducing Demetrio's silent contemplation, the
wife says: "¡Es tu padre, hijo, es tu padre!" (III, 75).

With emphasis on the names given to the relationship between
them, her words deepen the meaning of the man's gazing upon
the little boy. The pantomine is followed by María Antonia's
remark, which stimulates the spectators' imagination and
cements the bond between the two figures holding hands:
"¡Mírenlo! No puede negar las facciones del tata: los mismos
ojos, la misma boca . . . " (III, 76). The word "tata"
establishes yet another link between the father and his son:
their Indian blood.

When Demetrio's wife begs him not to go out to battle,
his words say one thing and his actions another:

> (Desprendiéndola cariñosamente, pero decidido,
> acaricia la mejilla de su hijo y dice:)
> Pancracio, vámonos que ya están aquí los
> carranclanes (III, 77).

Demetrio, on the surface, is concerned with business only,
but his pain at separation is made visible.

After Demetrio has left, his wife shows through pantomine
alone her extreme agitation:

> (. . . La mujer, tremendamente agitada, va y viene
> sin salir del mismo sitio, . . .) (III, 78).

The woman exhibits the most typical activity associated with
anxiety.

At the close of Cuadro IV, Pintada demonstrates without
words emotion strong enough to make her kill. Crazed by the
laughter of those who have heard Demetrio tell her to leave
and by Margarito's refusal to stand by her, she looks all
around, grabs the dagger strapped to her leg, and hurls herself upon Camila (III, 62). Pintada's frantic scanning of
the room and the sudden movements with which she draws her
knife and attacks Camila, are standard signs of extreme
rage. Camila runs off stage (III, 62), manifesting a universal symptom of great fear. Camila's flight, facilitating
the off-stage representation of her murder, greatly reduces
the potential sensationalism of the scene. The spectators,
not excited by graphic violence, might more easily contemplate
the consequences and antecedents of the homicide.

When Pancracio and La Codorniz bring Pintada back in,
Demetrio orders them to kill her. Her reaction is both verbal
and visual:

> LA PINTADA
> ¡Ustedes no, desgraciados! ¡Mátame tú, Demetrio!
> (Le tiende el puñal ensangrentado, desgarra
> bruscamente sus ropas y le muestra su pecho des-
> nudo . . .) (III, 63).

Pintada's words prove her defiant bravery, as does the symbolic
gesture of baring her chest, in a signal that she will offer
no resistance.

Demetrio seizes the dagger, revealing his extreme agitation, then performs an ambiguous act. If it is grief that causes him to spare Pintada, the script calls for no grimacing or wiping of his eyes. Demetrio's lowering of the knife is not coupled with any other sign of emotion except his command that Pintada leave, spoken "con voz apagada y ronca" (III, 63).

Two good examples of dialog which takes the place of animation are in Cuadro VI. María Antonia, atop the huge boulder, verbally describes Demetrio's arrival (III, 73-74), and Demetrio's wife, upon the same boulder, relays the news of his death as if she were repeating messages shouted to her from a distance by María Antonia (III, 80). Indirect representation of both events allows the playwright to complete Cuadro VI in just one scene of moderate length.

Another example of indirect revelation is in Cuadro II, where the outcome of Luis Cervantes' "confession" by the bogus priest is reported. The spectators hear that result as Demetrio learns it, first from Anastasio and then from Pancracio:

DEMETRIO

. . . .
¿Qué sucedió, pues, con el curro?

ANASTASIO

Que se está riendo del cuatro que le puso. Es repicolargo, pero verdá de Dios que no viene a lo que usted piensa. . . .

PANCRACIO

(Entrando.)
No le pudimos sacar nada en claro (III, 35).

The other episodes of Luis' inquisition were portrayed first-hand: his capture and first interrogation, Demetrio's choice of a method to discover his motives, and the formal inquest by Demetrio and the others. The "confession" by la Codorniz, which takes place in an unspecified off-stage place to which Anastasio has led Cervantes, is rendered more suspenseful by indirect, delayed revelation of its outcome.

The drama contains one example of an incident dramatized directly and later reported verbally by one of the participants to a character who was not present. In Cuadro II, when Camila brings him a bowl of milk, Demetrio playfully seizes her arm; she is forced to struggle to escape his grasp. In Cuadro III Camila describes the incident to Luis Cervantes:

. . . oye, curro, . . . si vieras qué malo es el hombre Demetrio; cuando le llevo el champurrao, me agarra rejuerte, juerte, de una mano y comienza a pellizcarme (III, 47).

The single incident of Cuadro II has been multiplied into a regular occurrence, either in fact or in Camila's imagination. Whether or not it is an exaggeration calculated to make Cervantes jealous, the verbal account is an embellishment of an incident, previously revealed to the spectators, which Luis Cervantes did not witness.

In Cuadro III, the author uses animation to relieve the tedium of the play's longest continuous dialog. Demetrio and Luis' discussion of their respective ideas about the Revolution is interrupted by several small actions, closely interwoven with the conversation. After Demetrio's first long speech, Pancracio and Anastasio come in with bottles of beer. Everyone present opens one and begins to drink, as Demetrio continues telling how he became involved in the insurrection (III, 39). Venancio, at one point, interrupts the two men's conversation to applaud what Cervantes has said (III, 41). Luis' final long speech is broken by Pancracio's exit, muttering about such verbosity, and by Luis himself, who pauses to finish his beer (III, 42). The interpolated actions, lacking value of their own, give life to what might otherwise be a long, static interchange.

Los de abajo contains many examples of theatrical techniques used to enhance the exposition of dialog. Lighting is of primary importance in Cuadro I, which has no illumination except the simulated hearth and a candle, both inside the hut. The deep shadows on the rest of the stage serve to heighten the drama of the action. Lighting simulates early morning in Cuadros II and VI. In Cuadro IV, mirrors on the walls intensify the illumination of the indoor set.

Sound effects are used to anticipate the arrival of characters (the federales in Cuadro I, Pancracio and his prisoner Luis Cervantes in Cuadro II, Demetrio and his followers in Cuadro V). Sound effects also signify phenomena which the playwright does not reveal visually. That technique, used twice in Cuadro IV, represents el güero's shooting of the goblet from the waiter's head and Pintada's murder of Camila. In Cuadro VI, the spectators hear gunfire but never see any part of the battle in which Demetrio is killed.

Music is sometimes used as background, throughout Cuadro III and at the end of Cuadro VI. It also may be woven into the plot; there is a small orchestra in Cuadro IV, and Valderrama accompanies himself on the guitar in Cuadro V.

Costuming shows the mark of events upon some characters. Demetrio, dressed poorly in Cuadros I-III, looks affluent in Cuadro IV but poor again in Cuadro V. In Cuadro IV, costuming distinguishes prosperous men from unprosperous ones and feminine women (Camila and María Antonia) from one with many mannish characteristics (la Pintada).

Stage directions are extensively used to complement or flavor a character's words. The effusively apologetic huertista lieutenant stands at attention as he showers Demetrio with compliments; Demetrio shakes his leg as he tells Luis that it is healed; and the shameless Pintada's extended feet graze Demetrio's back as she tries to attract his attention.

The play shows a balance between dialog and animation.
Animation sometimes replaces speech, as in Cuadro VI, where
Demetrio's words refer mostly to business but his gestures
express his tenderness for his wife and son. Also in Cuadro
VI, words take the place of animation. The audience hears the
step-by-step account of Demetrio's return home entirely through
María Antonia's speeches. Similarly, the wife's words are
the only means of revealing Demetrio's death. Once she has
uttered the fact that he is dead, she says not another word.
Her dance-like actions portray her grief.

Characterization

Luis Cervantes

Several major characters develop quite complete personalities. Their words and actions reveal directly what they
are like. Only in rare cases are personality traits presented
through the comments of another character. One of the best-
developed figures of Los de abajo is Luis Cervantes.
The first impression which the spectator receives about
Cervantes is his outspoken arrogance. In his first speech,
delivered while he is still in the wings, Luis demonstrates
his feeling of indignation at his captors' rough treatment:
"me has destrozado un pie, bárbaro" (III, 21). With his next
words, Cervantes haughtily asks who is in charge (III, 21).
The question infers that neither Pancracio, Codorniz nor
Anastasio appears to him like a man with authority.
Luis seems surprised at the men's intense hatred for
federales: "Pero ¿no me entienden ustedes, pues?" (III, 22-23).
Ushered into Demetrio's hut, the outraged Luis shows the
rebel leader his foot as if demanding redress. Demetrio replies:
"¿Quien jijos de un tal por cual es usted?" (III, 23). That
question may be the playwright's way of underlining the fact
that only Luis' own word places him above his captors. Seen
on stage, Cervantes looks no more prosperous than the rebels.
He is in shirtsleeves, without a hat, dirty, with torn trousers (III, 21). When Venancio appears and asks the others,
they say the prisoner is "un mocho" (III, 23). In fact, Cervantes gives little information about himself--not even his
name--until he is presented to Demetrio.
Luis impresses the revolutionaries more with his deeds than
with his words. When brought before Demetrio to be sentenced
and "confessed" by the false priest, he is unable to dissuade
the rebel leader with his high-styled rhetoric. He is interrupted and escorted from the room (III, 33). When "confessed,"
however, Luis obviously sees through the trick and convinces
the men that he is not there to murder Demetrio. He has also
impressed Anastasio with his skill in curing his own foot, so
much that Anastasio suggests that Demetrio call him in (III,
35).

In Cuadro III, Luis solidifies Demetrio and Venancio's
favor. Venancio, in the first speech of the cuadro, calls
him "Luisito" (III, 37). In Cuadro II he is always "curro"
or "mocho." The spectator knows, before Luis says a word,
that he has won Venancio as a friend. No one else ever calls
him by name; throughout Cuadro III he is "curro" to everyone
except Venancio.

It is interesting to note how the author uncovers the
weakness of each revolutionary whom Luis proselytizes. Venancio
obviously desires prestige and wealth; in the opening dialog
of Cuadro III, Cervantes promises to obtain for him a phy-
sician's license, with a minimum of qualifications (III, 37).
It is Venancio who applauds at Luis' mention of "unos cuantos
milloncejos de pesos" (III, 41). Demetrio, on the other hand,
is unconvinced and asks his followers whether he should take
Luis' advice. Demetrio's weakness is his desire for the companionship of a woman. He reacts with delight when Cervantes
promises to win him favor in Camila's eyes (III, 45).

Luis himself, as is demonstrated in Cuadro IV, is moti-
vated by avarice. In a brief episode which interrupts the conflict between Camila and Pintada, Luis buys jewelry from la
Codorniz. When the agreed price has been set, Cervantes
hurriedly takes out a roll of bills which he gives to Codorniz;
then he gathers the jewelry "con ansiedad mal encubierta" (III,
57). Though his words do not indicate that he is impatient,
the author conveys that message through gestures.

Structurally, Luis is present only while the revolutionaries'
future is bright. In Cuadro V, when their dream has turned sour,
Cervantes' letter proves that he is in El Paso, Texas, where he
sought safety and comfort (III, 67).

El güero Margarito

He appears only in Cuadro IV. In the cantina he displays
his violent temper and cruel sense of humor. He refers to a
cold-blooded murder he committed (III, 54) and to the prison
term he served (III, 50). None of his private life is mentioned, nor is he represented as having a distinguished military record. What the other characters say about Margarito
sheds very little light on his personality. To Anastasio
he is "un amigo de veras" (III, 50) and "acabado" (III, 52).
Pintada, who also has known him previously, adds: "Ustedes
no saben todavía quién es este güero" (III, 51). He is a
very flat, under-developed character whose main role is to
provide vulgar entertainment throughout Cuadro IV. The
playwright surrounds him with mirth: Anastasio's delight at
seeing him (III, 50), Anastasio and Pintada's guffaws when
he knocks down the waiter who fails to bring him ice water
(III, 53), and the hilarious uproar which greets his cruel
pranks (III, 60). El güero is the only character whose role
is almost purely comic.

Valderrama

He first appears in Cuadro IV, where his eloquent description of Demetrio's heroics at Zacatecas (III, 48-49) and his flowery toast (III, 59) might link him with the bombastic Cervantes, in the mind of the spectator. In Cuadro IV, Valderrama has no individualized personality. In Cuadro V, however, he becomes the author's vehicle for conveying a mood of pessimism. Entering with Demetrio and the rest, Valderrama remains standing as they sit down, and declaims about the great number of crosses he has seen which mark the graves of the Revolution's victims (III, 64). He is to deliver his speech "tendiendo su mirada a lo lejos" (III, 64); that pose might lend sincerity to his words.

Valderrama, strumming a guitar, sings a melancholy song as distant church bells begin to ring. That sound reminds Demetrio and Anastasio of the jubilant welcome they used to receive in every town. Memories and the tender ballad affect everyone. When Valderrama finishes singing, no one says a word. Seeing that Demetrio's eyes have filled with tears, Valderrama embraces him: "¡Cómaselas, mi general, esas lágrimas son muy bellas!" (III, 70). Once again, Valderrama has been used to create a mood of depression, a prelude to the tragedy of Cuadro VI and necessary to explain why Demetrio reacts so listlessly when Pancracio enters with the news that the carrancistas are approaching.

Valderrama seems a "utility" character, inserted by the playwright for a specific purpose. He has no past, no origins which might explain his presence in Cuadro IV. Though he does not appear after Cuadro V, there is no explanation for his disappearance. Moreover, Valderrama has no relations of blood or friendship with any other character. His presence seems justified only by the playwright's requirements.

Demetrio's Wife

The wife appears only twice, in Cuadros I and VI, but is a major character in both. Structurally, her appearances coincide exclusively with Demetrio's private life. The stage directions dictate that she be dressed in a manner typical of rural Mexico:

> La mujer viste camisa de manta trigueña muy escotada y sin mangas, y chomite colorado de cenefa verde. Cuando se levanta, muestra desnudos sus pies y sus piernas, hasta la mitad de los tobillos (III, 10).

With her child always close by, in a cradle or strapped to her breast (in Cuadro I) or standing at her side (in Cuadro VI) she becomes a symbol of Mexican motherhood.

In Cuadro VI, repeated pious phrases are assigned to the wife, whose speeches establish a tone of religiosity which preludes Demetrio's final battle. Awaiting his arrival, she prays constantly:

₀ . . . ¡Madre mía de Jalpa, que sean ellos!

. . . .
¡Dulces nombres de Jesús, María y José! (III, 73).

. . . ₀ . . . . ₀ . . . .
¡Animas benditas del purgatorio, que sean ellos!
(III, 74).

The wife is left in charge of the souls of Demetrio, Pancracio and María Antonia, as they go out to battle₀ Her husband tells her: " . . . rézale a Dios por mí" (III, 78), and María Antonia adds: "Encomiéndenos a Dios" (III, 78). The wife is also the only positively known survivor of the conflict who remains in Mexico₀ Luis Cervantes is still alive but has fled to the United States₀ Demetrio and Pancracio are definitely dead; the fate of María Antonia and of Venancio is uncertain. Demetrio's wife has, therefore, a very special role as the only character left at the close of the play₀ The survival of Mexican motherhood is an optimistic ending for the play, a symbolic message that life will go on despite the revolutionary cataclysm.

María Antonia

The playwright's most skillful character development is seen upon careful examination of María Antonia, who appears or is alluded to in five of the six cuadros and evolves from a minor, comic figure to the play's most impressive female character.

In Cuadro II, María Antonia is nameless. She first appears for just a moment at the side of old Señá Remigia: " . . . muchacha flacucha y tuerta, falda de percal, camisa de manta, . ₀ . " (III, 24). The audience has no way of knowing her name, for it is Camila whom Remigia calls to bring water to Luis Cervantes.

The cuadro contains two passing references to María Antonia. Pancracio and Codorniz, leaving Cervantes alone with Camila, exchange the following comments:

PANCRACIO

. . . . ₀ . . . . . . ₀ . . . .
Oye, vale, ¿no vamos a ver si damos por
allí con la flaca de anoche?

CODORNIZ
No más jala tú primero (III, 25).

Summoned by Demetrio, the two men return, laughing heartily about some cross-eyed girl (III, 31). The playwright has underlined the only characteristics revealed so far: María Antonia is excessively thin, with crossed eyes.

She speaks for the first time late in Cuadro II. Seeing Camila outside the hut, eavesdropping on Luis' trial, María Antonia asks:

¿Qué estabas fisgando, tú?

. . . .
        ¡Ya te mueres por el curro! Pero sólo por
eso que ya lo van a fusilar (III, 34).

The remark seems cruel or at least irresponsible. With
Codorniz and Pancracio's ambiguous insinuations that María
Antonia may have been more than cordial to them, it is the
author's only hint as to her character.

María Antonia, never directly present in Cuadro III, is
mentioned only once. When Pancracio tells Cervantes that she
wants to dance with him, Demetrio insists that Luis comply.
Luis exits, bearing a smile of resignation (III, 43). His
reaction seems to underscore María Antonia's unattractiveness
once again. Neither her thin form nor her crossed eyes are
again mentioned in the rest of the play.

Though María Antonia's role in Cuadro IV is minor, her
lines reveal her personality more than in the previous cuadros.
Discussing Camila's stormy arrival and Cervantes' trickery,
she condemns Luis for misleading the girl (III, 52). For the
first time, María Antonia is portrayed as a person with opinions.
Whether she feels compassion for Camila or merely indignation
at the perfidious Luis, she has at last taken a stand.

In Cuadro IV, the playwright subtly informs the audience
that María Antonia and Pancracio have become lovers. When the
waiter takes everyone's order, María Antonia requests "lo
que Pancracio quera" (III, 51). Her subordination to his
will suggests the relationship between them. Their exuberant
love is illustrated when Demetrio announces his orders to proceed to Jalisco. Hearing Pancracio shout a lewd reference to
the tapatías, María Antonia begins to pinch him and the two
exit laughing merrily (III, 61). With just three short appearances, María Antonia has been expanded from an ugly village
wench, the butt of jokes, into a strong-minded woman, cherished
by a man, who feels deep joy in returning his love.

In Cuadro V, María Antonia appears for only a few minutes
and has just two speeches. Her exposure is, however, sufficient
to establish her as a brave and generous woman. Demetrio, now
close to home, asks Doña Nica if there is a way to send his
wife a message, instructing her to meet him two days hence at
a predetermined place. When the old woman says the roads are
unsafe for travel, María Antonia does not hesitate to offer her
services:

                    MARIA ANTONIA
        Yo voy, mi general, ¿por qué no me lo había
dicho?

                    DEMETRIO
        No, todavía de aquí es mucho jalón pa que te
lo aguantes.

                    MARIA ANTONIA
        Soy muy pata de perro; no más dígame lo que
tenga que icirle a la siñora y oritita mesmo me
voy (III, 66).

María Antonia blossoms into a full-fledged character with
a major role in Cuadro VI. There she is contrasted to
Demetrio's wife, mother of his child, with a prayer on her
lips and her thoughts always for her home and family. María
Antonia symbolizes the companion/helpmate, able as any man,
who accompanies Pancracio on his most dangerous mission.
Perched atop the huge boulder, watching the men arrive, she
cautions the wife not to attempt to climb up there with her:

> Ni esperanzas, mi alma; con una resbaladita
> va a parar a la eternidá. Es un barrancón
> retehorrible. ¡Yo, porque me crié como chiva!
> (III, 73).

María Antonia shouts risqué comments to Pancracio (III, 75),
while Demetrio's wife prays. She symbolizes a joyous romance
based on freedom, contrasted to the relationship, born of mu-
tual obligation, which exists between Demetrio and his wife.

When María Antonia last appears, her role is that of the
loyal female comrade, capable of facing any danger or hardship
to serve her lover. Shouting that Pancracio "tiene el pecho
abierto" (III, 80), she searches frantically for her water
skin and then races back to aid him.

María Antonia's last function is indirect. Demetrio's
wife, anxious to know his fate in the battle, scales the rock
and shouts as if to María Antonia. The wife continues shouting as if repeating a message she can scarcely hear, relaying
the information that Demetrio is dead (III, 80). The author
uses the device of relayed messages in order to represent the
off-stage death. The audience never hears María Antonia's
voice, only the wife's.

Even in the emotion-charged Cuadro VI, María Antonia
never shows a "feminine" sentiment. Her loyalty to Pancracio
and concern for him are portrayed as if she were a man, her
pride perhaps concealing her deepest feelings. To that end,
the author chooses that she shout jokes to Pancracio, expressing in that way her feelings upon seeing him again. When
he lies dying, María Antonia bursts on stage not to grieve but
to find her water skin. A potential display of emotion is
subordinated to a heroic act.

Of the women represented in Los de abajo, María Antonia
is the most admirably developed. She is shown as more re-
sourceful than Demetrio's wife, emotionally stronger and braver
than Camila, and more unselfish than Pintada. Not necessarily
superior to the others, she is a more imposing figure even than
Camila, who appears on stage more.

Temporal Progression

When Demetrio goes away, his son is an infant; upon the
father's return, he can walk at his mother's side. Time has
wrought a great change during Demetrio's absence. Another
very noticeable cleavage of time is seen in the costuming of

Cuadros IV and V. Demetrio and Venancio, as witnessed by their attire, have gone from poverty to affluence to poverty again. Time and events have altered the mood of the characters in Cuadro V. Their jubilance of Cuadro IV is suddenly gone.

One character evolves independently of any group, as a result of her experience in time: Camila. In Cuadro II she is a silly, love-stricken girl whose conversation with Luis Cervantes borders on banality:

> CAMILA
> Oiga, y ¿quién lo insiñó a curar?

> CERVANTES
> Soy estudiante de medicina.

> CAMILA
> ¡Ande! ¿De moo es que usté iba a ser dotor?

> CERVANTES
> Voy a serlo.

> CAMILA
> (Desternillándose de risa.)
> Pa morirse uno de risa (III, 28).

In Cuadro III, during her last meeting with Luis, Camila seems quite unchanged:

> Oye, curro, yo quero que me enseñes la "Adelita";
> ¿adivina pa qué? Pos pa cantarla muncho, muncho,
> cuando vayas ya muy lejos, cuando ya ni siquiera
> te acuerdes de mí . . . (III, 46-47).

In Cuadro IV, the experience of unreciprocated love has altered Camila vastly, maturing her and stifling her innocent, girlish charm:

> . . . ¡Míreme cómo estoy de encanijada todavía!
> Amanece y yo ni ganas del metate. La gorda se
> me hacía trapo en la boca . . . ¡y aquella pinción!
> . . . ¡aquella pinción! . . . (III, 55).

Luis Cervantes is unchanging, as are Pancracio, Codorniz and Anastasio. Demetrio's wife, seen in Cuadro VI, is no different than in Cuadro I. El güero Margarito, la Pintada and Valderrama all appear so briefly that there is no latitude for their evolution in time. María Antonia evolves not through experiences in time but through characterization. Demetrio evolves because of external events. Camila is the only character whose changes reflect her growing maturity. The playwright traces her development from adolescence to womanhood.

Conclusions

The central character present throughout the drama is
Demetrio Macías, who is forced to flee his home, exposed
to various adventures with new acquaintances, and finally
able to return to his wife just long enough to say good-by
before he goes out and is killed in battle. His life is
affected by Luis Cervantes, who heals his leg and shows him
how to profit from revolution. He loves and is loved by
young Camila, who is murdered by the jealous Pintada almost
as soon as their romance has begun.

The structure of Los de abajo retains its symmetry though
examined from several perspectives. The first and last cuadros
portray Demetrio at home, while the four interior units take
place during his public career. Two cuadros are set at home,
two in Camila's village, and two in other places. Cuadros I-III
portray the rise of Demetrio's fortunes, while Cuadros IV-VI
show him at the pinnacle of good fortune and then present his
decline.

Settings create an illusion of freedom or restriction and
enhance the build-up or release of dramatic tension. The most
confining set, Cuadro IV's cantina, is the scene for the play's
most powerful incident: Camila's murder. Ironically, Demetrio
meets death during Cuadro VI, which is the least confining set.

The playwright makes effective use of the techniques pe-
culiar to drama. Lighting, tailored to the needs of each
cuadro, also follows an over-all pattern. Illumination imitates the natural light of one day: from dawn to morning
light in Cuadros I and II, to full illumination in Cuadros
III-V, to "dusk" in Cuadro VI. Though the hour represented is
dawn, and the stage becomes brighter for Demetrio's arrival,
the light fades again as the wife silently mourns her husband.

Dialog at times takes the place of animation, particularly in Cuadro VI, where Demetrio's wife verbally reveals his
death in battle. To present her grief, the playwright chooses
animation over dialog. Without saying a word, she prostrates
herself upon the rock in a gesture symbolic of despair.

Several minor characters have a special function in the
play. Luis Cervantes, through his calculated program to gain
allies among his former captors, reveals Venancio's avarice and
Demetrio's need for feminine companionship. El güero Margarito's
cruel pranks, presented humorously, break the high dramatic
tension of Cuadro IV. Valderrama contributes more than any
other character to the mood of pessimism in Cuadro V, a prelude
to Demetrio's death in Cuadro VI. Demetrio's wife establishes
him as a private family man, before and after his public career,
and her religiosity augurs his death. María Antonia is the
author's greatest achievement in painstaking character development.

Events in Los de abajo progress in time, which is demonstrated as moving and as capable of affecting the characters.
Demetrio exchanges his peasant's clothing for prosperous-
looking attire, only to appear again dressed poorly. His
son, an infant in Cuadro I, is a toddler in Cuadro VI. One

character evolves in time independently from the others: the childish Camila, who through suffering becomes a woman.

Demetrio's death in battle is tragic in the sense that it constitutes one of the rare, unusual circumstances which distinguish tragedy. Los de abajo is not, however, high tragedy in the traditional sense of the term. Despite the renown he achieves, Demetrio is not of high station, so his misfortunes are not on the same level with Agamemnon's murder or Macbeth's loss of his throne. The ruin of commonplace characters is not as moving a spectacle as is the downfall of the mighty.

For the reasons cited above, Los de abajo can be only what we might call low tragedy. Demetrio's downfall and death are the result of influences beyond his control. In town to hear Sunday Mass and do his shopping for the week, Demetrio customarily drinks with his friends at an open-air cantina. On one occasion, when harrassed by Don Mónico, the local political chieftain, Demetrio spits in his face. Don Mónico is unforgiving and calls in government troops to obtain revenge, using as an excuse his alleged suspicions that Demetrio supports the recently-assassinated President Madero. Demetrio, through no volition of his own, has taken the first step toward fame and ultimate death. No longer an unknown peasant, he has gained a political reputation which will grow with his first victories over the government troops. For an unexplained reason, presumably the caprice of a local official, Demetrio has paid a price far in excess of his original misdemeanor. Rather than being jailed for a while, he has been treated like a politically dangerous activist. His successful efforts at self-defense have earned him such a reputation that he can no longer live in peace at home. The chain of events has been set in motion by the corruption of one man, Don Mónico, whose extreme actions also might be interpreted as symbolic of an unjust system of local law enforcement.

Demetrio is forced to leave home because of an unlucky coincidence. Two huertista soldiers chance upon his hut in the dark. They do not even realize where they are until they ask:

Por eso, pues, ¿en dónde diablos estamos? Oiga, señora, ¿cómo se llama este ranchito?

LA MUJER
Pos Limón, ¿cómo quiere que se llame?

SARGENTO
¿Lo oyó, mi teniente? Estamos en Limón, en la mera tierra del famoso Demetrio Macías (III, 16).

The wife, disclosing the name of the village, unintentionally betrays her husband. The enemy soldiers know that Demetrio lives there; so well-known is he that they recognize him when he enters the hut. His reputation, sufficient to make the intruders shrink away like cowards, offering him no resistance, is an asset only for the moment. Soon, he knows, the federales will be back with reinforcements. His fame is, in this case, his undoing. Sending his wife and child to his parents' home, he leaves them to join his men. Demetrio's separation from his family makes him a victim of a fame which he did not seek. Thus far, his life has been greatly affected by Don Mónico's ill will or churlishness and by the federales' stroke of good luck. The only decision Demetrio has made is to fight back rather than surrender to his adversaries. His determination is a virtue and his initial victories are a result of his men's bravery and skill. Each triumph, however, gains him more notoriety and makes more unlikely his chances of remaining with his wife. Nothing he can do will restore his domestic tranquility; his prowess has gained him life, liberty and continued liability to death or imprisonment.

Another stroke of misfortune profoundly changes Demetrio's life. Wounded in battle, he is brought to a small village for recuperation. There his platoon is joined by the huertista deserter Luis Cervantes, a medical student who restores Demetrio to health and thereby gains his confidence. Luis, disappointed at the rebels' obvious poverty, persuades them to affiliate themselves with Villa's more prosperous armies. Luis sees the Revolution as an opportunity for wealth, but knows he cannot become rich except in the company of revolutionaries in the mainstream of the campaign. With rhetoric which Demetrio does not completely understand, Cervantes convinces him to subordinate himself to a villista general in time to win accolades at the Battle of Zacatecas.

Cuadro IV portrays the celebration of that victory, and Cuadro V, the frustration which accompanies the triumph of the Revolution. The arrangement of the play powerfully underlines the defeat which comes to individuals despite an overall victory. In Cuadro V it becomes clear that only Luis Cervantes has profited from the Revolution, having taken the money he plundered and gone to the United States. Demetrio and his men are ragged and hungry, apparently braced for ultimate defeat and death. Giving few details of political circumstances, the text reveals only that the men are pursued by troops loyal to Carranza. The spectators, if they are familiar with the history of the Mexican Revolution, can provide the missing details. Demetrio and his men, by their decision to ally themselves with Natera, became villistas. Their non-political decision was interpreted politically by outsiders with whom they came in contact. When Villa rebelled against Carranza, Demetrio and his followers became unintentionally disloyal to the established government. Villa's defeat at Celaya placed them in grave danger, making them the quarry of the carrancistas.

A hero of high tragedy usually has made an error which directly causes his downfall. The mistake is a result of the hero's natural and inevitable action, a tragic flaw, involving no weakness or moral fault. In Demetrio's case, the erroneous decision is to continue engaging the carrancistas. He is not optimistic about the outcome, but he feels that for him and his men to disband and flee would be cowardly. To Demetrio, manly valor is a way of life. In Cuadro III he tells Luis

Cervantes of the conduct which his code requires, even in
frivolous matters:

> . . Pero que pasa el policía y vuelve a pasar,
> que se asoma el comisario y fisgan los auxiliares
> y que lo miran y paran oreja y comienzan a quitarle
> a usted su gusto. ¡Y usted no tiene la sangre de
> horchata, claro! A usted le da coraje, se levanta
> y les dice su justo precio . . . (III, 39).

That code, in Demetrio's system of values, takes precedence
over his safety and that of his men, even over his future as
a husband and father. Demetrio's worship of bravery is
directly responsible for his death in battle.

In several respects, Demetrio is a pitiable victim of
other characters' vices and of bad luck. Don Mónico over-
reacted to Demetrio's insult and Luis Cervantes used him for
his own purposes. The huertista lieutenant and sergeant who
stumble upon Demetrio's hut are not astute but merely for-
tunate at his expense. Adding to Demetrio's pathetic condition is the fact that he did not understand until too late
the political consequences of allying himself with the villistas. The kind of pity evoked in the spectators is, however,
proper to low tragedy.

Demetrio's tragic flaw, the personality trait which does
not permit him to avoid the battle in which he is killed, is
his devotion to bravery. Not unique with him, it seems to be
a trait of his social class. When the carrancistas open fire,
none of the peasants is struck with fear. Only the newly-
recruited city dwellers instinctively flee for safety:

> CODORNIZ
> (Entra jadeando.)
> Demetrio, hay tiroteo en la vanguardia. Los
> curros andan muy asustados y comienzan a pelarse
> (III, 77).

Steadfastness in the face of grave danger seems to be a
natural reaction of Demetrio and those like him. Within that
subgroup, stubborn valor is not a character fault but a way
of life. It is, then, a tragic flaw in the traditional sense.

Footnotes

[1]The text gives the year as 1916, almost certainly a misprint.

[2]The text erroneously assigns the words to Codorniz, who has the previous speech. Incidents of Cuadros V and VI suggest that María Antonia is Pancracio's woman. Further proof that there is a textual error is that Demetrio, immediately after María Antonia's exit, orders Codorniz to saddle a horse for Camila. Obviously Codorniz did not exit; in all likelihood it was Pancracio. When Pintada goes off stage to murder Camila, it is Pancracio and Codorniz who bring her back (III, 63). Codorniz left to saddle the horse, and Pancracio must have left with María Antonia.

CHAPTER III

A COMPARISON OF THE NOVEL AND THE PLAY

Edwin Muir has specified the qualities of dramatic novels which comprise their affinity to theater:

> . . . The confinement to one scene; the isolation of the characters; the unfolding development making towards an end; the conflict; the dénouement;
> . . .[1]

Though the incidents of Los de abajo take place in many scenes, they are consecutive and mutually exclusive. Nowhere in the novel does action occur at two sites simultaneously. The characters are isolated in that they appear in small groups and in chapters dedicated only to them. Rarely does an event take place amid a crowd. When large numbers of characters are present, the narrator relegates several of them to the background and concentrates on those whose role directly shapes the incident. An example is Chapter 12, Part II, which relates Camila's murder. Demetrio's entire brigade is present, saddling their horses. The soldiers become part of the background, their only function that of laughing at Pintada when Margarito declines to intercede for her. The only important characters are three: Demetrio, Camila, and la Pintada.

Action develops logically toward an end, though that end is not clearly defined until the latter chapters. A number of short-range goals (victory over Huerta, revenge against Don Mónico, acquisition of wealth, domination of Camila) are one by one achieved. It becomes apparent that the underlying goal, submerged in the early chapters, is Demetrio's return home. The inner conflict between his private dreams and his public aspirations is more crucial than the dispute between Pintada and Camila. The dénouement might be placed at the revelation of Demetrio's death.

Several episodes of the novel possess qualities which make them readily adaptable to theater. An example is Chapter 1, Part I, which details the intrusion of the federales. That incident forms the basis for the major scene of Cuadro I. In both the novel and the play, the visit of the enemy soldiers is presented in great detail and in one continuous segment. Each phase is revealed in the order in which it would logically occur, without flashbacks or anticipation. The action takes place in a limited area, the interior of a one-room hut; in both versions the federales' arrival and departure,

necessarily outside the hut, are presented entirely through
auditory images. The episode of the novel, containing a high
proportion of dialog, is easily adaptable to dramatic form.

Cuadro I, based on Chapters 1-3 of the novel, is not in
every way parallel to them. The very different substance and
arrangement of the scene which precedes the huertistas'
intrusion is due to the different demands of the respective
genres.

Many segments of the narrative appear to have passed directly to the play. In both Cuadro I and Chapter 1, Part I, the
federales' actions communicate the awe in which they hold
Demetrio. The huertista lieutenant and his sergeant immediately associate Demetrio with the name of his village, Limón.
When the wife tells them where they are, they utter unconvincing
platitudes which allude to their bravery. When Demetrio appears
in the doorway, the sergeant steps back in horror and the lieutenant, standing rigid, mouths solicitous formulas. In both
the novel and the play, Demetrio is very early endowed with a
mythlike quality suggested by his icy calm and by his silence
and motionlessness as the enemy mutter their apologies and
hurry away. The huertistas' reaction to Demetrio reinforces
his mythification. Demetrio's haughty reserve and the
federales' nervous agitation are in both versions manifested
principally through gestures which traditionally convey those
qualities.

Early in Cuadro I, Demetrio's wife verbally summarizes
past abuses of the federales, telling how they take away hus-
bands and fathers, then steal the peasants' livestock and
grain. Her description conveys the same information as would
a brief scene animating the enemy's excesses:

> . . . Hoy corren ustedes y mañana sólo Dios sabe
> lo que será de nosotros con estos condenados
> federales que donde dan con una se vuelven
> perros del mal: nos quitan maridos, padres,
> hijos . . . todo. Se roban nuestros puercos, nuestras
> gallinas, y el maicito que tenemos para pasar
> todo el año se lo echan a sus bestias. Y no
> paran hasta que nos queman nuestros jacales
> (III, 11).

The wife's speech is based on the words of an unidentified
serrano of Chapter 4, Part I, who speaks to the insurgents
carrying Demetrio on a stretcher as they pass through an
unspecified village:

> --¡Dios los bendiga! ¡Dios los ayude y los
> lleve por buen camino! . . . Ahora van ustedes;
> mañana correremos también nosotros, huyendo de
> la leva, perseguidos por estos condenados del
> gobierno, que nos han declarado guerra a muerte
> a todos los pobres; que nos roban nuestros
> puercos, nuestras gallinitas y hasta el maicito
> que tenemos para comer; que queman nuestras

casas y se llevan nuestras mujeres, y que, por
fin, donde dan con uno, allí lo acaban como si
fuera perro del mal (I, 328).

In the play, the speech of an unspecific person in an unidentified place is assigned to the wife, sitting in her hut
with Demetrio and his comrades. The group to whom the words
are directed remains the same, of course, or the speech would
lose its function as the plea of a helpless victim to would-
be avengers. The play, however, has no highly mobile scene
where Demetrio is carried by stretcher bearers. Accordingly,
the speech is assigned to a character who fits in with the
play's scenario. Placed as it is before the visit of the
federales, the wife's description is followed by a concrete
example of the abuses which she has mentioned.

  Cuadro II and Chapter 5, Part I, both describe the
arrival of Luis Cervantes as a prisoner of the rebels. In
both cases he communicates verbally, before appearing, that he
has been wounded in the foot. Luis' words call attention to the
bloodstain low on his leg, mentioned in the stage directions
and in the narration. In Cuadro II Luis' words immediately
precede his entrance, creating in the spectators an expectation
which is gratified by the red blotch on the actor's trousers:

> CERVANTES
> (Sin aparecer aún en escena.)
> Me has destrozado un pie, bárbaro.
>
> (Saliendo de la sierra aparecen Pancracio y
> Cervantes. Este sin sombrero, en camisa; el pan-
> talón desgarrado y con una mancha de sangre cerca
> de un pie; . . .) (III, 21).

In Chapter 5 Luis' words, as yet unidentified as to who
speaks them, are not contiguous with his appearance:

> -- ¡Estúpido! . . . ¡Me has destrozado un pie!
> La voz se oyó clara y distinta en las inmedia-
> ciones (I, 330).

In the novel, Luis' vociferous complaint and the narrator's
description are separate revelations of the same phenomenon.
The narrator does not, like the playwright, use one clue to
call attention to the other. It is interesting to note that
only the narrator pays so close attention to detail as to
specify a fresh bloodstain. His observation is perhaps from
the vantage point of Codorniz and Anastasio, who witness the
prisoner's arrival. It is not feasible, on stage, to present
details observable only at very close range.

  When Cervantes is first brought in as Pancracio's prisoner, in Chapter 5, Part I, the narrator does not describe his
personality. Luis' words, however, suggest arrogance. His
first question to his captors is: "¿Quién es aquí el jefe?"
(I, 330). When Pancracio prepares his rifle, as if to shoot

him in cold blood, Luis demands: "¿Pero qué clase de brutos
son ustedes?" (I, 331). Brought before Demetrio, he does not
introduce himself before seeking redress for what he considers
unjust treatment:

> --¡Una infamia, mi jefe, mire usted, . . .
> mire usted!--pronunció Luis Cervantes, mostrando
> las manchas de sangre en su pantalón y su boca y
> su nariz abotagadas (I, 331).

In the play as in the novel, Cervantes insults Pancracio while
still off stage: "Me has destrozado un pie, bárbaro" (III, 21).
When he asks who is in charge, stage directions call for him to
sound "altivo" (III, 21). As in the novel, when Pancracio
seems about to execute him, he reacts with arrogant indignation.
The dramatist indicates an attitude through stage directions:

> CERVANTES
> (Exasperado.)
> ¿Qué especie de brutos son ustedes, pues?
> (III, 22).

When presented to Demetrio, Cervantes states his grievance without introducing himself:

> ¡Mire usted, mi jefe! (Mostrando su pie herido.)
> ¿No es esto una infamia? (III, 23).

In the novel, Cervantes' arrogance is conveyed indirectly,
through the reactions of his captors. The following passage
illustrates the technique:

> . . . .
> Entonces habló el desconocido.
> --¿Quién es aquí el jefe?
> Anastasio levantó la cabeza con altivez
> enfrentándosele.
> El tono del mozo bajó un tanto (I, 330-331).

In the drama, both characters' voices are altered. Cervantes'
speech directly portrays haughtiness, reinforced by Anastasio's
reply:

> CERVANTES
> (Altivo.)
> ¿Quién es aquí, pues, el jefe?

> ANASTASIO
> (Con insolencia.)
> ¿Qué quiere con el jefe? (III, 21).

Drama involves auditory stimuli which prose fiction lacks.
The playwright employs the vehicle at his disposal to convey
Luis' personality.

In Cuadro II, when Demetrio tells Camila what a melodious voice she has, she lowers her head and leaves the hut (I, 30). Her reaction conveys the idea that she is modest or shy. Those qualities are expressed indirectly through narration in Chapter 7, Part I, where Camila brings Demetrio an earthen vessel full of goat's milk:

> Agradecido, sonrió Demetrio, se incorporó y, tomando la vasija de barro, comenzó a dar pequeños sorbos, sin quitar los ojos de la muchacha.
> Ella, inquieta, bajó los suyos.
> --¿Cómo te llamas?
> --Camila.
> --Me cuadra el nombre, pero más la tonadita.
> Camila se cubrió de rubor, y como él intentara asirla por un puño, asustada, tomó la vasija vacía y se escapó más que de prisa (I, 335).

In both cases a universal sign is used to show modesty. Since it would be impractical for the playwright to indicate a blush, which perhaps no actress can summon at will, he chooses a gesture which conveys the same emotion.

In Chapter 14, Part I, Luis Cervantes advises Camila to offer her affection to Demetrio, who will soon be able to give her wealth and prestige. The consequences of his advice may be placed in three categories: Camila's actions, her words and the narrator's intervention. The girl reacts defensively to Luis' words:

> Para que no le viera los ojos, Camila los levantó hacia el azul del cielo . . . (I, 350).

The narrator then inserts a lyric symbol of Camila's fallen hopes:

> . . . Una hoja seca se desprendió de las alturas del tajo y, balanceándose en el aire lentamente, cayó como mariposita muerta a sus pies (I, 350).

Camila stoops to pick up the leaf and, without looking directly at Luis, pronounces her only speech:

> --¡Ay, curro . . . si vieras qué feo siento que tú me digas eso! . . . Si yo a ti es al que quero . . . pero a ti no más . . . Vete, curro; vete, que no sé por qué me da tanta vergüenza . . . ¡Vete, vete! . . . (I, 350-351).

Camila throws away the dried leaf which she has crushed in her hands, then covers her face with a corner of her apron. The text does not suggest for how long she remain like that before opening her eyes and finding Luis gone. There follows a detailed description of the sunset hour and of Camila's reflection in the brook. Only after gazing at herself,

138

dressed to please Luis, does she burst into tears.
That incident, as presented in Cuadro III, transpires in
less time. There is no stylization of Nature to reflect Camila's
heartbreak, which is conveyed by her words, the tone of her voice,
and her actions:

CAMILA

(Con la voz apagada.)
¡Si vieras qué feo siento que tú me digas eso,
curro! . . . Si yo al que mero quero es a ti. (Se
cubre la cara con la punta de su rebozo.) Vete, curro,
vete, porque ora ya te tengo muncha vergüenza.
(Luis Cervantes se aleja sonriendo y cabizbajo,
y Camila, en cuanto se queda sola, prorrumpe en llanto.)
(III, 47).

To arrange for a leaf to fall at Camila's feet or for a bird
to burst into mournful song in accompaniment to her tears, as
in the novel, would create an unwanted distraction in the
theater. The playwright could, however, stylize Luis' rejection of Camila by decreasing the illumination or specifying
appropriate music in the background. The fact that he does
not, represents an artistic decision to present the incident
with a minimum of authorial management.
In Cuadro IV and in Chapter 1, Part II, Demetrio's almost
disdainful reserve when introduced to la Pintada and to el
güero Margarito contributes to the inaccessibility essential to
his mythification or heroification. In both works it is the
last presentation of that side of Demetrio's character. The
incidents are quite alike in the two works, although heroification in the play is more nearly unmitigated by signs of Demetrio's weaknesses. The major differences between the corresponding episodes explain why Demetrio's role as a legendary hero
is stronger than in the novel.
As the curtain rises for Cuadro IV, Valderrama is reciting
Demetrio's feats of bravery during the Battle of Zacatecas.
Demetrio, seated at Valderrama's table, remains silent and un-
responsive throughout the glowing account. His invulnerability
to praise seems awesome. In the novel, that description of
Demetrio's exploits is told by Alberto Solís to a one-man
audience, Luis Cervantes, in Chapter 21, Part I, the chapter
preceding that which corresponds to the opening scene of Cuadro
IV. The transition from Part I to Part II, interrupting the
immediacy of Solís' description, virtually invalidates it as
a contributing factor in Demetrio's aloofness. In Chapter 1,
Demetrio's vanity begins to erode his inscrutability. First
Margarito and then la Pintada refer to Demetrio's anticipated
promotion from colonel to general:

Demetrio, envanecido por las felicitaciones que
comenzaron a lloverle, mandó que sirvieran champaña
(I, 372).

No such softening of his icy reserve is suggested in Cuadro
IV, where he speaks seldom and only a few words each time.
When Margarito sits down at the table, Demetrio claps his
hands to summon the waiter and asks his companions: "¿Qué
toman?" (III, 50). Later he orders more beer for everyone.
His mood does not seem as expansive as if he requested champagne, symbolic of celebration. The austerity contributed by
Valderrama's story is due in part to the demands of the play.
Cuadro III is staged in an open space conducive to the
philosophical discussion between Demetrio and Luis, and Cuadro
IV, in the saloon where events may build to Pintada's murder
of Camila. Any description of Demetrio's prowess at Zacatecas
logically belongs at the beginning of Cuadro IV, where it has
a double function. Placed first in the cuadro, it becomes a
summary of an unrepresented event. It also is the occasion
for Demetrio's promotion and the resulting banquet which interrupts the mounting rivalry between Pintada and Camila, heightening audience expectation. It is not, however, structurally
necessary that Demetrio be present to hear and appear unaffected
by the tale of his exploits. He could enter after Valderrama's
speech, did the playwright not wish to underline his extreme
aloofness. The scene is governed by the requirements of the
work and by the author's artistic intent.

That one of Cervantes' vices is avarice is demonstrated
in both the novel and the play. In Chapter 6, Part II, his
eyes gleam when Demetrio offers him a fine pocket watch in
return for bringing Camila to join them (I, 386); in Chapter
11, Part II, Cervantes is so eager to buy a hoard of jewelry
that Codorniz decides not to sell (I, 394-395). In Cuadro IV
a similar transaction is revealed. Cervantes hurriedly takes
out a roll of bills and picks up the jewelry "con ansiedad mal
encubierta" (III, 57). While the narrator of the novel relies
on a greedy gleam in the character's eyes, the playwright sub-
stitutes hurried motions to denote avarice. The available
point of view dictates the difference in technique; the theater
cannot get close enough to a character to capture the gleam in
his eye. In Cuadro IV, the author chooses hurried movements
of the hands to communicate Luis' excessive eagerness.

In Chapter 12, Part II, and in Cuadro IV, Pintada asks
Margarito to side with her against Demetrio, obtaining permis-
sion for her to stay on. In both cases el güero abandons
her, provoking hilarity among the troops and driving Pintada
to such exacerbation that she kills Camila. In the novel,
part of the humor of the exchange lies in Margarito's condition
when he appears:

> . . . Acababa de levantarse; sus ojos azules se
> perdían bajo unos párpados hinchados y su voz
> estaba ronca. Se informó del sucedido y, acer-
> cándose a la Pintada, le dijo con mucha gravedad:
> --Sí, me parece muy bien que ya te largues
> mucho a la . . . ¡A todos nos tienes hartos!
> (I, 398).

In the play, his words sustain the comic effect:

EL GÜERO

> (Con mucha sorna.)
> Sí, Pintada, me parece muy bien lo que te ha
> dicho mi general Macías. Lárgate mucho al infierno,
> que a todos nos tienes hartos (III, 62).

Margarito is on stage at all times. He has just been the center of attention, forcing the short man to perform a dance.
His appearance, not subject to change, cannot contribute humor
to the incident in the play. The word infierno replaces the
ellipse found in the novel. In the theater, the author does
not normally leave out words and trust to the audience's imagination. Any such omission will be attributed to the character;
the author does not choose that Margarito use such a technique
in his speech.

In Cuadro IV and in Chapter 1, Part II, la Pintada's bawdy
nature is demonstrated by her actions. Sitting on the bar,
close behind Demetrio, she attracts his attention by stretching
out her legs and grazing his back. Her manner of dress also
characterizes her. In the play her gaudy attire reveals her
brash nature and almost manly self-assertion:

> . . . un vestido de seda de vivísimos colores,
> pésimamente ajustado a su cuerpo, medias azules
> y zapatillas de raso blanco. Muchas cuentas y
> avalorios relumbrosos adornan su traje. Se
> cubre con un gran sombrero galoneado y muestra
> carrilleras ajustadas a la cintura y cruzadas
> sobre el pecho (III, 48).

The details of her dress seem inspired by the description in
Chapter 5, Part II:

> . . . Muy ufana, lucía vestido de seda y grandes
> arracadas de oro; . . . Llevaba revólver al pecho
> y una cartuchera cruzada sobre la cabeza de la
> silla (I, 381).

Pintada, very much at ease in the cantina, is out of place in
fine clothes. The gown, expensive but ill-fitting, makes
her seem awkward. The huge sombrero, normally a man's gar-
ment, and the weapons are testimony to Pintada's unfemininity.
She is at first impression an unattractive woman, admirable
only for her bravery, which she asserts later in the cuadro.
By encouraging disfavor for Pintada, the playwright builds
sympathy for Camila, even before the women's feud is introduced.

In Chapter 12, Part II, Demetrio accedes to Camila's wishes
and orders Pintada to stay behind when the brigade moves on.
Pintada's outraged epithets, left to the reader's imagination,
are complemented by narrative summary:

-- ¿Qué estás diciendo?--exclamó ella con
asombro--. ¿ Es decir, que tú me corres? ¡Ja, ja,
ja! . . . ¡Pues qué . . . tal serás tú si te andas
creyendo de los chismes de esa . . . !
    Y la Pintada insultó a Camila, a Demetrio, a
Luis Cervantes y a cuantos le vinieron a las mientes,
con tal energía y novedad, que la tropa oyó injurias
e insolencias que no había sospechado siquiera.
    Demetrio esperó largo rato con paciencia;
pero como ella no diera trazas de acabar, con mucha
calma dijo a un soldado:
    --Echa fuera esa borracha.
    -- ¡Güero Margarito! ¡Güero de mi vida! ¡Ven
a defenderme de estos . . . ! ¡Anda, güerito de mi
corazón! . . . ¡Ven a enseñarles que tú eres hombre
de veras y ellos no son más que unos hijos de . . . !
    Y gesticulaba, pateaba y daba de gritos (I, 398).

The narrator's reference to the originality of Pintada's insults, probably an exaggeration, contributes extrinsic humor
to the incident. The passage is rich in contrasts: the
narrator's apparent amusement at Pintada's expense, counter
to her own uncontrollable rage, and immediately preceding
the grisly murder. The narrator's levity anticipates that of
the bystanders, who guffaw when Margarito refuses to come to
Pintada's defense. The laughter might mislead the reader into
believing that the woman's rage will go for naught. Therefore, Pintada's sudden murder of Camila might produce more of
a shock. Another strong contrast is that between Demetrio's
calm and Pintada's extreme anger.
    In Cuadro IV, the playwright prescribes no shrieking or
stamping of feet to visualize Pintada's rage. Presumably she
is to shout as she delivers rather measured insults:

LA PINTADA
    Pero oye, piojo resucitado, ¿pos qué te estás
creyendo, pues? ¿Es decir que tú me corres a mí?
¡Pos qué poco hombre serás si te has creído de esa
infeliz garraleta! (Sañalando a Camila.)

DEMETRIO
Echen fuera a esa borracha.

LA PINTADA
(Fuera de sí.)
    Güero Margarito, ¿qué no oyes cómo me está
insultando este hilacho mugroso, limosnero con
pistola? Ven a defenderme y a enseñarle que
eres hombre . . . (III, 62).

The stage directions "fuera de sí" leave to the discretion of
the director how graphic Pintada's anger is to be. As in the
novel, it is contrasted to Demetrio's apparent calm. Nothing
in the scene is humorous, and the troops' laughter seems

unjustified. Perhaps it carries over from the raucous banquet scene, just completed. The play, with a murder scene less hyperbolic than that of the novel, encourages the viewer to see the incident not from the bystanders' point of view but perhaps from that of one of the principals.

After la Pintada murders Camila, Demetrio orders his men to kill her. In the novel she demonstrates pride, fearlessness and a sense of justice:

> Dos soldados se arrojaron sobre la Pintada
> que, esgrimiendo el puñal, no les permitió tocarla.
> --¡Ustedes no, infelices! . . . Mátame tú,
> Demetrio--se adelantó, entregó su arma, irguió el
> pecho y dejó caer los brazos (I, 399).

By dropping her arms to her side, a sign that she waives the right to defend herself, Pintada seems to acknowledge that death at Demetrio's hand would be a just punishment. In the drama, Pintada's attitude is more ambiguous than in the novel:

> (Entran Pancracio y la Codorniz, que la traen
> bien trincada.)
>
>   LA PINTADA
> ¡Ustedes no, desgraciados! ¡Mátame tú, Demetrio!
>   (Le tiende el puñal ensangrentado, desgarra
> bruscamente sus ropas y le muestra se pecho des-
> nudo . . .) (III, 63).

It is not apparent what the actress is to do with her hands. Dropping them to her side would, as in the novel, indicate non-resistance to a just revenge. If, on the other hand, the actress continues to clutch at her dress, that gesture might suggest fear or defiance.

In Cuadro VI the playwright shows that the joy of Demetrio and his wife, seeing each other again, is silent and profound:

> (Entran Demetrio y Pancracio. Éste abraza a
> María Antonia y aquél a su mujer. Ella se mantiene
> en sus brazos, ahogando su llanto en silencio.)
> (III, 75).

The couple's long embrace communicates their deep emotion, especially when contrasted to the greeting María Antonia gives Pancracio. The exuberance of their love, already well established, suggests a rather animated reunion. The actress who plays Demetrio's wife might tremble convulsively from time to time, imitating stifled sobs.

Chapter 6, Part III, recounts Demetrio's homecoming differently:

La mujer de Demetrio Macías, loca de alegría,
salió a encontrarlo por la vereda de la sierra,
llevando de la mano al niño。
。。．．。。。。。．．。。。．．．．．．。．．
Se abrazaron y permanecieron mudos; ella embar-
gada por los sollozos y las lágrimas (I, 415).

The reunion is more openly emotional than in the play。 In
the absence of another couple whose love contrasts with that
of Demetrio, it is the wife who reacts with joy at Demetrio's
arrival. In the play, she merely allows herself to be em-
braced. In both versions, Demetrio's silence indicates his
own deep feelings。 The principal difference between the corresponding incidents is María Antonia's intervention in the
drama. The playwright uses four characters to convey the
emotions of a homecoming. In the novel, where only two characters produce the effect, the wife reacts more graphically.
    Some incidents, like the huertista's intrusion into De-
metrio's hut, are presented virtually the same way in the
play as in the novel. At times only one minor detail is omitted because it is inappropriate for the theater。 An example
is the bloodstain on Cervantes' leg when he is captured. Although the novelist mentions that it is fresh, as it logically would be, the playwright does not insist that the actor appear on stage with a still-damp stain. From the distance of
their seats, unaided by any mediator, the spectators would
not appreciate that detail.
    The immediacy of the theater sometimes dictates which
signs may be used to convey an emotion. When Luis Cervantes
is characterized as greedy in the novel, the gleam in his
eye is interpreted by the narrator。 With only an unmediated
sign to convey that notion, the playwright establishes avarice
through hurried movements of the actor's hands.
    The lack of psychological introspection in the theater
limits the actors' capacities to convey emotion. When
Camila is to appear modest, the playwright refrains from
prescribing a blush and indicates that the actress lower her
eyes. That difference between the novel and the play is
dictated by the demands of the genre.
    In Cuadro II, as in Chapter 5, Part I, the recently-cap-
tured Luis Cervantes displays arrogance。 Communicated by
the reactions of his captors in the novel, his haughtiness
in the drama is conveyed by his and the revolutionaries'
altered tones of voice. Drama has an auditory capacity,
lacking in narrative, which the playwright uses to expand the
representation of a trait。
    The scenario of the play limits what can be presented on
stage at a given moment. In the novel, when el güero Margarito
refuses to defend Pintada against Demetrio, the humor is sustained by his appearance, still half asleep and possibly not
fully recovered from heavy drinking。 In Cuadro IV, Margarito
is already on stage and cannot re-appear. For that reason,
humor can come only from the words he speaks to Pintada。
    The scenario does not provide for the revolutionaries to

pass through a village where an unidentified serrano might bless them and ask them to take revenge on the abusive federales. The playwright, who could assign that speech to any one of a number of characters, anywhere in the first three cuadros, placed it where it would be reinforced by a dramatized abuse by the federales. In this case the speech, assigned to Demetrio's wife, is more closely integrated into the scenario than into the narrative plan of the novel.

In the play, Demetrio's aloofness in the cantina scene is underlined by his presence in silence as Valderrama relates his brilliant prowess in a battle. The scenario may have obliged the author to place that description on Cuadro IV, where it summarizes an incident which logically must have taken place during the interval after Cuadro III. The author also exercises his artistic will, arranging that Demetrio be present during Valderrama's story, rather than entering after its conclusion. Artistic will also accounts for Pintada's ill-fitting dress in Cuadro IV, making her seem instantly out of place in the elegant gown; the absence of authorial manage-ment or stylization at the close of Cuadro III, when Luis Cer-vantes rejects Camila; and the lack of humor in the murder scene, shifting the point of view from the bystanders to the principals.

A previous arrangement of the scenario may affect a sub-sequent incident, as in the case of Demetrio's reunion with his wife. María Antonia has already been committed to presence when Demetrio returns home; it was she who volunteered to take a message. She and the wife describe Demetrio's indirect ar-rival. Since it has been established that Pancracio is María Antonia's lover, he appears with Demetrio. The emotional home-coming is effected through a sharp contrast between the exuber-ant joy of Pancracio and María Antonia and the unspeaking ten-derness between Demetrio and his wife.

In summary: a writer has available to him, in novelistic fiction, perspectives from which one could not present incidents on a stage. In the theater, the esthetic vantage point is never that of one person standing close to another. The spectator is only a spectator, denied a close-up view of the portrayed events. Therefore, a playwright dispenses with minute details which, presented directly and uninterpreted, would go unnoticed. Another limitation of the theater is the capacity of the actors, who cannot reveal their inner emotions except through direct exterior manifestations. A blush, uninterpreted, as by the narrator of a novel, would fail as a sign of modesty or embarrassment. Some signs of emotion are not, then, presentable on stage.

Conversely, the dramatist has at his disposal the gamut of auditory phenomena. A single sound can convey in an instant an impression which might require a sentence or paragraph of narrative explanation in a novel. The theater also can con-vey subtle visual impressions which may subliminally affect the audience's opinion about a given incident. The narrator of a novel can hardly manipulate so unobtrusively his readers' minds. Finally, in the study of a work which exists both in

novelistic and in the theatrical form, one will find significant changes occasioned by differences between the narrative
organization and the scenario. Bearing in mind these and
other similar considerations, we shall analyze the most significant differences between the novel and the play.

Contrasts between the Novel and the Play

Differences between the novel and the drama are sometimes
a function of genre characteristics and sometimes a result of
the author's will. Demetrio's odyssey, broadly similar in the
two versions, is developed differently. There are essential
distinctions in structure, settings, illumination, music, and
costuming. Stage directions, sometimes based upon a corresponding narrative passage of the novel, may reflect a unique interpretation of an incident. Dialog is varied by changing the
wording, the speaker or the context in which the speech is
delivered. The characters most unlike their image in the novel
are Camila, Luis, Margarito, and especially Valderrama. Alberto
Solís is deleted and three female characters are expanded from
minor roles in the novel: Doña Nica, Demetrio's wife, and
María Antonia. Of prime interest in this section are the reasons
for each change and their consequences in the play.

Demetrio: Differences in Exposition

Chapter 1, Part I, of the novel reveals Demetrio in a
family situation, alone at home with his wife and infant son.
In Cuadro I, on the other hand, Anastasio and la Codorniz share
a meal with him. After an opening discussion about the food,
the men begin to talk about their political situation: the
abuses of the federales and past victories over them, the arrival of new recruits, the persecution of Don Mónico and preparations for a forthcoming skirmish. The political background
of the plot is established prior to the exposition of Demetrio's
personality or the introduction of his semi-legendary renown.
The revised order gives the spectator a different impression
than one might receive by reading the novel. There Demetrio
is first defined as a distinct personality, then placed within a political milieu which is revealed in Chapters 2-4,
Part I. In the drama, he is inserted into circumstances already established. In the presence of secondary characters who
talk about events beyond the confines of his hut, Demetrio
seems a public man from the outset. There is not, as in the
novel, a passage during which he is just a man. Demetrio's
circumstance is revealed at the outset of Cuadro I because to
disclose it later would involve lengthy verbal explanations
or flashbacks, which the playwright decided not to employ.
The scenario, arranged to facilitate early presentation of
the milieu, occasions characterization of Demetrio which
is unlike that of the novel.

In the novel Demetrio is revealed in brief intimate
moments with Camila and with his wife. In Chapter 10, Part II,

he calls Camila his "mujer" and spends the night with her at a
peaceful farm. His grief over her death, in Chapter 13, Part
II, attests to the depth of his feeling. Similarly in Chapter
6, Part III, a sudden thunderstorm forces Demetrio and his wife
to take shelter in a small cavern. The narrator gives the impression that they are together there, with their son, for a
significant period of time. Although elapsed time is not
specifically mentioned, the passage suggests a detailed contemplation of distant landmarks:

> . . . Y todo era serranía: ondulaciones de cerros
> que suceden a cerros, más cerros circundados de
> montañas y éstas encerradas en una muralla de
> sierra . . . (I, 416).

The repetition of words and the allusion to distance in space,
in itself non-essential to the passage where it occurs, implies
by analogy that the thunderstorm is of at least moderate duration.

In Cuadro IV of the play, where Camila has taken her place
at Demetrio's side, they are never alone and exchange only a few
words. Throughout most of the cuadro attention is focused away
from them. No illusion of intimacy is created; even Demetrio's
grief is demonstrated only by a wavering hand and hoarse voice,
as he orders Pintada to leave. Likewise, in Cuadro VI, Demetrio's reunion with his wife is presented entirely on stage and
comprises only a few speeches before he is gone. Moreover,
that exchange emphasizes him as a property owner and father,
not a husband. Demetrio, whose tender moments with women are
few in the novel, is shown in no intimate situation in the
play. Within the dramatic arrangement of Cuadro IV, which
consists of scenes representing a growth of tension between
Camila and Pintada, alternated with humorous diversions which
complement that rivalry, there is no appropriate place for
intimacy between Demetrio and Camila. Any exchange between
them exacerbates Pintada's jealousy, so that their tenderness
toward each other would either cause the action to climax
prematurely or would be too pathetic in contrast to the merriment of the interludes. Similarly, in Cuadro VI, an unhurried
reunion of Demetrio and his wife would too deeply affect the
cyclic tempo upon which the cuadro's structure is built. In
both cases, to present Demetrio in an intimate conversation
would undermine the organization of the respective cuadros.

In Chapter 6, Part II, Luis Cervantes shows Demetrio his
hoard of jewelry, inviting him to take any items he wishes.
The answer enables the reader to penetrate deep into Demetrio's
psyche:

> --Déjelo todo para usted . . . ¡Si viera que
> no le tengo amor al dinero! . . . ¿Quiere que le
> diga la verdad? Pues yo, con que no me falte el
> trago y con traer una chamaquita que me cuadre,
> soy el hombre más feliz del mundo.

> --¡Ja, ja, ja! . . . ¡Qué mi general! . . .
> ¿Bueno, y por qué se aguanta a esa sierpe de la
> Pintada?
>   --Hombre, curro, me tiene harto; pero así
> soy. No me animo a decírselo . . . ése es mi
> genio. Mire, de que me cuadra una mujer, soy
> tan boca de palo, que si ella no comienza, . . .
> yo no me animo a nada . . . Ahí está Camila,
> la del ranchito . . . (I, 386).

Demetrio's confession is congruous with his extreme depression
after Camila's death. The brief tender moments he spends with
Camila and his wife, shortly before his definitive separation
from each, are rendered more pathetic in light of the above
passage.

In the play, where the scenario does not facilitate Demetrio's intimacy with his wife or with Camila, and where Demetrio
is never portrayed in mourning for his murdered lover, he reveals to Luis only his awkwardness with women:

> CERVANTES
> . . . Entre Camila y yo no hay ni ha habido nada.
> Ella al que quiere es a usted; pero le tiene
> miedo. (Riendo.)
>
> DEMETRIO
> ¡Es capaz que sí, curro! Siempre he sido muy boca
> de palo con las mujeres. Y si ellas no jalan
> primero . . . (III, 44-45).

Any mention of placing women among the most treasured objects
in life, as Demetrio does in the novel, might create in the
spectators a hope or expectation which the playwright could not
easily avoid frustrating. For that reason, only half of Demetrio's remark is used in the play. In both cases, what follows
is Luis' promise to help arrange an understanding between
Demetrio and Camila.

Demetrio's grief over Camila does not appear in the play
because the scenario makes it unfeasible. A display of depression like that of Chapter 13, Part II, would be an anti-clamactic
appendage to Cuadro IV, which is structured around the presentation of circumstances leading to Camila's death, alternated
with rather frivolous diversions. The resulting build-up of
tension would be impaired, did the cuadro not end with the murder itself. The anticipation of Demetrio's reunion with his
wife, very early in Cuadro V, makes inappropriate any nostalgia
about Camila, even in the scenes which evoke the past.

In both the novel and the play, Demetrio is the victim of
shifting political alliances which he does not understand, at
least not until his fate is sealed. The play does not include
one incident which is vitally important to an understanding of
Demetrio's motives as revealed in the novel. Nowhere in the
play does Demetrio avenge the injustice done him by his local
cacique, Don Mónico. To present that confrontation as in the

novel would require an additional cuadro devoted to little else.
Though it could be added, were the scenario considerably
altered, the playwright elected not to do so. A passing mention of Demetrio's having settled matters with Don Mónico
would, in an ideological sense, accomplish the same ends as a
full-blown incident. There is, however, no juncture where such
a revelation might be appropriate. It is in Cuadro III that
Demetrio explains to Luis how Don Mónico's persecution forced
him to take up arms; a report of revenge upon the cacique
would be out of place before or during Cuadro III, and might
suggest that Demetrio, his goal accomplished, should go home.
Cuadro IV begins with Valderrama's description of Demetrio's
prowess in battle, re-asserting the heroification of the protagonist. The news of a triumph over Don Mónico, inserted
after Valderrama's account, would de-mythify the hero by showing his human desire for revenge. Later in the cuadro, where
the only serious scenes are episodes in the rivalry between
Camila and Pintada, directly involving Demetrio, the conflict
between him and Don Mónico would complicate the action too much.
In Cuadro V, where there is no optimism except in Demetrio's
private life, news of a victory over the local cacique would
interrupt the pattern of defeat and discouragement.

The playwright's exclusion of Demetrio's revenge against
Don Mónico significantly affects the ideological message.
Demetrio, talking with his friends in Cuadro I and again with
Luis Cervantes in Cuadro III, declares that Don Mónico is to
blame for his leaving home and taking up arms. Demetrio's
personal goal, then, must be to kill Don Mónico or strip him
of his position. The triumph of the Revolution might occasion
Don Mónico's downfall; but the cacique is not mentioned after
Cuadro III. Demetrio's personal goal of revenge may go unful-
filled. If that is the case, he accomplishes little in his
revolutionary career. He does not amass a hoard of money, or
loses what he acquired, failing to make good on the advice Luis
Cervantes gave him. In contrast, however, the possibility that
Don Mónico has been spared eliminates the bitter irony of the
novel, where triumph over his enemy benefits Demetrio very
little and does not make his home safe again for him. The
play's lack of a resolution of the rivalry between Demetrio and
his detractor is only one of a series of ambiguities concerning
political questions. The case of Don Mónico reinforces the
de-emphasis of ideology in the play, composed after the Revolution. In the novel, written while the conflict still raged,
there is an effort to set forth an ideological motivation.

The novel progressively reveals Demetrio Macías both in
his private life and in his public career. In the play, the
incidents selected tend to subordinate the man to the soldier.
He is never revealed independent of the Revolution, nor is he
placed in an intimate situation either with his wife or with
Camila. In the drama, Demetrio is a military leader, judge,
friend, head of family, and father; the dramatic arrangement
does not lend itself to the development of his role as a
husband or lover.

Contrasts: The Structure

Of the forty-two chapters of Los de abajo, elements of
at least twenty-nine are directly utilized in the theatrical
adaptation. Material is at times presented in sequences different from those of the novel, effecting significant changes
in the exposition. The content of some chapters is omitted
and some unique scenes are introduced, especially in Cuadros
V and VI.
Chapter 1, Part I, introduces Demetrio as a family man
whose home is violated by the federales. After their intrusion and as a result of it, he joins his disciples who await
him in the sierra near his village. Chapter 2 describes the
preparations for a skirmish with the enemy; Chapter 3, the
battle itself; and Chapter 4, the consequences of that battle.
Chapter 1 treats Demetrio as a private individual, his life
interrupted by political events. In Chapter 2 his public life
is detailed. Chapter 3 integrates Demetrio's circumstance
with that of the conflict which at that moment afflicts his
nation, while Chapter 4 examines the impact of the conflict on
the lives of Demetrio and other peasants like him. Throughout
the first four chapters, rather generalized references to the
war become increasingly specific and affect a growing number
of characters more and more personally.
The process of exposition in Cuadro I is reversed from that
of the novel. The opening scene, a dinnertime conversation
among Demetrio, his wife and two of his disciples, sets forth
the effect of the Revolution on their lives. Following is a
discussion of Demetrio's public life, detailing what he has
done and will do to meet the new challenge. Last in the cuadro
is a specific example of enemy intruders invading Demetrio's
home and upsetting his domestic life. The exposition in Cuadro
I concentrates on specific, personal effects of the Revolution.
In the sense that it isolates Demetrio from other victims of
the war, the cuadro has a hermetic quality.
A noteworthy feature of Cuadro II is the fragmentation of
Demetrio's decision to test Luis Cervantes' truthfulness, his
interview with the prisoner and his verdict of acquittal. In
the novel, the entire process appears in a continuous passage
of Chapter 7. In the drama, Demetrio first orders Codorniz
to pose as a priest; Señá Remigia then enters to perform a folk
cure on Demetrio's leg, in material adapted from Chapter 9.
Following is the pretended death sentence of the prisoner,
whom Pancracio leads away. The outcome of his "confession"
is not revealed until after a brief exchange between Camila
and María Antonia and Demetrio's grabbing of Camila's wrist.
Only then is Cervantes exonerated. The fragmentation of the
incident adds dramatic tension not present in the novel. The
establishment of Luis' innocence, material from Chapter 7, is
immediately followed by a decision to call him in for treatment of Demetrio's leg. In the novel, that does not happen
until Chapter 10, Part I. Placement of the action immediately after Luis' exoneration reinforces the rebels' acceptance
of him, providing stylistic preparation for his proselytizing
in Cuadro III.

In Cuadro III, more faithful than any other to the corresponding chapters of the novel, a departure from them creates a different effect. Demetrio's veiled allusion to Camila (Chapter 14, Part I) and his request that Luis bring her to him (Chapter 6, Part II) are combined in the same conversation. That technique accelerates the action over its pace in the novel, facilitating the early introduction of the rivalry with Pintada in Cuadro IV.

In Part II of the novel, el güero Margarito's cruel abuses structurally separate individual encounters between Pintada and Camila, heightening the suspense leading up to the murder. In Cuadro IV, the interlude which postpones the inevitable violence is Demetrio's promotion banquet, during which Margarito performs the same relatively harmless pranks recorded in Chapter 13, part II. In the novel, humor is found in Chapter 3, very early in Part II. The playwright inserts the comic incident at the end of the cuadro, where it contrasts in a startling manner with the violence which follows.

Chapters 1-5, Part III, are structured chronologically. They record the men's discouragement, the result of ill fortune, followed by the news of Pancho Villa's disaster. The troops then approach Demetrio's home village, step by step. There is a logical progression toward his reunion with his wife. The structure of Cuadro V, by contrast, is built upon a rhythm of emotions. The cuadro opens with a mood of pessimism, established by Valderrama's speech about crosses. Following is an episode denoting hope: María Antonia's promise to seek out Demetrio's wife and tell her he will soon be home. On the heels of hope comes humor: Venancio's reading of his letter from Luis Cervantes. The psychological rhythm then swings back to pessimism and finally to bitterness. The men reminisce about bygone pleasures, then begin to complain about the recruitment of ex-federales. Pancracio's announcement that the enemy is very near, which triggers no emotional reaction in Demetrio, creates a mood of despair just prior to Demetrio's homecoming in Cuadro VI. The impression of foreboding, reinforced by the rhythm of pessimism/optimism/pessimism, is stronger than in the novel, with its unbroken gloom and sparse references to future emergencies. Rhythm is a convenient device for presenting in one unbroken scene events which in the novel occur successively over a time period of several days or perhaps weeks. To create the illusion of chronological succession in a play, it would be necessary to change the set in mid-cuadro, to fade the illumination or at least to empty the stage of characters from time to time. Such transitions would require a very rigid control of the illusion of passing time, so that too much does not appear to go by during the cuadro, impairing the pattern of accelerated events. To avoid such technical problems, the playwright synthesized into a rhythmic structure the events he chose for Cuadro V.

Cuadro VI, based on mere fragments of the brief Chapters 6 and 7, elaborates upon a skeleton of the events they relate. Demetrio's death is studied from the point of view of the living, a significant departure from the exposition in the novel. He does not die "in a vacuum," as in Chapter 7; his death affects

his wife, who silently grieves for him. In the play, the last
figure revealed is not the dead protagonist but his bereaved
wife. The drama, including a sequel to Demetrio's death, lacks
the terse finality of the novel. Off-stage presentation of
Demetrio's death is effected through pre-arranged messengers,
the wife and María Antonia, already on stage when Demetrio
arrives. The presence of Pancracio, for whom María Antonia
ventures to the battle front, makes her journey there seem
like a natural thing to do. It also seems natural for Demetrio's
wife, already identified as having awaited him at home, to stay
behind and be absent from his side when she receives news of
his death. Through careful construction of the cuadro, the
playwright creates an effective death scene very different from
the one in Chapter 7, Part III.

The novel's forty-two chapters are distributed among the
three parts in the ratio of 3:2:1. In the play, by contrast,
three cuadros derive from Part I, one from Part II, and two
from Part III. Part I, an introduction to the basic personal
and ideological subplots of the novel, serves the same purpose
in the play. Part II, an exposition of the revolutionaries'
physical impact on non-combatants, is greatly de-emphasized.
Expanded consideration is given to the material of Part III,
an analysis of the psychological effect of the Revolution on
participants and civilians alike. The increased emphasis has
made of the play a study of the emotional duress which the
revolutionaries undergo. That aspect of the conflict, touched
upon in the novel while the conflict still raged, is expanded
in the adaptation written when the military phase of the Revolution had become history.

Though the play contains roughly the same events as the
novel, they are presented differently. Cuadro I reverses the
order in which events are presented, while Cuadro II establishes
a rhythm of waxing and waning tension surrounding Luis Cervantes'
trial, creating suspense not present in the novel. Cuadro IV
inserts the humor of Demetrio's banquet and of el güero
Margarito's pranks immediately before the tragic murder of
Camila. No such sharp contrast exists in the novel. Cuadros
V and VI present in a new way the events of Part III. Only
Cuadro III follows closely the exposition of the novel.

In the play the content of Part II is de-emphasized and
that of Part III is given increased importance. Through that
shift of emphasis, the drama becomes something which the novel
is not: a study of the effects of civil war on human personalities.

The Background in Time and Place

Though the same events are described in the play as in
the novel, not all occur in comparable sites. The differences
constitute minor or major changes in the flavor of the incidents.

The interior of Demetrio's hut, in Cuadro I, has decora-
tions and accessories typical of Central Mexico. Most specific
is the portrait of Nuestra Señora de Jalpa, which fixes the
location in the southern portion of the state of Zacatecas. No

such descriptions orient the reader of Chapter 1, Part I.
Throughout the novel, it is not the interiors but the outdoor
sites which are specifically Mexican. However, descriptions
tend to be abstract, for the novel possesses a Nature-oriented
lyricism which the play lacks.

The split set of Cuadro II (the exterior of one hut and
the interior of another) divides into two categories the
actions performed there. The central personal incident (Luis
and Camila's conversation) occurs outside the hut on the left,
and the principal event (Luis' trial) takes place inside the
hut on the right. The exposed interior, with no furnishings
except Demetrio's cot, restricts the activities which can occur
there. No food is prepared or eaten, nor do normal daily
activities take place. Demetrio, isolated, is confined to
special roles: judge of Cervantes, commander of his men and
occasional contender for Camila's favor. In the novel, the
hut where Demetrio convalesces and to which he is confined
during Chapters 5-10, Part I, belongs specifically to Señá
Remigia, who is shown in pursuit of her daily concerns. In
Chapter 9 she prepares her corn meal and gossips with her
neighbors. The hut, as developed in the novel, has little of
the special, reserved status given it in the drama. The
limited amount of space available in a split set has significantly influenced the episodes presented there.

In Chapter 21, Part I, Alberto Solís sits on a hilltop
overlooking Zacatecas as he describes Demetrio's heroics in
the battle for that city, the last engagements of which are
still taking place below. Solís' account, immediate in time
and place, is only one step removed from a narrative description of the events as they happen. Temporal and spatial
immediacy are not factors in that narration as presented in
Cuadro IV, where Valderrama tells it to an audience seated in
a cantina. On the other hand, Demetrio himself is present,
listening in silence to the report of his own heroics. Achieving
relevance on a personal level, the playwright changes the circumstance of an incident without undermining its impact.

Demetrio's death, in Chapter 7, Part III, takes place outdoors in an ironic setting. He is revealed at an undetermined
point after the end of his life, surrounded by a grandiose
Nature, no element of which reflects his death. No reaction to
his removal is included in the novel. In Cuadro VI, Demetrio's
death is specific in time but occurs at an indeterminable point
in space. Excluding Nature from the exposition, the playwright
concentrates on the pained reaction of Demetrio's wife. The
result is the achievement of a more personalized death scene.

The spatial limitations of the theater do not facilitate
the illusion of an overwhelming Nature which would make man
seem insignificant. Nowhere is a colossal element of Nature
introduced except in Cuadro VI, where the enormous boulder,
scaled by María Antonia and later by Demetrio's wife, lends
them increased stature. The narrator of the novel frequently
presents characters as if they were smaller than life; the
playwright, after presenting his figures in their natural size
throughout the first five cuadros, uses Nature to make them seem

larger in the sixth. The characters of the play, never made to appear insignificant, seem responsible for their own destinies and less nearly pawns of an inexorable force than in the novel.

In Cuadro IV, a rather large group of characters, including nameless "extras," is confined to one room when Camila's murder takes place. They are figurative prisoners of the event; the closed room perhaps symbolizes their inability to prevent Pintada's deed or to escape from it. In Chapter 12, Part II, Demetrio approaches Pintada as the troops are saddling their horses, and tells her she is not to accompany them farther. Their exchange and the woman's violent reaction obviously occur somewhere out of doors. The site of the murder, unspecific and no longer symbolic, does not color the incident. No narrative management, comparable to the circumstance of Cuadro IV, increases the impact of the homicide.

In Chapter 7, Part III, Demetrio's dead body is revealed at the foot of an enormous cliff which confines him to the extent that it overshadows him. Moreover, his resting place is identified. His death is not presented visually in the play, where he goes off stage to a place which must be conjectured. That he is dead appears certain; there is no reason to believe the wife to be an unreliable messenger. However, the absence of a death scene fixed in space changes the nature of the psychological impact of Demetrio's removal. The viewer experiences Demetrio's death, one step removed, through the wife's grieved reactions.

In the play, Camila's death is presented under more spatial restriction than in the novel. Demetrio's, on the other hand, occurs in a completely non-confining hypothetical site unrevealed by the playwright. Those significant alterations make Camila's murder more visually dramatic, while Demetrio's death in battle is presented as a psychological phenomenon. Change in the confinement of the milieu greatly affects the nature of both incidents.

Stage Techniques versus Narrative Description

Contrasts in Lighting

Stage directions occasionally specify the illumination for scenes. Except in Cuadro II, with its simulated transition from dawn to morning light, illumination is used to increase the effect of a key incident: darkness for Demetrio's separation from his wife, in Cuadro I; the heightened illumination of mirrors for Camila's murder, in Cuadro IV; and a symbolic "dusk" for Demetrio's death in Cuadro VI. In each case the playwright has altered for dramatic purposes the illumination as given in the novel.

Though the huertista intruders come at night, in Chapter 1, Part I, the narrator points out that there is moonlight as Demetrio and his wife trudge off in opposite directions:

"La luna poblaba de sombras vagas la montaña" (I, 322).
The purpose of that semi-illumination is to fix a visual
image in Demetrio's mind:

> En cada risco y en cada chaparro, Demetrio seguía
> mirando la silueta dolorida de una mujer con su
> niño en los brazos (I, 322).

Total darkness would preclude that vision, which Demetrio recalls in Chapter 5, Part II. He spares the lives of Don
Mónico and his family but burns their house to the ground,
just as his house was burned on that moonlit night. The
confrontation with Don Mónico is not included in the play, and
Demetrio is not made to recall how his wife looked on the
night of their separation. Near-total darkness outside the
hut is, therefore, practical in Cuadro I. Its effect is to
turn Demetrio and his wife into anonymous shapes, maintaining
the mythlike aura with which he has been surrounded and turning
her into a generalized, suffering mother figure.
Camila's murder, committed indoors and in a room where
the bright lights are multiplied by mirrors on the walls, occurs
in a visually confusing set designed to increase the dramatic
effect of the deed. The murder, presented off stage and therefore less graphically than in the novel, is made equally impressive through "management" of the scene where it occurs.
The area is enclosed and lighted more brightly. The violent
act itself carries the impact in Chapter 12, Part II; in Cuadro
IV, the place where the crime occurs is partially responsible
for the dramatic effect. The playwright takes advantage of the
theater's potential for subliminal suggestion through subtle
visual stimuli.
Demetrio's death, as presented in Part III, is revealed in
the full light of day, in a sun-drenched setting. The playwright dims the illumination, creating a symbolic "dusk."
The death is communicated mainly through the words of Demetrio's
wife; the playwright underlines her announcement with stylized
lighting. As the narrator contrasts life and death, the playwright represents those two forces symbolically, in light and
darkness. Illumination in the play, when it differs from that
of the novel, enhances the imagery of the new work.

Contrasts in Music

Music is an important feature of both the novel and the
play, contributing to a number of different moods. In Chapter
1, Part I, as well as in Cuadro I, the drunken huertista lieutenant's refrain conveys his objectionable behavior. In
Chapter 3, Part III, and in Cuadro V, Valderrama's nostalgic
song intensifies the melancholy of the other characters. Only
in these two instances is music used the same in the two versions.
Cuadro IV contains Demetrio's banquet, adapted from Chapters 3 and 13, Part II. In the play, the role of music is
expanded and extensively incorporated into the action; in the

novel it forms part of an unperceivable background of which
the reader is reminded from time to time. The novel contains
two references to an orchestra at the banquet. When Demetrio
asks the reason for "el afinar de cuerdas y latones en el patio
de la casa" (I, 376) Cervantes announces the celebration of
his new rank. The narrator pauses to introduce the beautiful
girl whom Luis has brought to the banquet, then marks with
music the commencement of festivities: "Rompió la orquesta
una rumbosa marcha taurina. Los soldados bramaron de alegría"
(I, 377). There is humor in the animal sounds of the men,
emphasized by bullfight music.

The playwright creates a spectacular beginning to the banquet: Valderrama, Margarito and la Pintada are to enter, followed by a five-piece orchestra playing "La Adelita," a song
which typifies the revolutionary epoch. The orchestra participates in the merriment, playing dianas after Valderrama's
rhetorical toast.

The most extensive expansion of musical accompaniment
occurs toward the close of the banquet scene, when el güero
forces a short man to dance "Los enanos." The orchestra plays
appropriate music, creating a more comic situation than in
Chapter 13, Part II, where the hilarity of Margarito's pranks
is not as contagious as in the play.

In Chapter 13, Part II, music intensifies the impression
of Demetrio's grief over the loss of Camila. He sings the same
verse over and over:

> En la medianía del cuerpo
> una daga me metió,
> sin saber por qué
> ni por qué sé yo . . . (I, 399).

The narrator alludes to those words in Chapter 3, Part III,
establishing a structural link with Part II and reinforcing
the idea that Demetrio's depression is partly from grief over
Camila. The refrain does not appear in the play, where the
scenario does not allow for a display of Demetrio's sadness
at losing his mistress.

The revelation of Demetrio's death is an instance where
music is used in the drama but not in the novel. The wife
has relayed the message that he is dead and has pantomined her
despair. As the curtain descends, a mouth organ plays "La
Adelita" softly, as if from a distance. If interpreted as
meaning eternal life for Demetrio, it fulfills a function performed by the narrator in Part III. The dove in Chapter 6 and
the cliff at the bottom of which Demetrio lies dead, "enorme y
suntuosa como pórtico de vieja catedral" (I, 418), are both
intimations of life after death. The religious theme in the
play is conveyed through music and through the wife's pious
utterances. The playwright makes use of a tangible stimulus
which, in the novel, would be only a suggestion to the reader's
imagination.

Contrasts in Costuming

The attire of the characters, in both the novel and the play, establishes their Mexican nationality and their station in life. In Cuadro IV, the playwright communicates through costuming that a gulf has opened between Demetrio and several of his men. He is dressed to look affluent, while they appear as humble as ever. That difference does not appear to exist in Part II of the novel. In Chapter 1 the narrator describes the enlisted men in general:

> Hombres manchados de tierra, de humo y de
> sudor; de barbas crespas y alborotadas caballeras,
> cubiertos de andrajos mugrientos . . . (I, 370).

Later the dress of the officers is established:

> Menudearon las estrellas y las barras en sombreros
> de todas formas y matices; grandes pañuelos de seda
> al cuello, anillos de gruesos brillantes y pesadas
> leopoldinas de oro (I, 372).

There are simply two groups of soldiers, most of them Natera's men. Demetrio and his disciples are not characterized either as well-dressed or as ragged. In Chapter 5 the narrator comments that Anastasio and Pancracio are the highest-ranking officers under Demetrio. He is attired elegantly, but not in contrast to his old friends, whose dress is never revealed. The novel, unlike the play, never employs costuming to set Demetrio apart from his disciples. In Cuadro V the playwright prescribes that all the characters dress poorly, contrasting with their handsome attire of Cuadro IV. That technique calls attention to the difficult times they have endured. The characters of Part III are also shabbily dressed:

> La polvareda ondulosa e interminable se prolongaba
> por las opuestas direcciones de la vereda, en un hormi-
> guero de sombreros de palma, viejos kakis mugrientos,
> frazadas musgas . . . (I, 407).

The narrator is not necessarily underlining a new situation, for he has consistently described the rebels in similar terms. He does not single out Demetrio or any other specific character as dressing that way; the description applies to the troops in general. In Part III, narrative passages and not clothing sustain the message of defeat and despair. The manner of dress is more generalized and less packed with meaning in the novel than in the play. Costume in the theater is unavoidable and therefore many times unobtrusive, even when prescribed with a special intent. In a novel, on the other hand, mention of the characters' attire is the exception rather than the rule. Including costume, the narrator must necessarily give it relative prominence. Development of a hierarchy of dress might overshadow an incident which merits the reader's prime consideration.

Illumination, music, and costuming are all specified from time to time in narrative passages of the novel. The fact that all are employed more extensively in the play than in the novel reflects the nature of the two media. The key problem for the novelist is the duration of an image: a gunshot, a dog's bark or the crowing of a cock occur, are noticed, and may or may not color the reader's interpretation of events subsequently described. Indeed, such sound effects are used similarly in the two versions of Los de abajo. Lighting, sustained music or a character's attire, on the other hand, are present throughout a given incident and may color its every phase. The novelist may mention that the walls of a cantina are lined with mirrors or that a chieftain is more ostentatiously dressed than his men; but those facts do not affect subsequent incidents unless the narrator re-introduces them. The reader is not expected to remember the mirrors or the differentiated costumes and view each event with them in mind. In the theater, the mirrors or costumes are continuously present for the audience to interpret as it wishes. The result is a more subtle stimulus. In Cuadro V, for example, Demetrio's shabby clothing, presented without comment, creates an impression on any viewer who remembers how he was dressed in Cuadro IV. A novelist, striving for a similar effect, might have to remind his readers of Demetrio's clothing from time to time. That procedure might result in a distraction from the central incident. In summary: illumination, music, and costuming have a more pervasive influence in the representational mode of the theater than in the descriptive mode of narration.

Stage Directions versus Narrative Passages

Many times a character's stance or gestures are as eloquent as his words. The playwright sometimes prescribes gestures or poses designated in the novel; on occasion he invents an action which surrounds a character's words with new meaning.

When Demetrio re-enters his hut, interrupting the huertista lieutenant's amorous advances to his wife, the officer makes approximately the same effusive speech in the play as in the novel. However, his words in Cuadro I make him appear more ridiculous because he stands at attention while speaking them, as though addressing a superior. The playwright, adding a pose of deference, creates a new source of humor. The lieutenant merely stands still in Chapter 1, Part I: "El teniente se puso de pie y enmudeció, quedóse frío e inmóvil como una estatua" (I, 322). Though the intent is in both cases comic, novelistic narration is limited in that it cannot present an action in time. Though the lieutenant is described as standing at attention in both versions, only in the theater can he be visualized in that continuing position as he speaks. Theatrical humor, in this case, achieves an immediacy which in the novel would depend heavily on the readers' imaginations.

Camila's elliptical conversation in Chapter 8, Part I,
is a rich source of humor. Only her questions and answers are
recorded in a technique which suggests disdainful silence
or terse replies from the other participant, Luis Cervantes.
The effect is to make Camila seem ridiculous. Though she
is equally garrulous in Cuadro II, the playwright cannot conceal Luis' replies. Using a visual technique to convey the
absurdity of Camila's position, he assigns to her exaggerated
gestures which do not appear in the novel. Her words,
accompanied by those movements, take on new meaning.

In Chapter 7, Part I, Demetrio orders Luis Cervantes to
be led off for "confession" and perhaps execution. His command is carried out in a rather matter-of-fact way:

> Anastasio, impasible como siempre, tomó con
> suavidad el brazo de Cervantes.
> --Véngase pa acá, curro . . . (I, 336).

In Cuadro II, though he utters almost the same words, Anastasio's
compliance is quite humorous because of a gesture inappropriate
to the occasion:

> (Tomándolo suavemente por un brazo y con
> cordialidad.)
> Véngase por acá, curro (III, 33).

"Cordiality" is more humorous than mere lack of emotion.
In Cuadro III Venancio, enthused by Cervantes' gospel
of self-gain through revolution, is to applaud and exclaim:

> ¡Luisito ha dicho una verdad del tamaño de la
> parroquia! (III, 41).

That speech is based on Chapter 13, Part I:

> --¡Luisito ha dicho una verdad como un templo!--
> exclamó con entusiasmo el barbero Venancio (I, 348).

The clapping of his hands in the play, calling attention to
Venancio's speech and making it more emphatic, makes use of
the instant impressions available in the theater.
In Cuadro VI Demetrio's wife drops to her knees, embraces
his waist and begs him not to leave. Her position of supplication adds force to her plea. The action is an expansion of
Chapter 6, Part III, which does not specify the wife's movements as she utters her request. The narrator quotes the
words, similar to those of the play, and adds: "Y se deja
sacudir de nuevo por el llanto" (I, 416). The wife's desperation, interiorized in the novel and exteriorized in the play,
demonstrates the capacities and limitations of each art form.
Prose fiction cannot present a gesture which affects a speech
from beginning to end, just as the theater cannot exhibit a
character's inward turmoil.
Although characters often recite approximately the same
words in the two versions of Los de abajo, their speeches

frequently make different impressions. The reason is the accompanying stage directions for the play, often a departure from what the narrator indicates in the novel. A gesture or inflection of voice heavily affects the meaning of words which a character recites.

Contrasts in Dialog

Variations in Wording

Many speeches of the play can be traced to the novel; in most cases there is a difference in the wording, minor or major, which does not substantially change what the character says. A few speeches, however, contain important changes in the wording.

The playwright most frequently alters a speech for comic effect, inserting more picturesque language or underlining humor already present. He strengthens an incipient play on words by the huertista lieutenant in Chapter 1, Part I. Demetrio's wife enters dragging her dead dog, Palomo, and reproaching the federales for having shot the animal. A pun lies hidden in the lieutenant's reply, weakened by an intervening comment:

> --¡Mira no más qué chapetes, sargento! . . .
> Mi alma, no te enojes, yo te juro volverte tu
> casa un palomar; . . . (I, 321).

In Cuadro I, where the play on words comes after a long interruption, the key word is repeated for a more vivid effect:

> ¡Mira no más que cachetes, mi sargento! Un
> peroncito para morderlo. No te enojes, mi chatita,
> que si te murió un palomo yo te voy a poner un
> palomar (III, 16).

In this case, the theatrical adaptation casts light upon an ambiguous passage of the novel.

The theatrical adaptation of Luis Cervantes' arrival exhibits less picturesque language than the same account in the novel. In Chapter 5, Part I, when Pancracio leads his prisoner into view, Anastasio asks what has happened. Pancracio replies:

> --Yo estoy de centinela, oí ruido entre las
> yerbas y grité: "¿Quién vive?" "Carranzo," me
> respondió este vale . . . "¿Carranzo . . . ? No
> conozco yo a ese gallo . . . " Y toma tu Carranzo:
> le metí un plomazo en una pata . . . (I, 330).

Humor lies in the words vale, gallo, toma, plomazo, and pata. The description is graphic, made vivid by the initial use of the present tense and by the direct quotes. Of course, the

incorrect rendition of Carranza's name is an ironic joke
obvious only to the narrator and the reader. Presumably,
neither Anastasio nor Codorniz can correct Pancracio's error.
In Cuadro II, when Anastasio asks what has happened, Pancracio gives a less colorful reply:

> Le di el vive y me respondió "Carranzo." "Toma
> tu Carranzo." Le metí un plomo en la pata. Yo no sé
> quién es ese Carranzo (III, 21).

The passage in the novel depends for clarity upon quotation
marks, impossible to indicate in a speech delivered on stage.
For the actor to use two voices would add a farcical touch
which the author might not intend; a short pause to suggest a
quote from another character might go unnoticed by the spectators, and a longer pause might only make the speaker seem
slow-witted. The theater requires a signal, in this case the
word respondió, to announce a quote. Overused, it would create
awkward dialog. The totally auditory nature of theatrical
dialog necessitates less complication than the printed page
of a novel tolerates. At times that limitation restricts the
playwright's options.

Later in the presentation of Cervantes' capture, a matter-
of-fact narrative revelation becomes a colorfully colloquial
speech. In the novel, Demetrio's intervention is presented
indirectly:

> En efecto, Demetrio quiso informarse de lo que
> ocurría e hizo que le llevaran al prisionero (I, 331).

In the play Venancio appears in the doorway of Demetrio's hut
and interrupts the other characters: "¿Qué bulla tienen?
. . . " (III, 23). The playwright must, of course, reveal
through dialog that Demetrio wants to know the reason for the
commotion. Choosing Venancio rather than Demetrio himself to
interrupt the raucous confrontation, the playwright not only
provides a transition to Demetrio's first encounter with Luis
but also reveals to the audience that Demetrio may be too badly wounded to get out of bed. That fact is reaffirmed when
Demetrio remains lying down though Luis has been brought inside the hut. The author has overcome two kinds of obstacles:
those imposed by genre limitations and those created by scenario.

Cervantes, presented to Demetrio, does not stop to introduce himself before complaining vociferously about the treatment he has received. Demetrio, unimpressed, demands: "--Por
eso, pues, ¿quién jijos de un . . . es usté? . . . " (I, 331).
The unessential por eso and pues suggest informal speech, and
the ellipse allows the reader to complete the epithet in his
imagination. In the theatrical version, where everyday speech
is conveyed by the actor's intonation and where the second half
of a well-known phrase is not customarily left unspoken (unless
that be a sign of the character's volition), the corresponding
passage is more terse: "¿Quién jijos de un tal por cual es
usted?" (III, 23).

In Cuadro IV el güero Margarito performs three cruel
stunts as his "toast" to Demetrio. The first is to shoot a
goblet of tequila from the head of a waiter. Twice, using
highly colorful language, he warns his victim to stand still:

> Quieto, muchacho, porque voy a romper esa copa
> y si te bulles te rompo el alma.
>
> No te buigas . . . que te voy a retratar (III, 59).

The humor of the first speech lies in the use of bullirse for
"moverse" and in the exaggerated expression "romperle a uno el
alma." The second quote is comic because of the vulgar pronunciation of "huirse" and the new interpretation of retratar.
In Chapter 13, Part II, Margarito only warns the waiter, in
somewhat less picturesque language: "--¡A tu lugar . . .
tasajo! O de veras te meto una calientita" (I, 400).

In Chapter 12, Part II, when Demetrio sends Pintada away,
her reaction is abstracted in the narrative portions of the
passage. The narrator humorously summarizes Pintada's most
picturesque phrases, leaving only her mildest language:

> -- ¿Qué estás diciendo?--exclamó ella con asombro--.
> ¿Es decir, que tú me corres? ¡Ja, ja, ja! . . .¡Pues
> qué . . . tal serás tú si te andas creyendo de los
> chismes de esa . . . !
> Y la Pintada insultó a Camila, a Demetrio, a Luis
> Cervantes y a cuantos le vinieron a las mientes, con
> tal energía y novedad, que la tropa oyó injurias e
> insolencias que no había sospechado siquiera.
>
> --¡Güero Margarito! ¡Güero de mi vida! ¡Ven
> a defenderme de estos . . . ! ¡Anda, güerito de
> mi corazón! . . . Ven a enseñarles que tú eres
> hombre de veras y ellos no son más que unos hijos
> de . . . !
> Y gesticulaba, pateaba y daba de gritos (I, 398).

In Cuadro IV, Pintada's epithets are concrete and impressive
if not humorous:

> LA PINTADA
> ¿Pero oye, piojo resucitado, pos qué te estás
> creyendo, pues? ¿Es decir que tú me corres a mí?
> ¡Pos qué poco hombre serás si te has creído de esa
> infeliz garraleta! (Señalando a Camila.)
>
> DEMETRIO
> Echen fuera a esa borracha.
>
> LA PINTADA
> (Fuera de sí.)
> Güero Margarito, ¿qué no oyes cómo me está
> insultando este hilacho mugroso, limosnero con pis-
> tola? Ven a defenderme y a enseñarle que eres hombre
> . . . (III, 62).

Another humorous revision is in Luis Cervantes' letter, where the young medic reneges on his vow to make Venancio a doctor. In Chapter 1, Part III, he writes in rather matter-of-fact language:

> Me parece difícil, amigo Venancio, que pueda usted obtener el título de médico que ambiciona tanto aquí en los Estados Unidos, por más que haya reunido suficiente oro y plata para comprarlo (I, 406).

In Cuadro V Venancio interprets the letter aloud in a more colorful manner:

> "Me parece difícil, querido Venancio, que aquí pueda conseguir el título que ambiciona, por más plata que traiga, porque aquí se jila de otra modo . . . " (III, 68).

Part of the humor is in Venancio's pronunciation of the collo-quial jilar for "hilar."

Cervantes frequently appears insincere when speaking of politics or ideologies because his thoughts are expressed in eloquent but hollow rhetorical phrases. Arguing for his life in Demetrio's hut, he declares in the novel:

> . . . ¿Yo qué me gano con que la revolución triunfe o no?
>
> . . . .
> --La revolución beneficia al pobre, al ignorante, al que toda su vida ha sido esclavo, a los infelices que ni siquiera saben que si lo son es porque el rico convierte en oro las lágrimas, el sudor y la sangre de los pobres . . . (I, 336).

During the corresponding scene in Cuadro II, he speaks clearly and forcibly, without Independence Day oratory:

> . . . si quiero luchar es sólo por el bien de ustedes, los de su clase. ¿Yo qué gano ni qué pierdo con que la revolución gane o pierda? Su triunfo le aprovecha a los pobres, a los ignorantes, a los que no han podido salir de una vida de esclavos, porque a los ricos les conviene tenerlos así para explotarlos mejor . . . (III, 33).

Luis, stating his views in simple terms, appears to believe what he says.

A speech meant to be read must satisfy different require-ments than one designed for recitation. A specific social level of speech, in prose fiction, must be imitated by means of narrative comment or imitation of erroneous pronunciation through phonetic spelling. In the theater, the actor's intona-tion reproduces the desired level of speech. Similarly, a

novelist may omit words from dialog, allowing the reader to fill
in the blanks; in the theater, unless the character himself
is to omit a word, every phrase must be recited intact. Other
considerations of genre affect the nature of dialog in the
novel and in the theater. In some cases, though, altered
wording reflects the author's volition.

Speeches by a Different Speaker

The interpretation given to words depends on the person
who says them. A character giving his own story makes a
greater impression than another character who talks about him;
also the words of a character closely related to another carry
deeper meaning than those of a stranger. An example of that
phenomenon is evident in the theatrical adaptation of the words
of unidentified serranos in Chapter 4, Part I, who give their
blessing to Demetrio and his men:

> Y los serranos, después de estrecharles fuerte-
> mente las manos encallecidas, exclamaban:
> --¡Dios los bendiga! ¡Dios los ayude y los
> lleve por buen camino! . . . (I, 328).

In the play that blessing is uttered by Demetrio's wife. Private rather than public, it is emotionally more moving. It
is reminiscent of the ritual, older than El Cid and Jimena,
in which a wife blesses her husband before he rides off to
battle.
In Chapter 13, Part I, Demetrio tells how Don Mónico
accused him as a maderista and he was nearly captured by
government troops:

> . . . Pero como no faltan amigos, hubo quien me
> lo avisara a tiempo, y cuando los federales
> vinieron a Limón, yo ya me había pelado (I, 347).

The statement is quite impersonal, omitting the name of the
friend who saved Demetrio from prison. In Cuadro III Anastasio interrupts Demetrio's story:

> Pero cuando uno tiene buenas amistades. . . .
> Yo se lo advertí todo a tiempo y cuando los federales
> llegaron, mi compadre se les había pelado (III, 39).

Assignment of that part of the account to the character who
performed the act, shifts the emphasis from the secondary
action, Demetrio's escape, to what is most important, the
warning. Anastasio's intervention is a graphic representation
of comradeship, shown rather than told.
The weight of a speech is influenced not only by the
speaker but equally by the audience. In Chapter 7, Part III,
Demetrio recognizes the Canyon of Juchipila, where he fought
his first battle. He tells his new recruits:

> --En esta misma sierra . . . yo, solo con
> veinte hombres, les hice más de quinientas bajas
> a los federales . . . (I, 417).

The recently-arrived men become serious, thinking about the perils of war:

> . . . ¿Conque si el enemigo, en vez de estar a dos
> días de camino todavía, les fuera resultando escon-
> dido entre las malezas de aquel formidable barranco,
> por cuyo fondo se han aventurado? . . .
> Y cuando comienza un tiroteo lejano . . . ni
> siquiera se sorprenden ya (I, 417).

The speaker is a military leader, and the audience, his troops. The words are a stylistic prelude to real events which will occur very soon. In Cuadro VI, after Demetrio has left for his final battle, Venancio enters to put his medicine kit in a safe place. Demetrio's wife asks him:

LA MUJER
¿Son muchos los enemigos?

VENANCIO
Un titipuchal.

LA MUJER
¡Acabarán con ustedes!

VENANCIO
En esta misma sierra, con veinte hombres no más,
les hicimos quinientas bajas a los federales . . .

LA MUJER
Pero aquéllos eran federales . . . (III, 78-79).

Venancio's reminiscence is more personal than Demetrio's because his audience is not a batallion but one person--his commander's wife, whom he tries to reassure with his idle boast.

Speeches in a Different Context

On two occasions, the playwright adapts from the novel dialog which he uses in a context so different that a speech becomes less effective. In Cuadro II, for example, la Codorniz has heard a rifle shot and tries to wake Anastasio Montañés, who says: "Ya te dije que los muertos no se aparecen" (III, 20). Codorniz insists: "No, ya no he vuelto a soñar a los ahorcados . . ." (III, 20). The reference becomes clearer if one examines the novel; it may be that the author assumed that most spectators of his play would have read the novel or would be familiar with the atrocities of the Revolution. In Chapter 4, Part I, the troops come upon the bodies of two comrades who were captured by the huertistas and hanged. Codorniz is particularly shaken by the incident:

La Codorniz no se apartaba un instante de
Anastasio. Las siluetas de los ahorcados, con
el cuello fláccido, los brazos pendientes,
rígidas las piernas, suavemente mecidos por el
viento, no se borraban de su memoria (I, 328).

In that context, Codorniz' remark about not again dreaming
about the hanged men is highly effective when it appears in
Chapter 5. In the drama "los ahorcados" are revealed only
after Codorniz' reference and only in passing. When Venancio
asks who Luis Cervantes is, Anastasio says:

Un mocho. Uno de los federales que ayer
hirieron a Demetrio y colgaron a Serapio y a
Antonio (III, 23).

Another remark out of context is found in Cuadro III,
where Demetrio enters and asks Luis: "¿Qué hace por acá tan
triste, curro?" (III, 37). The question is less effective
than in the novel, for Cervantes can be seen to have been
conversing enthusiastically with Venancio, who has even in-
vited him to share a drink. The question is more pertinent
in Chapter 12, Part I, where Luis is described as sitting
alone on a high rock, gazing into the distance and trying to
overcome his boredom. It is Anastasio, not Demetrio, who
approaches him and asks why he is so sad (I, 344). The speech,
like that in the novel but placed without obvious antecedents
in Cuadro III, refers to a situation not adequately visualized
there. These isolated remarks with a more defined context
in the novel than in the play may be indications of Azuela's
constancy in characterization. Codorniz is apparently impres-
sionable, suffering nightmares about his hanged comrades; Luis
Cervantes is apparently moody, at least until he persuades
Demetrio to help him pursue wealth through revolution. Sketchy
though their antecedents may be, the above-cited incidents
establish character traits not previously or subsequently con-
tradicted in the play.

The play omits much dialog found in the novel and includes
speeches not found there, especially in Cuadros V and VI.
Dialog may be used as is, paraphrased, or assigned to a different speaker in a different context. Such techniques may
obey the demands of the genre or the scenario of the new work;
they may at times reflect the author's artistic will. Extensively re-worked dialog enhances the play's value as an independent
work.

Contrasts in Characterization

Camila

In both the novel and the play, Camila matures from a
girl to a woman; in both she demonstrates courage and

decisiveness. She is, however, characterized differently
in the two versions, partly because of their differing arrangements of incidents and partly because of the author's intent.
In Chapter 8, Part I, and in Cuadro II, where Camila
talks with Luis for the first time, she appears talkative and
giddy. In both cases, Luis' uncommunicativeness makes Camila
seem absurd by contrast. In the play, however, she demonstrates great concern over the possibility that he may be
executed. After reassuring herself that Luis is not a government sympathizer, Camila boldly intervenes with Demetrio in
an effort to save the prisoner's life. It is structurally impossible for her to display her boldness by defending Luis in
the novel, where he is exonerated before she meets him. For
that reason, Camila seems at first a foolish adolescent with
no redeeming virtue save her modesty, which she demonstrates
when Demetrio makes an overture toward her. In both the novel
and the play, she flirtatiously asks Luis to teach her "La
Adelita," then tries to make him jealous by exaggerating Demetrio's interest in her. In both versions, crushed by Luis'
disregard for her, she makes a womanly declaration of her love
for him and, too proud to weep in his presence, orders him to
leave her alone. Chapter 15, Part I, of the novel expands
upon Camila's emotional pain in a sequence not represented in
the play. At the close of Cuadro III, however, as at the end
of Part I, Camila's pain has made her less naïve and closer
to womanhood.
In Chapter 7, Part II, and in Cuadro IV, Camila reveals
her heartbreak to the outwardly sympathetic Pintada. In both
cases, Luis' callous trickery has already been disclosed. An
important difference, however, can be seen in the nature of
Camila's decision not to feign illness so that Pintada can
help her return to her village. In the novel, Pintada's plan
and Camila's rejection of it are not consecutive but in separate chapters. In Chapter 7, Part II, Pintada consistently
pretends friendliness; neither Camila nor the reader senses
animosity. Even in Chapter 8, where Camila disregards Pintada's unsubtle prompting and declares that she will go with
Demetrio if he so wishes, there is little anticipation of the
danger she is in:

> La Pintada se puso negra y se le inflamaron
> los carrillos; pero no dijo nada y se alejó a mon-
> tar la yegua que le estaba ensillando el güero
> Margarito (I, 389).

In Cuadro IV, Camila readily confesses that she is beginning
to feel at ease with Demetrio. Pintada discards her veneer
of good will and draws a knife, ordering Camila to leave
immediately. Camila's act of crossing the stage to sit with
Demetrio at his table constitutes, then, open defiance despite
grave peril. In the novel Camila does not seem courageous
at all, but merely resolute. The exchange in Chapter 8 implies
that she has just decided to remain with Demetrio rather than
accept Pintada's kind offer. The demands of the theater have
probably influenced the scene in the play, condensed from two

incidents of the novel. A complicated action is usually accelerated in the theater, lest the story line be undramatizable because of its extreme length. In the play, every aspect of the women's rivalry is quickly established and subsequently developed.

In the novel, where Camila does not work boldly to save Cervantes' life, she does become a champion of the oppressed and a critic of the rebels' atrocities. In Chapter 9, Part II, Camila complains to Demetrio about Margarito's treatment of his prisoner; in Chapter 11, she persuades Demetrio to order restitution for a poor peasant from whom the soldiers stole a year's supply of corn; in Chapter 12, she becomes indignant upon hearing how Margarito refuted Demetrio's written instructions and beat the peasant with his sword.

Camila's attacks upon Margarito, which in the novel convey the growing discord between her and Pintada, serve the secondary purpose of making Camila seem out of place among the revolutionaries. No one but she is moved to compassion or outrage at Margarito's cruelties. In Chapter 9, Part II, when Camila tells him how Margarito has tortured his prisoner, Demetrio only furrows his brow and says nothing. It seems that Demetrio, who does not himself commit acts of torture, has learned to accept them as part of the Revolution. Indeed the narrator, describing the prisoner in a highly de-personalized manner and concentrating on his grotesque obesity and subhuman reaction to fear, implies no compassion for him. Camila's outcry is incongruous, for only she sees Margarito's behavior as barbarous.

In Chapter 11, Part II, the peasant whose grain has been stolen presents his plea:

> . . . tímidamente, entró y expuso a Demetrio su queja. Los soldados acababan de "limpiarlo." Ni un grano de maíz le habían dejado.
> --Pos pa qué se dejan--le respondió Demetrio con indolencia.
> Luego el hombre insistió con lamentos y lloriqueos, y Luis Cervantes se dispuso a echarlo fuera insolentemente. Pero Camila intervino:
> -- ¡Ande, don Demetrio, no sea uste también mal alma; dele una orden pa que le devuelvan su maíz! . . .
> Luis Cervantes tuvo que obedecer; escribió unos renglones, y Demetrio, al calce, puso un garabato (I, 396).

In this passage, the narrator's use of the adverbs con indolencia and insolentemente constitute unfavorable commentary about the attitudes of Demetrio and Luis. Camila is not made to seem so out of place as in Chapter 9.

In Chapter 12, Anastasio tells Demetrio how Margarito mistreated the man sent to reclaim his corn. Anastasio's words imply only a slight reaction to el güero's reckless act:

--Ande, compadre, ni le he contado . . . ¡Qué
travieso es de veras el güero Margarito! . . .
(I, 396).

The mild reproach _travieso_ and Anastasio's delay in telling
Demetrio what happened indicate only perfunctory opposition
to Margarito. Pintada overreacts to one extreme and Camila
to the other:

La Pintada se caía de risa.
Y Camila, sin poderse contener, dijo:
--¡Viejo condenado, tan mala entraña! . . .
¡Con razón no lo puedo ver! (I, 397).

In this final example, neither Camila nor Pintada exhibits
the customary reaction to Margarito's brash deeds. Whereas
most characters merely tolerate _el güero_, no one but Camila
becomes angry at him and no one but Pintada celebrates his
acts.

In a sense Camila, obviously unlike the revolutionaries,
dies because she does not belong with them. In the play, by
contrast, it is Pintada, grotesque in her ill-fitting finery,
who is made to seem out of place.

In Chapter 12, Part II, Pintada unties Camila's braids
and causes her to fall from her horse, cutting her forehead
on the stones. When Luis Cervantes offers to dress her wound,
Camila tells him:

--¿De usté? . . . ¡Aunque me estuviera
muriendo! . . . ¡Ni agua! . . . (I, 397).

That exchange underlines how Camila's love for Luis has
turned to hate, partially explaining why she remained with
Demetrio. Though the play contains no positive evidence that
Camila ever despises Luis, stage directions do at one point
suggest that she avoid contact with him. In Cuadro IV, Pintada has threatened Camila and left the table:

. . . Después de un momento de estupor, Camila
se levanta y va a sentarse a la mesa de Demetrio,
en el momento en que Cervantes lo deja . . . (III,
56).

That subtle indication that Camila now avoids Luis may be a
part of her transferral of affection to Demetrio.

In summary, the play portrays Camila as less a silly
girl than the novel. Accordingly, her process of maturation
is less pronounced in the drama. Naïve in some respects but
also bold and determined, the theatrical Camila has, from the
outset, virtues which might help her develop into an admirable
woman. She is indeed admirable in Part II and in Cuadro IV,
where she overcomes her fear of Pintada and asserts her right
to Demetrio's favor. The dramatic organization of the play
makes possible Camila's intervention on Luis' behalf and ele-
vates her above a purely comic role in Cuadro II.

Luis Cervantes

Cervantes, the <u>huertista</u> who deserts to join revolutionaries and then convinces them to make themselves rich through
rebellion, has basically the same personality in the play as
in the novel. He is a verbose charlatan, schooled in hollow
rhetoric, greedy, and calculating. His best quality, loyalty
to Demetrio, can be seen in both versions. The play shows him
as a different man in two respects: he appears more truthful
and more prone to use his new comrades to achieve his selfish
goals.

In the novel, Luis' great lie is claiming that the <u>federales</u>
forcibly inducted him into their ranks because of his articles
supporting the rebels. In his paraphrased thoughts of Chapter
6, Part I, the truth about him is revealed:

> . . . él no había sabido apreciar a su debido tiempo
> la distancia que hay de manejar el escalpelo, fulminar
> latrofacciosos desde las columnas de un diario pro-
> vinciano, a venir a buscarlos con el fusil en las
> manos a sus propias guaridas (I, 332).

Since Luis makes no such confession in the play, there is no
indication that he was not indeed conscripted by the government. Exposition of a character's inner thoughts is not
dramatizable except through a soliloquy, a technique never
used in <u>Los de abajo</u>.

The playwright emphasizes and re-emphasizes Luis' use
of his friends for his own benefit, a fault not made so prominent in the novel. Luis appears to single out two characters whom he dupes constantly: Camila and Venancio. In the
novel, Camila's infatuation with him seems doubly ridiculous
because of her naiveté and because Luis is shown doing nothing
to encourage it. In Chapter 8, Part I, the narrator records
no words of Luis directed at the girl. The elliptical conversation, containing only Camila's comments, reinforces the
impression of Cervantes' silence. When he looks at her, his
reaction is one of displeasure. In Chapter 11 the narrator
alludes several times to Luis' annoyance at the girl's constant attentions:

> La muchacha andaba inquieta de días atrás, y
> sus melindres y reticencias habían acabado por
> fastidiar al mozo, . . . (I, 342).

> Luis Cervantes plégo el ceño con enojo manifiesto
> y se puso de nuevo a curarse sin hacer más caso de
> ella (I, 343).

> Luis Cervantes, distraído, con su indiferencia en-
> valentó a Camila, . . . (I, 343).

Sus palabras hacían en Luis Cervantes el efecto de
una punta de acero resbalando por las paredes de
una redoma (I, 343).

In Cuadro II Cervantes, sustaining an extended conversation
with Camila, appears less indifferent than in the novel. He
caresses her, attempting to find out if the rebels are carrying large amounts of money. At the close of their conversation Luis touches her again:

> (Acabando de vendarse y acariciando a Camila,
> que hace un mohín de vergüenza.)
>   Eres de veras muy simpática, prietita (III, 29).

His use of the familiar term prietita and Camila's display
of embarrassment are evidence that he does not behave indif-
ferently toward her. Apparently she does not recognize his
attitude of condescension. Just as a reader of the novel
receives the impression that Camila tricks herself, believing
that she can reach an understanding with Luis, the spectator
of the play might be convinced that Cervantes takes advantage
of her naiveté. In an effort to obtain information, he has
led her to believe that she appeals to him.
     In both the novel and the play, Luis assures Demetrio
that Camila cares for him but is afraid in his presence.
In the play, Demetrio promises him a reward for securing her
favor. That arrangement is not recorded until Chapter 6,
Part II, of the novel. In both versions, Cervantes dashes
Camila's romantic dreams in their last interview. In each he
thanks her for her solicitous kindness, saying she has been
like a sister to him. He then advises her to accept Demetrio's
affection, seizing the opportunity for wealth and prestige.
With the antecedents as presented in the novel, Luis' advice
might appear to be out of sincere concern for Camila. He
has lied, telling Demetrio the girl secretly loves him; but
there is not yet even an implicit reward in delivering the
girl to the rebel chief. Cervantes' falsehood might be considered benevolent. In the play, on the other hand, Demetrio
has sworn to show his gratitude if Luis will persuade the
girl to accept his love. Just before his farewell to Camila,
he and Cervantes exchange the following remarks:

> CERVANTES
> Le prometo que yo se la hago buena, mi jefe.
>
> DEMETRIO
> (Mostrando su dentadura muy blanca, en la risa
> más ingenua.)
>   ¿De veras? ¡Mire que yo no soy de los que se
> dan nunca por bien servidos! (III, 45).

No other arrangements intervene before Cuadro IV, where Cervantes has tricked Camila into joining the brigade. In the
play, the impression is given that Luis, in hopes of a reward,

callously advises Camila to attach herself to Demetrio. The
scenario requires that Demetrio express a concrete interest in
Camila and that Luis be clearly willing to procure her for
him, prior to the revelations of Cuadro IV.

Both the novel and the drama contain the opinions of
other characters about Luis' deception of Camila. In Chapter 7, Part II, la Codorniz has told how he and Cervantes
brought the girl back. Several of the men then comment on
the occurrence. Venancio, to whom Luis has made glowing promises, defends him. El güero Margarito treats the incident
as a great joke, while two unidentified soldiers seem re-
proachful of Cervantes:

> --Yo creo--opinó con mucha gravedad Venancio--
> que si Camila amaneció en la cama de Demetrio, sólo
> fue por una equivocación. Bebimos mucho . . .
> ¡Acuérdense! . . . Se nos subieron los espíritus
> alcohólicos a la cabeza y todo perdimos el sentido.
> --¡Qué espíritus alcohólicos ni qué! . . . Fue
> una cosa convenida entre el curro y el general.
> --¡Claro! . . . Pa mí el tal curro no es más
> que un . . .
> --A mí no me gusta hablar de los amigos en
> ausencia--dijo el güero Margarito--; pero sí sé
> decirles que de dos novias que le he conocido, una
> ha sido para . . . mí y la otra para el general
> . . .
> Y prorrumpieron en carcajadas (I, 387).

Though it is impossible to know whether the men criticize
Luis' deception or his apparent lack of manly interest in
women, Margarito's joke suggests the latter interpretation.

In Cuadro IV, seated at a table, several characters discuss the same event. As in the novel, Venancio defends Cervantes. María Antonia condemns him, while Pancracio voices
skepticism:

> VENANCIO
> . . . .
> Yo creo que si Camila ameneció en la cama de
> Demetrio fue por equivocación. Bebimos mucho y los
> espíritus alcohólicos . . .

> PANCRACIO
> ¡Anda al diablo con los espíritus alcohólicos!
> Todo fue cosa convenida con el gurro.

> MARÍA ANTONIA
> Eso mesmo digo yo.

> PANCRACIO
> Pero quien mejor lo sabe es la Codorniz, que
> fue con él a traerla.

CODORNIZ
A mí me dijo Demetrio: "Ensilla tu caballo y
la yegua mora y vas con el curro a una comisión."
Llegamos al ranchito, metiéndose el sol.   "Vuélvete
con la yegua mora--me dijo el curro en la madrugada--
y espérame a media legua de aquí."   Así lo hice, y
al ratito ahí no más que va llegando con Camila, él
en ancas.

MARÍA ANTONIA
¿Y qué cara venía poniendo ella?

CODORNIZ
Alegre como una sonaja, de no pararle la boca.

MARÍA ANTONIA
¡Y miren cómo ora no arrienda a ver a naiden!
Pa mí que el tal curro no es más que un . . .

VENANCIO
No, Luisito es muy buena persona y lo que sucede
es que ustedes a la bondad la llaman . . . (III, 52-53).

The conversation is quite serious, compared to that of the
novel, and not at all ribald. It seems likely that what María
Antonia denounces is Luis' trickery. That notion is strengthened
by the playwright's insertion of a woman, likely to represent
compassion for Camila and resentment toward her deceiver.
    In Chapter 14, Part I, Camila is emotionally devastated
by Luis' advice that she become Demetrio's mistress. She confesses her love for him, then covers her face. When she again
opens her eyes he is gone. The narrator removes Cervantes from
the scene of grief, having made no effort to categorize his
feelings. In Cuadro III the playwright expresses Luis' sen-
timents at that moment:

        (Luis Cervantes se aleja sonriendo y cabizbajo,
    y Camila, en cuanto se queda sola, prorrumpe en
    llanto.)   (III, 47).

The smile is most likely to represent Luis' pride or satisfaction upon having accomplished at least part of what he
wanted: incurring Demetrio's debt of gratitude. He seems
more self-seeking than in the novel.
    Luis' letter to Venancio is an obvious attempt at exploit-
ation. Suggesting that the two of them open a Mexican restaurant in El Paso, he expects Venancio to supply the capital
while he furnishes ambiguous "knowledge of the city." The
narrator of the novel presents Luis' letter without comment,
allowing the reader to draw his own conclusion. In the drama
Venancio reads the letter not to himself but aloud to his
comrades, who interrupt with sarcastic comments which underline Luis' trickery and ridicule Venancio's gullibility.
Demetrio makes a bitter remark when the letter is finished:

"A ese curro debíamos haberlo fusilado. No más nos vino a
tantear" (III, 69). A severely critical remark, contrasting
sharply with the jokes of the other bystanders, it places
in a new perspective Cervantes' cynical opportunism. In
the theater, a character's acts are condemned through the
reactions of other characters.

The play de-emphasizes one of Cervantes' faults, as presented in the novel, while underlining another. It is never
indicated that he lies to his captors, for the dialog never
contradicts his claim that he was forced to join the huertistas
or that he wrote pro-revolutionary articles in a newspaper.
The novel includes a synthesis of Luis' thoughts, necessarily
absent from the play, which proves that he is in fact a one-
time supporter of Huerta who volunteered to help put down the
rebellion. Though a third party could reveal Luis' past, or
he himself could confess it, the play contains no such dis-
closures. Duplicity which Luis keeps to himself is not dramatizable within the scenario of Los de abajo.

Cervantes' use of his new friends for his own purposes,
insinuated in the novel, is heavily underlined in the drama.
He encourages Camila's infatuation with him, fondling her to
obtain information. When Demetrio promises him a reward for
securing Camila's affections, Luis breaks off with her and goes
away smiling. The round of jokes and Demetrio's harsh remark
emphasize the self-seeking tone of Luis' letter to Venancio.
Recreated ten or twelve years after his conception, Cervantes
is a more nearly-perfect opportunist than in his original form.

El güero Margarito

El güero, irresponsible and irrepressible, entertains his
fellow revolutionaries in the play just as in the novel. More
than any other character he spreads exuberant, boisterous hap-
piness. That, in the drama, is his entire function.

In the novel Margarito commits ruthless acts, much more
violent than shooting the glass from the waiter's head or
firing at the short, fat man's feet to make him dance. In
Chapter 11, Part II, his neglect and abuse cause the death of
his prisoner, a man he has held captive purely out of malig-
nant curiosity. In Chapter 12 he refutes Demetrio's written
order that he return several bushels of corn to a poor peasant,
beating the innocent man with his sword. In Chapter 13 he
not only refuses to pay a bill in a cantina but breaks every
glass behind the bar. No such extreme act is included in
the play, where Margarito is not a source of contention
between Pintada and Camila. No act of his brings a reaction
of disgust from Camila or a pugnacious defense from Pintada.
He intervenes only to side with Demetrio, agreeing that Pintada should leave the brigade.

Margarito, in the play, does not react unemotionally to
death. He makes no irreverent comment after Camila's death.
El güero, who enhances the jubilation of the banquet scene,
never violates the general mood as he sometimes does in the
novel.

Margarito's "toasts" to Demetrio's promotion, in a context different from that of the novel, seem frivolous in comparison. They fulfill two functions: stylistically they contribute to the hilarity of the banquet scene, and structurally, they form a contrast with the grim murder which follows. But their purpose is not, as in Chapter 13, Part II, to cheer a depressed comrade.

In the novel, Cervantes' letter mentions that Margarito has committed suicide; no such revelation is included in the play. Though his origins are adequately documented, at the beginning of Cuadro IV, he disappears without explanation after that cuadro. The exclusion of his suicide eliminates a view of him as a human being with shortcomings, leaving him a "flat" character.

El güero Margarito, as presented in the novel, typifies the revolutionary personality. He is pleasure-oriented, finding joy in every event. He is generous, valuing friendship above material gain. His faults are a lack of self-discipline, an ungovernable temper which cools as quickly as it becomes inflamed, and a sadistic curiosity. His mixture of virtues and vices makes him a perfect revolutionary, the character most "at home" with the conflict. In the play he is too narrowly-developed to be an insurgent par excellence. He seems only a self-appointed entertainer with a flair for disruptive pranks. The scenario has reduced Margarito's role, limiting every side of his personality except his extroversion and quick temper.

Valderrama

Valderrama is the character most unlike his image in the novel. His appearance in Cuadro IV shows a very different side of his personality. In the opening speech of the cuadro he describes Demetrio's heroics at Zacatecas, indicating beyond a doubt that he was among the combatants. Presence on a battlefield is a contradiction of Valderrama as he is in the novel, who "siempre que de fusilar se hablaba, sabía perderse lejos y durante todo el día" (I, 409). Concluding his story, Valderrama declares: "¡Qué bonito soldado es usted, Demetrio Macías! ¡Qué machitos son sus muchachos!" (III, 49). That statement would never be uttered by the Valderrama of Chapter 3, Part III, who expresses violent indignation at the spectacle of a cock fight. The playwright's choice of Valderrama to praise Demetrio's bravery characterizes him very differently from his role in the novel.

Valderrama's declaration of love for the Revolution, regardless who wins or loses, does not appear in the play. Toasting Demetrio in Cuadro IV, he takes a doctrinal stand:

Mi general Macías: uno mi voz con entusiasmo a
la de sus abnegados y bravos camaradas, para felicitarlo
y felicitarnos por el triunfo de nuestra causa, que es
el triunfo de la Justicia, y porque sean un hecho los
ideales y anhelos de redención de este nuestro pueblo
sufrido y noble, siempre sacrificado y traicionado siempre
(III, 59).

In this speech Valderrama appears as insincere as Luis Cervantes, the only other character who mouths high-blown
rhetoric. Eulogizing the fallen heroes of Juchipila, in
Cuadro V, he drinks in rapid succession several glasses of
wine and then stations himself in the doorway to begin his
speech. Halfway through he bends down with exaggerated gravity, kneels and kisses the ground. The stage directions suggest that his speech is perhaps not to be interpreted as
sincere; it may be the result of wine and of Valderrama's
desire to be the center of attention. He seems aware of his
audience, not so self-engrossed as when, kneeling in a similar
pose, he recites the corresponding speech in Chapter 4, Part
III:

> . . . Ya a la vista de Juchipila, Valderrama echa
> pie a tierra, se inclina, dobla la rodilla y
> gravemente besa el suelo. Los soldados pasan sin
> detenerse. Unos ríen del loco y otros le dicen
> alguna cuchufleta.
> Valderrama, sin oír a nadie, reza su oración
> solemnemente . . . (I, 412).

Valderrama's oblivion to other people is, in the novel, an
indication of his extreme introversion. He wanders off to
talk with the trees, the mountains or the sky, something which
the set of Cuadro V would not permit him to do. Only when
he declaims about the crosses, in the opening speech of Cuadro
V, is he to recite his words "tendiendo su mirada a lo lejos"
(III, 64). Further undermining of his role as a "loco cuerdo"
is his apparent readiness to participate in the activities of
the men. His eyewitness account of the Battle of Zacatecas
is evidence that he is less introverted than in the novel.
Praising the dead heroes of Juchipila, he calls them "los
únicos que fueron buenos" (III, 70). A voice shouts: "Porque
no tuvieron tiempo de ser malos" (III, 70). Instead of laughing and asking his detractor for a drink, as in Chapter 4,
Part III, Valderrama calls him "imbécil" (III, 70). His
readiness to communicate with other characters humanizes him
beyond his role in Part III.

The narrator of the novel points out the obscurity of
Valderrama's origins and destination, including both in the
same paragraph. In the play, no explanation is given for his
appearance or for the fact that he does not appear again
after Cuadro V. De-emphasis of the mystery surrounding him
further weakens the prophet's role he played in the novel.

Valderrama, whose actions enhance the mood of depression
in Cuadro V, does not suggest the madness or illogic of the
times. In the play, the theme of madness in the scenes
corresponding to Part III of the novel is not stylistically
underlined. The rhythmic organization of Cuadro V conceals
the illogical essence of the characters' actions. Their sudden shifts from euphoria to depression to bitterness seem a
function not of their condition but of an over-all plan.
Valderrama is a less unique character in the drama than

in the novel. He is neither insane nor prophetic, but only a
drifting minstrel who seems to enjoy the attention of his comrades. Not insulated from the other characters as in the
novel, he goes into battle with them, participates in Demetrio's banquet and interrupts Venancio to insult him for his
gullibility in not seeing the inconsistencies in Luis Cervantes'
letter. If compared to his role as developed in the novel,
Valderrama is recognizable only in a few speeches and actions,
all presented in a different context. No other character
is changed more in the adaptation than Valderrama.

A Character Deleted: Alberto Solís

Though Solís never appears in the play, his description
of Demetrio's exploits at the Battle of Zacatecas is assigned
to another character, to Valderrama in Cuadro IV. In the
novel, Solís makes predictions about events subsequently
described in Part II: pillage of the homes of non-combatants
and the murder of innocent bystanders. Cuadro IV, which
corresponds to Part II, contains descriptions of past homi-
cides and a fleeting reference to avances. For the most part,
however, the novel's scenes of plunder have been eliminated
from the play. Solís' function of anticipating future incidents is, therefore, inappropriate to the drama.

Solís' exclusion might be considered in relation to
Valderrama's vastly-altered personality. In the novel they
are alike in two respects: both love the conflict despite
elements which they detest, and both see it from a special
vantage point. In the play there is no figure who expresses
a subjective, illogical love for the conflict and no impartial
observer. The result of the "normalization" of Valderrama
and the elimination of Solís is that the Revolution never
seems to be, as in the novel, a force stronger than the participants. Alberto Solís, whose dire predictions would seem
fanciful in a work where they do not materialize, is excluded
as a prophetic observer of the Revolution.

Characters Expanded

Doña Nica

Though no character in the novel is named Doña Nica, she
is identifiable as a nameless old hag in Chapter 5, Part III.
The narrator describes the troops' foraging for food in the
ruined city of Juchipila:

> . . . Un solo fonducho está abierto y en seguida
> se aprieta. No hay frijoles, no hay tortillas:
> puro chile picado y sal corriente. En vano los
> jefes muestran sus bolsillos reventando de billetes
> o quieren ponerse amenazadores.
> --¡Papeles, sí! . . . ¡Eso nos han traído
> ustedes! . . . ¡Pos eso coman! . . . --dice la
> fondera, una viejota insolente, con una enorme

cicatriz en la cara, quien cuenta que "ya durmió
en el petate del muerto para no morirse de un susto" (I, 415).

The playwright specifies, in the stage directions for Cuadro
V, that Doña Nica be "una viejota con enorme cicatriz en la
cara" (III, 53). The other points of reference are two
speeches the old woman makes:

PANCRACIO
Buígase, vieja, que aquí traigo dinero pa que
se pague hasta las ganas.

DOÑA NICA
¡Hum! ¡Papeles! Pos papeles coman . . .

PANCRACIO
Con papeles y sin papeles, nos da lo que
tenga o se la lleva la . . . corriente.

DOÑA NICA
(Lanzando una carcajada hombruna.)
¡Hum! No me pele los ojos. Míreme esta
cicatriz . . . es porque ya dormí en el petate del
muerto, pa no morirme de un susto (III, 64-65).

In the novel her squalid appearance and ugly disposition
complement the desolation described in the chapter; she
functions as a symbol. In the play Doña Nica, equally squalid,
is the only character on stage at the beginning and at the end
of the cuadro. Her wretched figure is in harmony with the
dilapidated set. She also plays an additional role, unique
to the drama. Doña Nica is a key character in the de-mythification of Demetrio Macías in Cuadro V, the preparation for his
homecoming and death in Cuadro VI. Reacting to him as a
civilian and old friend, apparently unimpressed by his reputation, the old woman comes out to greet him:

¡Don Demetrio! ¡Alma mía de usted! ¡Pos qué
esperanzas tenía ya de volverlo a ver! Ande, venga
y deme un abrazo muy apretado. ¡Cuánto gusto va a
darle a su siñora! . . . (III, 65).

The moment the old woman sees Demetrio, she thinks of his wife
and his imminent homecoming. She is used to re-introduce
Demetrio as a private citizen. Her words and Demetrio's attire, similar to that which he wears in Cuadros I-III, are
visual suggestions that his career has run full circle.
Doña Nica forms the bridge between Demetrio and his wife,
whom she sees regularly. If Demetrio's first step toward home
is Camila's death, the second is the insertion of the old
woman. In the play, where Demetrio's step-by-step return
home is more precisely elaborated than in the novel, the scenario requires that Doña Nica's intervention be more extensive.

Doña Nica's third function in the drama is to supply a
preliminary suggestion that Demetrio's battle with the carrancistas may be his last. The troops exit boisterously, leaving
the old woman alone. She stands in the doorway of her tumble-
down quiosco and watches them go away, with a compassionate
look in her eyes. She then exclaims: "¡Pobrecitos! ¿Quién
los volverá a ver?" (III, 72). The play, unlike the novel,
calls for several anticipations of a battle in which Demetrio
will probably be defeated. Pancracio's announcement that the
carrancistas are near and Doña Nica's exclamation of despair
increase the potential pathos of Cuadro VI, with its strong
suggestion that Demetrio, when he takes leave of his wife,
will never again see her. That undercurrent of finality is
more highly developed than in Chapter 6, Part III, where the
wife's plea ("¡El corazón me avisa que ahora te va a suceder
algo!" (I, 416)) might be interpreted as normal apprehension
perhaps unfounded. Doña Nica's last remark is, then, part
of the playwright's intent to establish a strong bittersweet
mood for Demetrio's homecoming.

Demetrio's Wife

Since Chapter 1 of Part I and Chapters 6-7, Part III,
are each expanded into cuadros in the play, Demetrio's wife,
who appears only there, is given an expanded role. Her appearances are longer than in the novel and substantially
different.

The wife, with her child always nearby, is a mother
figure in both versions of Los de abajo. The playwright's
emphasis on her attire makes her a specifically Mexican
mother, more than in the novel.

Chapters 6 and 7, Part III, contain religious symbols:
the silver-breasted swallow, flying through rays of sun after
the thunderstorm; and the cliff at the bottom of which Demetrio's corpse is revealed. The narrator compares it to the
portal of an ancient cathedral. Those images are unpresentable
in Cuadro VI, where the pious utterances of Demetrio's wife
suggest the religious tone.

In the novel, action stops after the revelation of
Demetrio's death. The narrator does not mention the widow
nor any other survivor. In the play, the last action is
not Demetrio's death but his wife's reaction to it. More than
a survivor, she is the patroness of the dead. Both Demetrio
and María Antonia, going to the battlefield, ask her to pray
for them. In the novel, the wife does not hold in trust the
welfare of the souls of the departed.

The play ends more optimistically than the novel, because
a human survivor of the Revolution is presented. In Chapter
7, Part III, only locusts, doves and grazing cattle remain,
while at the end of Cuadro VI, a typically Mexican mother
and her child are left. Animal life, which would on the stage
be an unconvincing symbol of continued vitality despite the
protagonist's death, is replaced by symbols which suggest that
vitality to an audience.

María Antonia

As presented in the novel, she is a purely comic character usually placed in ridicule by other characters and, in
one passage, by the narrator.

When introduced in Chapter 10, Part I, María Antonia has
noticed Camila's new infatuation with Luis Cervantes. She
shouts a rather crude taunt, is answered in kind by Camila,
and responds with another jibe:

>   --¡Epa, tú! . . . Dale los polvos de amor . . .
> A ver si ansina cai . . .
>   --¡Pior! . . . Ésa será usté . . .
>   --¡Si yo quijiera! . . . Pero, ¡fuche!, les
> tengo asco a los curros . . . (I, 338).

Their exchange seems a good-natured give-and-take, not cruel
or in earnest. María Antonia is never shown in a serious
moment.

María Antonia appears several times in Chapter 15, Part
I, which describes the troops' departure from her village.
Her farewell contrasts humorously with the blessings and good
wishes of other village women:

>   --Dios los tenga de su santa mano--dijo una
> vieja.
>   --Dios los bendiga y los lleve por buen camino--
> dijeron otras. Y María Antonia, muy borracha:
>   --¡Qué güelvan pronto . . . pero repronto!
> . . . (I, 351).

In the next paragraph the narrator gives his only description of her:

> . . . aunque cacariza y con una nube en un ojo tenía
> muy mala fama, tan mala que se aseguraba que no había
> varón que no la hubiese conocido entre los jarales
> del río, . . . (I, 351).

That revelation, side-by-side with the biased physical description, seems more nearly ridicule than moral condemnation.

María Antonia, cheerful at the troops' departure, reacts
differently from the other villagers. The men and women are
depressed at the end of the fiesta atmosphere which has pre-
vailed during the soldiers' stay; Camila is disconsolate because Luis Cervantes has rejected her and gone away. María
Antonia tries to prod her out of her depression:

>   --¡Epa, tú! . . . ¿Qué es eso? . . . ¿Qué haces
> en el rincón con el rebozo liado a la cabeza? . . .
> ¡Huy! . . . ¿Llorando? . . . ¡Mira qué ojos! ¡Ya
> pareces hechicera! ¡Vaya . . . no te apures! . . .
> No hay dolor que al alma llegue, que a los tres días
> no se acabe (I, 351-352).

María Antonia laughs aloud when Camila bursts into tears,
seeing the troops' silhouettes in the distance. She seems
to be the antithesis of melancholy, a character who finds
something good in every event and does not understand heartbreak. Her role in the novel, that of cheering her friends,
is somewhat like that of el güero Margarito in the play.
María Antonia is mentioned in a ribald allusion by el
Meco in Chapter 19, Part I:

> --Hombre, sí, Pancracio; traite a la tuerta
> María Antonia, que por acá hace mucho frío . . .
> (I, 364).

Two other passages suggest a passing romance between Pancracio
and María Antonia. In Chapter 14, Part I, he speaks of the
imminent departure from the village:

> --Pos nos iremos--exclamó Pancracio y dio
> un aullido--; pero lo que es yo ya no me voy solo
> . . . Tengo mi amor y me lo llevo (I, 349).

In Chapter 7, Part II, la Codorniz describes his trip to the
village, with Luis Cervantes, to bring back Camila:

> . . . Nos dio posada la tuerta María Antonia . . .
> Que cómo estás tanto, Pancracio . . . (I, 386-387).

In the play, the hinted love interest between Pancracio
and María Antonia is developed into a full-blown romance.
The relationship between them is carefree and jubilant, not
unlike the personality developed for María Antonia in the novel.
When Demetrio announces that the brigade must leave for Jalisco,
Pancracio makes an obscene remark about las tapatías. He and
María Antonia exit laughing, tickling one another.
María Antonia plays a more serious role in the drama than
in the novel. In Cuadro V she demonstrates loyalty and bravery,
venturing out alone over dangerous back trails to bring
Demetrio's wife the message that he is returning home. In
Cuadro VI she is Pancracio's helpmate, as able as any man,
going with him into battle and tending him when he lies dying.
María Antonia's last function is that of messenger.
Demetrio's wife, alone on stage, reveals his death as if she
were receiving the news from María Antonia. Her key role in
the cuadros which correspond to Part III of the novel dictates
that her function be more than comic. In the novel she constitutes the principal source of low humor in Part I, the
least dramatic of the three parts. Such a flat character is
she that she does not appear in chapters describing the tension-
frought incidents of Parts II and III. In the play, María
Antonia's role, comic in Cuadros II-IV, is expanded thereafter. Bridging the gap between Demetrio's public and private
lives, she prefigures his homecoming.
Eight major characters undergo significant changes in the
adaptation of the novel into a theatrical work. Camila is not
initially a comic character as in the novel; Luis Cervantes

suffers an altered personality; el güero Margarito and Valderrama have simplified roles, and Alberto Solís is
eliminated. Three female characters are expanded from minor
roles in the novel: Doña Nica, Demetrio's wife, and María
Antonia.

Camila's maturation is less abrupt in the play than in
the novel. The dramatic organization facilities her intervention in Luis' behalf, a bold act which forms the basis
for her subsequent defiance of Pintada and assertion of her
right to Demetrio's attentions.

Luis Cervantes, in the play, is less a liar than in the
novel and more obviously uses his new comrades for his own
purposes. In Cuadro II no evidence is presented to suggest
that Cervantes has lied about how he joined the huertistas
or against which side he wrote his newspaper articles. The
playwright points out how Luis dupes Camila, feigning affection to pump her for information, and Venancio, writing
thinly-veiled extortions. The cynical comments of the characters who interrupt Venancio's reading of the letter berate
his gullibility, but Demetrio makes a bitter remark attacking
Luis.

El güero Margarito's only function, in the play, is to
provide a rowdy diversion from the conflict of Cuadro IV.
None of his ruthless acts from the novel is retained. He is
no longer a catalyst in the rivalry between Camila and Pintada,
for he commits no deeds to warrant Camila's contempt.

Valderrama is more changed than any other character. In
the play, he expresses no love for the Revolution as an independent force. He is not a prophet but more nearly an entertainer, neither introverted nor insane. Not himself illogical
as in the novel, Valderrama reflects the rhythmic logic of the
events of Cuadro V.

None of the acts which Alberto Solís predicts in the novel
is represented in the play; he himself is excluded. With Solís'
absence and the weakening of Valderrama, the Revolution is no
longer a force independent of the combatants or superior to
them.

Doña Nica, expanded from an anonymous old hag in Part
II, is a squalid figure in harmony with the set of Cuadro V.
She is the key character in the de-militarization of Demetrio,
a prelude to his homecoming and death. Doña Nica also gives
the initial warning that Demetrio is going out to his last
battle.

Demetrio's wife takes on greater importance because the
chapters in which she appears are expanded into Cuadros I and
VI. She carries the religiosity of Cuadro VI, with a prayer
constantly on her lips. The other characters commend their
souls to her as they leave for battle. The only survivor
upon whom the playwright concentrates, Demetrio's wife is the
key figure in an ending with visual imagery different from
that of the novel.

María Antonia, expanded from the purely comic role she
plays in the novel, takes on a more serious function in the
drama. She is Demetrio's loyal disciple and a fearless helpmate to Pancracio.

There is a pattern in the re-characterization of the
novel when adapted for the theater. Major characters like
Demetrio and Camila remain virtually the same. The most
important secondary character, Luis Cervantes, is substantially changed, while the others are reduced. Tertiary
figures like Demetrio's wife are given expanded roles. The
similar circumstance of the works lies in the ancillary characters: Pancracio, Anastasio, and Codorniz. They, determined
by the plot and never influencing it, are unchanged in the
adaptation. Their actions provide the stable circumstances
in which the protagonists move.

Summary: The Novel versus the Play

The novel Los de abajo is readily adaptable for the theater.
Many incidents are presented step by step in great detail and
in their entirety. Their length is appropriate for one scene
on stage. These incidents take place in one limited place and
involve few characters. A high proportion of dialog makes
them readily dramatizable. Indeed, the novel may be considered dramatic, according to Muir's definition.
The story of Demetrio is quite alike in both versions.
From the outset of each, he is endowed with a mythlike quality
which is gradually dispelled. His complete humanization is a
prelude to his death.
Frequently, when the stage directions prescribe that a
character convey a thought through pantomine rather than words,
they reflect a choice already made in the novel. Camila's
reactions proclaim her modesty, never mentioned in the play
or in the novel, just as Pintada's pantomine shows her rage
when el güero Margarito refuses to side with her against
Demetrio.
Both versions of Los de abajo portray Luis Cervantes as
arrogant, an insincere flatterer, materialistic, and greedy.
In the play those traits are presented through dialog and
external signs, and in the novel, more frequently through
narration.
Nearly everyone respects el güero Margarito and finds him
an enjoyable companion. In the play his personality is developed
through his own actions. In the novel it is exposed through
the actions of Margarito's victims and through what other
characters say about him.
La Pintada's bawdy nature is revealed by her words and
actions when she first appears. Her last act, the same in
both versions, is revealed differently. In the novel, the
narrator alludes to Pintada's obscene reaction when Demetrio
sends her away. The dialog, very mild, becomes more explicit
in the play, where words replace pantomine in depicting
Pintada's rage.
The respective versions contain some differences in the
exposition of Demetrio's odyssey. The novel progressively reveals Demetrio on two simultaneous planes: his private life
and his public career, analyzed alternately. In the play, by

contrast, the incidents selected subordinate the man to the
soldier. He is not revealed independent of the Revolution.

The play presents the same basic events as does the
novel but within a different structural framework. Cuadro I
reverses the order in which events are introduced in the
novel; Cuadro II fragments Luis Cervantes' trial for the sake
of dramatic tension; Cuadro IV contrasts the humorous banquet
scene with the grisly murder which immediately follows it.
The events of Cuadro V are not presented chronologically, as
in the novel, but rhythmically. Cuadro III presents few inno-
vations, and Cuadro VI is so original that its structure cannot be compared with that of any part of the novel.

The content of Part II is de-emphasized and that of Part
III, greatly expanded. The play thereby becomes a study of
the effects of the Revolution on human personalities.

In the play, the background in space and time is quite
different from that of the novel. While the playwright
establishes Mexican-ness through identifiable interiors, the
novelist chooses lyricized Mexican exteriors.

Camila's murder, in Cuadro IV, occurs in a restricting
indoor set which contributes spatially to the dramatic
tension. The corresponding passage of the novel occurs outdoors and does not confine the characters. Similarly, the
effect of Demetrio's death, in an unrevealed site, is
achieved differently.

Illumination, specified in very broad terms in the novel,
is altered for three crucial incidents of the play. When
Demetrio and his wife go their separate ways, after the intrusion by the federales, the playwright calls for darkness which
lends the characters anonymity rather than moonlight which,
in the novel, allows Demetrio to look back and see his wife's
pained silhouette. Camila's murder takes place in a cantina
with mirrors on the walls, creating dazzling light which increases the dramatic impact of the homicide. No such authorial
"management" of the murder episode can be detected in Chapter
12, Part II. In the novel, Demetrio's death occurs under a
bright sun, and in the play, during a symbolic twilight.

Music, in the play, is more completely integrated into
the banquet scene than in the novel. It adds to Margarito's
pranks a hilarity which they lack in Chapter 13, Part II.
In Cuadro VI the playwright adds an original use of music:
the sound of a distant mouth organ, which symbolizes Demetrio's
life after death. One instance of music used in the novel but
not in the play is the refrain which Demetrio sings while
grieving for Camila. Her death occurs at the very end of
Cuadro IV, and Demetrio's sorrow is only fleetingly suggested
in the play.

Costuming carries a message in the drama which it does
not suggest in the novel. In Cuadro IV, their different
attire usually segregates one group of Demetrio's followers
from the other. In Cuadro V, a drastic change in all the
characters' dress reveals that they have experienced misfortune.

Different gestures accompanying a similar speech leave a
different impression in the play than in the novel. A character

may seem more sincere or more absurd because of his gestures
or the tone of his voice.

Much of the novel's dialog is omitted in the play, which
contains some original speeches. The playwright may vary the
words of a speech, assign it to a different speaker or place
it in a changed context in order to achieve an original effect.

Several characters undergo a personality change in the
process of adaptation for the theater. Camila, when first
presented, shows more adult traits than in the novel. Luis
Cervantes, less a liar, appears more cynical in using his
friends. El güero Margarito, narrowed, is still entertaining
but not fully enough developed to typify the revolutionary
spirit as he does in the novel. Valderrama, no longer insane
or prophetic, is an extrovert who participates in his comrades'
activities. With the weakening of Valderrama and Alberto
Solís' deletion from the play, no character makes the Revolution seem like a force superior to the participants.

Three female characters with minor roles in the novel
play a very significant role in the play. Doña Nica, expanded from a nameless old hag who appears very briefly in
Part III, is the key figure in the process which converts
Demetrio from a public to a private man; she also serves as
part of the stylistic preparation for his death. Demetrio's
wife becomes the only identified survivor of the Revolution;
in the novel, the narrator reveals none. The wife's role
interprets differently the optimistic ending of the novel.
The last expanded female character is María Antonia, who grows
from a comic role in the novel to a well-developed personality
in the play. She is a messenger of Demetrio's death.

The novel's structure fits loosely within a temporal framework. Events are presented either condensed into a few pages
or distributed among two or more episodes separated by intervening incidents. Integral or fragmented presentation depends
upon the nature of the event as it might occur in life.
Events in the drama are presented temporally insomuch as they
occur in order and progress logically; however, the structure
of individual events is rhythmic. Manipulated into flowing
and ebbing cycles are Cervantes' trial, the rivalry between
Camila and Pintada, and the events of Cuadro V which achieve
the "personalization" of Demetrio. Only one major subplot
is developed temporally, as in the novel: the one-sided
romance between Luis and Camila.

The novel contains various elements: Demetrio's private
and public lives, insights into the thoughts of secondary
characters like Cervantes and Solís, descriptions of battles,
vignettes of typical activities of the revolutionaries,
cuadros costumbristas, and analyses of semi-historical events.
Each element is the principal content of a few chapters or
of many. A reader must look beyond the basic unit of the
chapter to perceive which elements are most important. The
play, by contrast, is undivided beyond the six cuadros. In
each, the most important element is the progress of Demetrio's
private or public career. Since much of the novel's secondary
plot content is unrepresented in the drama and the structure
is greatly simplified, Demetrio's life is made to stand out

stronger than in the novel. Camila's murder, for instance, the dominant event of Cuadro IV, does not in the novel rise high above other incidents of the corresponding Part II, divided into fourteen chapters which examine a variety of subjects.

An important message of the novel is that the Revolution is an independent force, controlling the destinies of the participants, whose individual actions affect its course very little. The narrator develops that concept through frequent anonymity and miniaturization of combatants, through the philosophies expressed by Solís, Valderrama and others, and by means of narrative comment. In the play, characters are infrequently anonymous and cannot be made smaller than life. Solís does not appear; Valderrama is not presented as a soothsayer. No authorial management suggests that the characters are helpless before the cataclysmic power of the Revolution. It is a scaled-down phenomenon, manageable by the characters and in fact influenced by them. If the Revolution is the protagonist of the novel, the revolutionaries themselves are protagonists of the play.

Footnotes

[1]Muir, <u>The Structure of the Novel</u>, p. 147.

CONCLUSIONS

The novel Los de abajo demonstrates considerable mobility
of setting, including incidents which occur while the troops
are on the open road. Demetrio and his followers visit a
succession of cities and enter a number of different houses
and buildings. The narrator, with a sketchy description
of each new place, makes each one real to the reader by presenting in convincing circumstances some event which occurs
there. The action of the play, taking place in just six different settings, is restricted by the limitations inherent to
its naturalistic sets. In each cuadro the scenery and props
suggest concretely the place where the action is to evolve.
The interiors and exteriors of huts, the outskirts of the
village, the dining room of the cantina, the kiosk in the
small town, and the ledge of Cuadro VI will not in all likelihood be mistaken for anything else. The characters do not
further identify the settings except to specify that a hut
belongs to Demetrio or to Señá Remigia, that Doña Nica's open-
air restaurant is in Juchipila, and similar details which may
complement an incident but are unnecessary for identification
of the set.
The cuadros are not internally subdivided, with no transitions through lighting and, except in Cuadro I, no emptying
of the stage before a new episode begins. That arrangement
severely restricts the number of major incidents which can be
presented in the play. Examples of pillage and cruelty are
omitted, while battles are presented indirectly in summary,
in a passing reference or not at all. No limitation inherent
to the theater precludes representation of a battle, which
might be viewed from a command post or a small sector of the
front. The dramatist's choice of settings in Los de abajo,
however, does not facilitate battle scenes except through
messengers and auditory effects, as in Cuadro VI. The author's
de-emphasis of battles, in a play which describes events of
the Revolution, suggests that combat is not to him the most
important aspect of the struggle.
A characteristic common to theatrical works greatly
limits the presentation of episodes which take place along a
trail, as the troops move from one city to another. They cannot be portrayed in progressive motion, much less on horse-
back as in the novel. The playwright chooses not to depict
the men simply at rest along the trail, a workable technique
but apparently not, in his judgment, deserving of the major
part of a cuadro.
Characters amid a raging battle display a rather narrow
range of emotions: anxiety, fear, depression, rage, bravado--
all of which appear during the indirect representation of the

187

battle in Cuadro VI. All are short-lived emotions, not usually sustained during a long episode, which leave few traces once they are spent. In the play, most scenes allow the development of longer-term psychological phenomena such as romantic love and political indoctrination.

The novel contains psychological expositions of several characters, revealing thoughts and emotions which contradict their outward behavior. Such subject matter is not dramatizable in a play like Los de abajo, which lacks soliloquies and asides.

From time to time the narrator intervenes in a passage of the novel, inserting natural symbols or an unmediated comment. Representation on the stage of elements of Nature would distract from the essential action; unmediated comment could not be employed in the theater except through a dramatized narrator. The dramatist does, however, manipulate some incidents through symbolic illumination or appropriate music.

Throughout the novel Los de abajo are found narrative paraphrases of dialog and elliptical conversations, both well-established novelistic techniques. In the theater, dialog can be quoted second-hand but not effectively paraphrased. An elliptical or one-sided conversation is dramatizable as one half of a telephone conversation or as a repetition of phrases shouted from a distance by a conjectured off-stage character. Also, for comic effect, one character may be limited to meaningful gestures which another interprets verbally, monopolizing a conversation.

The novel can choose its perspective, so remote that a man seems only an inch high or so close that a gleam in his eye is a meaningful sign. Since the perspective of the theater is relatively unchanging, varied points of view must be achieved by other means: intensity of illumination, tone of voice, costume, gestures or position on stage.

Imagery in a novel is a fleeting phenomenon; mentioned at the beginning of an episode, it may or may not affect that episode from beginning to end. Only if a reader keeps the image in mind can it flavor the incident in conjunction with which the narrator introduces it. In drama, by contrast, visual or auditory imagery is in evidence until the playwright removes it. So immediate is the theater that an image may be very subtle and still potent. Pantomine, likewise, is more direct than the most vivid narrative exposition.

If two specific works be compared, one a novel and the other a play, the differences between them result not only from genre characteristics but also from their contrasting organizations. In the case of the two versions of Los de abajo, the play's scenario makes demands very different from those of the narrative sequence of the novel.

The playwright, in planning the framework for Los de abajo, chose to create just six cuadros with no interior divisions. He thus limited his exposition to a maximum of six major episodes and six to twelve or perhaps fifteen minor incidents. Obliged to pick very carefully among the episodes presented in the novel, the playwright seems to have chosen first those which might be considered indispensable: Demetrio's

separation from his wife, his homecoming, and his death in
battle. He also included incidents most directly presentable
on stage: romantic conversations between Camila and Luis,
and the philosophical debate between Luis and Demetrio. That
choice required the insertion of factorial incidents which
would achieve believability for the personal confrontations;
examples are Luis' capture and the process through which he
gains the revolutionaries' confidence. Episodes not directly
dramatizable in their entirety, such as Pintada's murder of
Camila and Margarito's hilarious pranks, are confined to
Cuadro IV. There the spectators are conditioned to a visual
and auditory spectacle unlike the material of any other cuadro.

The playwright seems to have preferred incidents which set
forth the characters' normal personality traits, over those
which reveal their reactions in an emergency or exceptional
situation. Evidence of that preference is the de-emphasis of
plunder and cruelty, very prevalent in Part II of the novel,
and of all battles except the indispensable final skirmish
in which Demetrio is killed. The characters are made to reveal under relatively normal circumstances their true personalities, except in isolated scenes like Pintada's stabbing of
Camila and confrontation with Demetrio, and the extreme agitation of María Antonia and Demetrio's wife during the final
battle. The playwright's artistic will is seen in his choice
of the material to be presented and in his decision to structure it simply so that each important episode stands out strongly in a subdivision devoted largely to it.

An examination of details reveals the potentials and
limitations of each genre. The narrator's indirect exposition
of many incidents, through artistic deformation or suggestive
symbolism, is one of the novel's most noteworthy features. By
contrast, direct visual and auditory imagery contributes greatly to the artistry of the play. Both works exhibit vivid
events and lively dialog.

In addition to the author's intentional choices and those
made for him by the requirements of the respective genres,
are the limitations imposed upon him by the expository sequence of each work. The novel obeys one structural pattern,
and the play, another; the differences between them account
for much of the individuality of the respective versions of
Los de abajo.

SELECTED BIBLIOGRAPHY

No attempt is made to include a complete bibliography of Azuela, already available in sources such as the Obras completas, Volume III, and Leal. As the Introduction points out, this dissertation investigates a dramatic work which the critics have ignored. Extensive citation of the available criticism of the novel, in the first chapter, would create an imbalance with the analysis of the play, which must of course be done without reference to critics. For that reason, the bibliography is quite brief and includes a number of theoretical works which lead to pertinent original observations.

Primary Work

Azuela, Mariano. Obras completas. 3 vols. Foreword by Francisco Monterde. "Letras Mexicanas" Series. México: Fondo de Cultura Económica, 1958-60.

Works Cited

Booth, Wayne C. The Rhetoric of Fiction. Chicago: University of Chicago Press, 1961.

Englekirk, John E. "The 'Discovery' of Los de abajo." Hispania, XVIII (1935), 53-62.

Englekirk, John E., and Kiddle, Lawrence B. Foreword to Los de abajo, by Mariano Azuela. New York: Appleton-Century-Crofts, 1939.

González, Manuel Pedro. Trayectoria de la novela en México. México: Botas, 1951.

Leal, Luis. Mariano Azuela, vida y obra. México: Ediciones Andrea, 1961.

Muir, Edwin. The Structure of the Novel. New York: Harcourt and Brace, 1929.

Works Consulted

Barry, Jackson G. Dramatic Structure: The Shaping of Experience. Berkeley: University of California Press, 1970.

Brushwood, John S. *Mexico in Its Novel*. Austin: University of Texas Press, 1966.

Frank, Joseph. "Spatial Forms in Modern Literature." *Sewanee Review*, LIII (1945), 221-240, 433-456, 643-653.

Menton, Seymour. "La estructura épica de *Los de abajo* y un prólogo especulativo." *Hispania*, L (1967), 1001-1011.

Meyerhoff, Hans. *Time in Literature*. Berkeley: University of California Press, 1955.

Morton, F. Rand. *Los novelistas de la Revolución mexicana*. México: Editorial Cultura, 1949.

Olson, Elder. *Tragedy and the Theory of Drama*. Detroit: Wayne State University Press, 1961.

Pupo-Walker, C. Enrique. "*Los de abajo* y la pintura de Orozco: un caso de correspondencias estéticas." *Cuadernos Americanos*, XXVI, No. 5 (1967), 237-254.

Spell, Jefferson Rea. *Contemporary Spanish American Fiction*. Chapel Hill: University of North Carolina Press, 1944.

Torres Ríoseco, Arturo. *Los novelistas de la tierra*. Berkeley: University of California Press, 1941.